Red Navy at Sea:
Soviet Naval Operations
on the High Seas, 1956–1980

About the Book and Author

Red Navy at Sea:
Soviet Naval Operations on the High Seas, 1956–1980
Bruce W. Watson

This is the only book to offer a detailed chronology of modern Soviet naval operations set within the framework of long-range Soviet foreign and domestic policy. This context is important because it puts the navy in its proper place as a significant cog in the gigantic machinery of Soviet "grand strategy." Commander Watson argues that the Soviet Navy's physical configuration, strategy, and operations reflect a long-term "upgrading" pattern, designed to create an equal-partner status in the total balance of Soviet military forces. Changes in the navy's activities are not merely pragmatic reactions to momentary crises or shifts in world power trends. The navy has played an integral part in implementing the four strategic long-range goals of Soviet policy: defense of the Soviet Union, enhancement of its international position, establishment and maintenance of Soviet military superiority internationally, and the promotion of other Communist revolutions.

Commander Watson discusses in detail Soviet naval operations in all of the world's oceans. He provides new insight into the dimensions of Soviet naval presence and port visit activity, using vast amounts of statistical material gathered from his original research. The text is supplemented by maps, photographs, and extensive tabular documentation.

Dr. Bruce W. Watson is presently a commander in the United States Navy. He teaches at the Defense Intelligence School in Washington, D.C. Dr. Watson holds a doctorate in Russian area studies from Georgetown University and is also a member of its adjunct staff, lecturing on Soviet naval and maritime affairs.

Soviet naval port visit to Boston, 1975. (U.S. Navy, R. Woods)

Red Navy at Sea:
Soviet Naval Operations
on the High Seas, 1956–1980

Bruce W. Watson

Westview Press • Boulder, Colorado

Arms and Armour Press/Royal United Services
Institute for Defence Studies • London

This volume is included in Westview Special Studies on the Soviet Union and Eastern Europe.

Material quoted from Elmo Zumwalt, *On Watch,* copyright © 1976 by Elmo Zumwalt is reprinted by permission of TIMES BOOKS, a division of Quadrangle/The New York Times Book Co., Inc.

Published in the United States of America in 1982 by Westview Press, Inc., 5500 Central Avenue, Boulder, Colorado 80301. Frederick A. Praeger, President and Publisher.

Published in Great Britain in 1982 by Arms and Armour Press, 2-6 Hampstead High Street, London NW3 1QQ, and at 4-12 Tattersails Lane, Melbourne, Victoria 3000, Australia, in cooperation with the Royal United Services Institute for Defence Studies, Whitehall, London SW1A 2ET.

Library of Congress Catalog Card Number: 81-21948
ISBN (U.S.): 0-86531-204-4
ISBN (U.K.): 0-85368-551-7   *8052424*

Printed and bound in the United States of America

For my wife, Susan

Contents

Part 3
The Pacific and Indian Oceans

Maps and Tables

xiii

Photographs

Preface

This is a history of Soviet naval operations on the high seas. It begins with the year 1956, when Admiral Sergei G. Gorshkov was appointed commander in chief of the Soviet Navy, and continues through 1980. Major emphasis is on the period since 1967, when operations began to increase in importance. Although much has been written on Soviet naval construction and selected operations, a comprehensive history of Soviet naval operations has not existed until now.

The Soviets have built and operated a modern navy that has contributed to Soviet progress toward certain long-range goals. The navy's mission has been to assist in implementing a Soviet policy aimed at achieving four long-range goals: defending the Soviet Union, enhancing the country's international position, establishing a preponderance of Soviet power in the international sphere, and promoting external political changes that are compatible with the Soviet system. The navy's tasks include participating in the nation's defense; posing a strategic threat to the United States; stationing naval power in strategic areas of the high seas in order to oppose U.S. naval power in periodic U.S.-Soviet confrontations; projecting naval power into the Atlantic, Pacific, and Indian oceans and the Mediterranean and Caribbean seas to assist in advancing Soviet influence in the Third World; harassing Western naval forces; making port visits; and accomplishing other politically motivated operations relevant to Soviet strategic goals.

The majority of studies on the Soviet Navy have assumed that it has been built and operated under the influence of relatively short-term goals and objectives. In that context, tactical changes frequently have been interpreted as major departures in Soviet planning. Thus many authors have argued that the navy is governed by sets of rules to which naval operations must conform so we should expect certain reactions to given sets of circumstances, and analyses of past reactions to discrete events should support the development of models to accurately predict future activities. These studies often depict the Soviet leadership as pragmatic, guided by an ad hoc strategy, and making maximum use of contemporary opportunities. Their authors generally ignore the influence of Marxist-Leninist ideology in Soviet military operations and the probable existence of a long-range strategy.

Dismissing these two factors can lead to faulty biases. For example, the appearance of new ships has been interpreted as a reflection of major strategy shifts, ignoring the fact that the Soviets have maintained an impressive construction program since 1956. Likewise, the marked uniformity in naval operations is often understated. For instance, the Soviet Navy has expanded its operations over increasingly larger areas of the world's oceans, and in all areas, these operations have been similar. The use of anchorages, the conformance of port visits to established patterns, the use of indigenous port facilities, and the consistency in force composition are all reflections of this similarity. Indeed, there appears to be a significant continuity in Soviet naval operations that has not been given sufficient attention.

This study examines that continuity and the long-range strategies I consider to be of prime importance in the Soviet Navy's operations since 1956. In this way, I hope to generate critical discussion of many of the current assumptions concerning the Soviet Navy.

Bruce W. Watson
Fairfax, Virginia

Acknowledgments

I wish to express my gratitude to several people for their invaluable assistance and support, which made this study possible. Foremost is the late Professor Joseph Schiebel of Georgetown University, whose theory of Soviet strategy is a basic premise of this work and whose support, encouragement, and guidance dominated its scope and thrust. I also wish to thank Professor Paul Holman of Georgetown University for his guidance, advice, and criticism.

I would also like to acknowledge the untiring efforts of my wife, Susan, and to thank her for her constant support, assistance, and encouragement, without which the completion of this work would not have been possible. I am indebted to my brother, Donald, who prepared all the maps that appear on the following pages; to Eugene Grant, who typed all the tables; to my parents, Wallace and Viola Watson, for a lifetime of encouragement, support, and guidance; and to my children, Bruce, Jr., Susan, and Jennifer, whose spontaneous examinations of my drafts and research materials — although unsettling — provided relief from an at-times arduous task. Finally, I would like to acknowledge, with great appreciation, James George, Dale Tahtinen, Gerald Hopple, Ida and Maurice Kramer, and Elizabeth and Louis Colonna for their advice and encouragement over the years.

This book is the culmination of a personal research program that has spanned a period of twelve years and has relied heavily on the assistance of many individuals. My appreciation for interviews goes to Admiral Thomas Moorer, U.S. Navy (Ret.); Admiral Elmo Zumwalt, U.S. Navy (Ret.); and Vice Admiral Gerald Miller, U.S. Navy (Ret.). I am also indebted to Rear Admiral John T. Parker, Rear Admiral John Butts, retired Captains Jack Hilton and Albert Steinbeck, and retired Lieutenant Commander Frank Colonna, all of the U.S. Navy, whose support and encouragement over the last twelve years were indispensable for this study.

B.W.W.

1
The Development and Purpose of the Soviet Navy

Since 1956, the Soviet Union, historically a land power, has been working toward challenging the United States for supremacy of the seas so that today it is one of the world's two leading sea powers — in some respects the leading sea power. Starting from a position of marked naval inferiority and with a gross national product approximately half that of the United States, the Soviets have built fleets of modern surface combatants and submarines and a modern naval air force. The Soviet Navy now operates on all of the world's oceans and major seas. Its ships and aircraft conduct sophisticated training exercises and an impressive port visit program, and the navy has gained access to port facilities in the Third World and has responded to several international crises.

In order to understand the history of Soviet naval operations since 1956 and to evaluate the effectiveness of the navy in fulfilling its assigned roles, it is necessary to examine first why the Soviet leadership built this navy and how it intends to use it.

Why the Navy Was Built

The Soviet Navy was built as a major instrument for attaining four long-range goals: (1) security from external threats and preservation of the ruling elite's unlimited power, (2) enhancement of the country's political position in the world community, (3) projection of Soviet power beyond national borders, and (4) a capability to change the international political system to suit Soviet purposes. Defense and the furtherance of a country's international position are typical national goals, and projecting power is normal for nations aspiring to world leadership. Thus, only the fourth goal is peculiar to the Soviet Union. This goal may embrace atavistic remnants of Leninism, which lost momentum in the post–World War II period but nonetheless has played a role in Soviet postwar strategy.[1]

The four goals were to be achieved through the manipulation of both long- and short-term adversary relationships among nations, some of which were discussed by Lenin as early as 1920.[2] In his speech to the Moscow cadres on December 6, 1920, he noted five antagonisms that would endure for decades. The first three—the United States vs. Japan, the United States vs. Europe, and Europe vs. Germany—were resolved, at least temporarily, by World War II.[3] The fourth was between the colonial powers and their colonies. Although Lenin was less specific concerning this struggle than he was in describing the first three, he implied that conflicts would occur in the colonial empires and that the Soviet Union should stand as defender of the world's oppressed peoples. Dissolution of the colonial empires also would weaken the "imperialist powers" and hasten the socialist revolution. The fifth antagonism, arising out of the hostility between capitalism and communism, was between the Soviet Union and the capitalist world. Lenin intended to downplay this conflict and work to exploit the other four in order to develop sufficient power to confront the United States successfully.[4]

The Nature of the Postwar Antagonisms

The Resolution of Old Issues

Prior to and during World War II, the Soviets used their army to support foreign policy. In Europe, for example, the threat posed by Nazi Germany was land based, and Soviet defense measures were focused on bolstering the army. The navy was little more than a coastal defense force, an adjunct of the army, and it was incapable of projecting significant naval power on the high seas. Although the Soviet Union emerged from World War II as a superpower, it remained preoccupied with the issues of that conflict in the immediate postwar years.

Soviet occupation of Eastern Europe transformed that region into a buffer zone, which precluded the West's using the area to apply strategic pressure to the Soviet Union. The Soviets, however, began using the area as a base from which to exert pressure on Western Europe. The Soviet policy—to forestall consolidation of the European continent by opposing Germany's political and military integration into Western Europe—led to postwar confrontations. But the U.S. decision to remain in Europe and assist in that area's reconstruction produced an Atlantic alliance that fostered consolidation and created a potential threat to the Soviet bloc. By 1954, the Soviets realized that their policy had failed, and in 1955, they normalized relations with West Germany. Defusing the German issue led to a reordering of Soviet priorities, which in turn favored the development of naval power.[5]

In the East, Soviet attention was concentrated on Northeast Asia. The victory of Chinese Communist forces in 1949 had reduced Western influence in the area. The new Chinese ruling elite was organizationally and philosophically closer to the Soviet Union than to the West, and China provided the Soviets with a base they could use to project their power into northeastern Asia, thus facilitating their support of indigenous national liberation movements against the European colonial powers.

To maintain its strategic position in China, the Soviet Union had to prevent Chinese reconciliation with the West. This aim was accomplished by manipulating the animosity between the People's Republic of China and the United States, in which Chinese and U.S. participation in the Korean War played an important role. The policy was successful for 20 years and denied the Chinese the freedom to exercise policy alternatives, thus securing the Soviet strategic position in Asia during this period.[6]

Although World War II shifted the balance of power from Europe to the Soviet Union and the United States, Germany and China remained focal points in the immediate postwar period. By 1954, however, the Soviet leadership was free to turn its attention to new postwar issues.

The Creation of New Issues

Though the Soviet Navy was an adjunct of the army in World War II, historically, there had been a considerable investment in naval development. Indeed, prior to the war, the Soviets had had ambitious naval plans that included construction of aircraft carriers. World War II interrupted these endeavors, but interest in naval construction returned in the postwar Stalinist period. Emphasis was placed on submarines and conventionally armed surface combatants. However, the Soviets were preoccupied with Europe and Northeast Asia and failed to fully appreciate the drastic changes caused by World War II. They failed to recognize that naval weapons and tactics had changed and that a different type of navy was now needed.

Stalin's death in 1953 marked the beginning of a strategic reorientation. One element of that reorientation was Khrushchev's influence on strategy until 1964 after his successful bid for the leadership. Another element was the Soviet realization that the main European and Chinese issues had been resolved, at least temporarily. The Soviets now saw the Third World as a new arena for conflict and the United States as the principal protagonist. Admiral Sergei G. Gorshkov, a proponent of submarines and small missile-armed combatants, was appointed head of the navy, and the Communist Party allotted funds for building a new navy at the Twentieth Party Congress in 1956.

Gorshkov's appointment reflects an integration of naval strategy and revised national aims. The Stalinist shipbuilding programs were halted, many of the large gun-armed surface combatants were scrapped, and the Soviets began to create a new type of navy, one that was more able to compete for influence in the Third World.[7] Two obstacles, however, stood between the Soviet Union and its Third World goals: the geographic isolation

Admiral of the Fleet of the Soviet Union Sergei G. Gorshkov, commander in chief of the Soviet Navy since 1956, is the architect of today's modern Soviet naval forces. (U.S. Navy, Lt. Col. Tiede, USMC)

of the USSR from Third World countries and the military power of the United States.

The Geographic Factor. / Geography had given the Soviet Union tactical advantages while its principal involvements were with Europe and China as both are contiguous to the USSR. Soviet territory provided a secure base, a sanctuary, from which foreign policy offensives, such as the 1939–1940 invasion of Finland and the occupation of the Baltic republics in 1940, could be launched and logistically supported.

For their projected incursions into the Third World, the Soviets needed to extend their traditional sanctuary concept to the high seas. This extension was accomplished by creating secure seaborne "enclaves" — Soviet merchant ships that could deliver arms and supplies to the "progressive" forces of the Third World. These merchant ships, which enjoy the protection of international maritime law, are theoretically inviolate. However, there are definite limits to their inviolability as the Cuban missile crisis and the bombing of Soviet ships in Haiphong Harbor during the Vietnam War have demonstrated. Nevertheless, the seaborne extension of Soviet sovereignty has been usually successful. The Soviets also have stationed naval power close to Third World areas of interest to protect the Soviet supply lines and, under certain conditions, to assist the "progressive" forces in activities compatible with Soviet strategic goals.

U.S. Military Power. / During its incursions into Europe and Asia, the Soviet Union had collided with Germany and, to a much lesser extent, with Japan. The confrontation had involved land-based forces, and geography had made the power of the Soviet Army relevant.

In the postwar U.S.-Soviet superpower relationship, the Soviet Army was not a military threat against U.S. territory, though it did remain a credible threat to U.S. interests in Europe. Furthermore, since the United States was a maritime power of the first order and projected its power through its navy, the Soviet Army was of limited value in blocking potential U.S. naval or air operations that threatened Soviet security. Indeed, Gorshkov has pointed to U.S. naval power as an important reason for the creation of the new Soviet Navy.

> Other pretenders to world domination—the U.S. imperialists—have sprung up to take the place of the smashed fascist Germany. In the last two decades, the policies of U.S. ruling circles have been aimed at organizing aggressive blocs directed against the Soviet Union and other socialist countries.
>
> Under these conditions, the Communist Party and the Soviet government have been compelled to devote much attention and manpower to increasing our state's defense capabilities. The country, by utilizing the advantages of the Soviet socialist system and the latest achievements of science and technology, has been able to produce qualitatively new armed forces in a short time. The navy has developed with all other branches.
>
> In their aggressive plans, the transoceanic imperialists are giving a leading role to their navies. For this reason, we too have been compelled to create a fleet capable of reliably protecting our motherland and guaranteeing its state interests on the seas and oceans.[8]

Gorshkov views U.S. policy in the postwar period as a consistently anti-Soviet "oceanic strategy" with heavy reliance on submarine-launched intercontinental ballistic missiles as the main instruments of "imperialist agression." In addition to orienting its military power against the USSR, the West, according to Gorshkov, has conducted a series of "local wars of imperialism," which includes every application of Western naval power since World War II. In all these encounters, he has averred, Western navies have been the primary vehicle for interjecting Western power, with the U.S. Navy the key to the Western alliance systems. In the Mediterranean, for example, the Sixth Fleet threatened Arab national liberation movements, and in the Pacific, U.S. naval power was used extensively in the Korean and Vietnam wars.[9]

It is true that the United States, through its naval power, has enjoyed many military advantages in the postwar period. Its navy poses a strategic threat to the Soviet Union, achieved initially by deploying aircraft carriers with long-range strike aircraft to waters near the Soviet Union and sustained by *Polaris* ballistic missile submarines and the *Poseidon* and *Trident* programs. Also, the United States enjoys strategic security. Its large numbers of nuclear weapons and delivery systems have effectively deterred a Soviet nuclear attack, and the U.S. sea frontiers and sea lines of communication have been protected by its massive naval power. Finally, because of its navy, the United States has had a significant capability to control and manage external crises, and the U.S. Navy has inhibited Soviet activities in the Third World, thus threatening long-range Soviet goals.

The Tasks of the New Soviet Navy

The U.S.-Soviet adversary relationship dictates that the Soviet Union must have a powerful navy and that this force should serve the four long-range goals mentioned earlier. To fulfill the first, assisting in the nation's strategic defense, an antisubmarine warfare capability has been developed to locate and, if circumstances require it, destroy both Western ballistic missile submarines targeted against the Soviet Union and Western attack submarines that could be directed against Soviet shipping and naval forces. Many classes of submarines and surface combatants and a naval air force have been created, and forces designed to destroy aircraft carriers and impressive coastal defenses have been built to safeguard the sea approaches to the USSR.

Next, the navy must pose a strategic threat against the Western powers, and a nuclear-powered submarine force equipped with ballistic missiles has been created to fulfill this mission. According to Gorshkov, those submarines are the prime reason for the navy's importance, and surface combatants and aircraft have been constructed to protect the submarine force. The navy's nuclear threat is reinforced by an antishipping force composed of submarines, surface combatants, and aircraft, which, if properly deployed, could threaten the security of the Western sea lanes.[10] As a deterrent to a Western use of nuclear weapons, the missile-armed submarines are an important part of the Soviet defensive structure.

The navy also needs to be able to influence the outcome of external crises, and it attempts to achieve this aim by dispatching naval forces to turbulent areas. The U.S. attack aircraft carrier task groups and attack submarines are the primary obstacles to this mission. In response to that element of U.S. seapower, a fleet of cruise missile–equipped submarines, a naval air force to provide reconnaissance and air defense, and a fleet of surface combatants with air defense, antisubmarine warfare, and antisurface warfare capabilities have been built.

Finally, the ability to act effectively in foreign crises, protect external interests, and extend Soviet influence throughout the world requires a true sea projection capability. This means having a navy that is able to make extended deployments to the Indian Ocean, the West African coast, and the Caribbean Sea in order to protect Soviet merchant shipping, exert pressure on selected Third World countries, and engage in military operations against shore targets. In addition, a fleet of efficient auxiliary ships is required to support the deployed forces, and amphibious warfare force is needed to carry Soviet power ashore.[11]

The New Soviet Navy's Targets

The modern Soviet Navy was started in 1956, and its subsequent operations have been directed on the one hand toward both "traditional" leaders and "progressive" factions in the Third World and on the other toward the United States. The navy has helped extend Soviet influence in the Third World by impressing on local leaders a sense of Soviet military superiority. It has maintained a presence in strategic Third World areas, made port visits, and conducted naval exercises, and it has been a primary force in exploiting crises. The Soviets also have provided military equipment to many Third World nations.

These actions have created the impression that the Soviet military is a thoroughly professional organization with vast amounts of superior military hardware. Whether by design or not, Soviet naval power has transmitted a twofold message. "Progressive" forces have been led to believe that the Soviet Union is prepared to support them, and they have been encouraged tacitly to initiate or continue actions aimed at extending socialism. "Traditional" leaders have been warned that socialism (and Soviet influence) is the wave of the future, which they should accept if they wish to stay in power.

So far as the navy is concerned, the Soviets appear to have had a dual approach to the United States: a nominal policy directed toward civilian policymakers, the news media, and the public and an operational policy aimed at U.S. naval personnel. Soviet officials have proclaimed that their navy exists solely for national defense and is designed for defensive operations only. This approach, in conjunction with the Soviets' advocacy of peaceful coexistence and détente, has persuaded large segments of the U.S. Congress, media, and public that the Soviet Navy is no threat to U.S. interests.

The operational policy has been a form of psychological warfare focused on Western naval personnel in general and the U.S. Navy in particular. Harassment and surveillance of U.S. forces afloat and extensive Soviet exercises convey an impression of an aggressive and a professional Soviet Navy. At the same time, U.S. naval analysts have reported large Soviet naval construction programs, increasingly professional operations, an expanding naval presence on the high seas, and a constantly increasing strategic threat from Soviet submarine-launched missiles. The intent of the Soviets may have been to foster an exaggerated perception of Soviet naval might and thus persuade U.S. naval leaders to recommend unwarranted concessions to the USSR.[12]

When the Soviets have not been able to translate their perceived naval threat into reality, they have not committed their forces to action (e.g., the failure of the Soviet Navy to react to the Suez crisis in 1956, the Lebanon crisis in 1958, the Cuban missile crisis in 1962, and the Vietnam War throughout the 1960s and early 1970s). Conversely, when the Soviet naval forces have been employed, they have performed assertively and professionally, giving the impression of an increasing challenge to U.S. naval power.

The Types of Soviet Naval Operations

Restraints on Soviet Naval Operations

In the early years, Soviet naval operations were limited primarily to the nation's sea approaches in the northern Atlantic and Pacific oceans. The Soviet Navy could not sustain operations in the Indian Ocean and the Caribbean Sea until the late 1960s, by which time great numbers of ships had been built. An additional restraint is the U.S. Navy. Whenever the odds against a successful projection of Soviet naval power are too great, Russian ships are not deployed.

A final restraint is the fact that conventional, as opposed to nuclear, naval power is of limited political or military effectiveness against a nation that is not dependent on the sea. Thus, in some cases when Soviet naval power has been used as a political tool to advance Soviet interests in a particular country, it has had to be coordinated with diplomatic, cultural, and social operations, and the navy is vulnerable to reverses in any of these nonmilitary areas. Perhaps the best example of this vulnerability is Egypt, where Soviet political influence and intrigues triggered President Sadat's pursuit of a more independent policy and resulted in the expulsion of the Soviet Navy from Alexandria in April 1976.

Soviet Naval Operations on the High Seas

Naval Presence. / Naval presence is the stationing of ships to maintain a force in a given area on an intermittent or a continuing basis. Developing the capability to sustain such a presence has improved the Soviet position vis-à-vis the United States as it has prevented the U.S. Navy from concentrating its attention on limited areas and has enhanced Soviet influence in Third World nations. This influence has been exerted along a broad front, and all maritime nations have had to adjust their policies accordingly.

Gorshkov demonstrated his appreciation of naval presence in furthering Soviet interests when he stated:

> the role of the navy is not limited to the execution of important missions in armed combat. While representing a formidable force in war, it has always been an instrument of policy of the imperialist states and an important support for diplomacy in peacetime owing to its inherent qualities which permit it to a greater degree than other branches of the armed forces to exert pressure on potential enemies without the direct employment of weaponry.[13]

The effects of naval presence are difficult to quantify and are often underrated. In the absence of any countervailing Western naval power, the deployment of a single combatant or amphibious ship to an area could assume a degree of importance that far outweighed that ship's military capabilities.

Establishing either an intermittent or a constant naval combatant presence has often been the first step toward permanent Soviet naval operations in an area. This presence is at first sustained by Soviet supply ships, which guarantee logistic independence from the coastal nations of the area. That provision for independence implies that the Soviets have anticipated an adverse reaction to the initial interjection of their naval power. Through a complex mixture of political, economic, cultural, social, and military actions, they then attempt to increase their influence. In the naval sphere, this increased influence has been accomplished by port visits. If the visits are successful, the use of port facilities and the conduct of political operations might result.

A principal purpose of Soviet naval presence, then, is to advance Soviet influence in an area that seems ripe for political penetration. The Czechoslovakian arms agreement with Egypt, for example (see Chapter 5, section on "The Aftermath of Suez"), was followed shortly by the establishment of a Mediterranean Squadron, which signaled a major Soviet offensive in the Middle East; the deployment of an Indian Ocean Squadron coincided with great Soviet interest in Somalia, Aden, Iraq, and India in the late

1960s; and the organization of the West African Force in 1970 and its dramatic enlargement in the years 1975–1977 coincided with Soviet-sponsored activity in Guinea and Angola. Inversely, the absence of significant Soviet naval operations along the coasts of South America and in the South Pacific from 1956 through 1980 can be attributed to a lack of Soviet diplomatic, cultural, or economic interest in those areas.

Often the Soviet naval presence has been aimed at individual Third World nations, but the ultimate target has been the United States. In theory, if the Soviets can either neutralize or control an area, the United States would be weakened: strategically, because it might be denied access to the area; diplomatically, because it could lose support in the United Nations and other international organizations; and most important, economically, because U.S. access to raw materials and markets for its goods could be cut off.

Naval Exercise Activity. / In 1956, the Soviet Navy had had little experience operating on the high seas and faced several problems. It was untested in combat and was confronted by the U.S. Navy, which had gained vast experience in modern naval operations in World War II and Korea. The Soviet Navy also had experienced periodic incidents of rebelliousness, demonstrated most vividly in the Kronstadt rebellion of 1921 and more recently in the mutiny of the crew of the *Krivak* guided missile frigate *Storozhevoy* in the Baltic in 1975. Another problem concerned equipment. Although the modern Soviet missile-armed combatants were impressive, the navy still had many ships that were inferior to those of the West through 1970. As a result of these deficiencies, it was imperative that the navy be seen as a professional organization, which would reduce its inherent liabilities.

Naval exercises provide a means of overcoming some of those limitations. Generally, the types of exercise activity—antisubmarine operations in the Norwegian Sea and antisubmarine and antiaircraft carrier warfare exercises in the Mediterranean Sea, for example—are relevant to the combat operations that would be likely in wartime. Thus, such exercises fulfill the navy's mission in three ways. They demonstrate Soviet naval capabilities to the United States and NATO, thus possibly enhancing the perceived threat. They also show the power of the navy to the littoral nations of the Mediterranean Sea and the Atlantic, Pacific, and Indian oceans, perhaps influencing the internal affairs of those nations in ways that will support the Soviet goal of exporting revolution. Finally, the exercises build professionalism.

Naval Patrols and Surveillance. / From 1956 through 1980, Soviet interest in Western naval movements grew. Intelligence collection, for the most part executed proficiently, has conveyed the impression of a tough, professional service determined to analyze Western strengths and weaknesses in order to counter the West successfully in wartime. Strategic patrols, conducted by ballistic missile submarines, have been targeted primarily against the United States with the aim of deterring the United States from using nuclear weapons. Nonstrategic patrols performed by surface ships, submarines, and aircraft have provided an early warning capability.

Soviet maritime surveillance has been conducted by submarines, surface ships, and aircraft. Aircraft have often flown from Third World bases and have carried out general reconnaissance over broad oceanic expanses. Intelligence collection ships have operated near the U.S. ballistic missile submarine bases at Charleston, Holy Loch, Rota, and Guam. U.S. naval ships have been under almost constant surveillance in the Norwegian, Baltic, and Black seas and the Sea of Japan. U.S. aircraft carriers have been monitored by surface combatants and submarines in the eastern Mediterranean Sea.[14]

These reconnaissance and surveillance operations have provided the Soviet Union with timely information on all U.S. naval movements, and they have reinforced the Soviet Navy's image as a powerful, professional organization capable of accomplishing its assigned missions.

Harassment. / Harassment is usually interpreted as operating a ship in deliberate violation of international maritime law to intimidate the crew of another ship. Prior to 1972, both the U.S. and the Soviet navies violated international maritime law. U.S. ships often cut in front of Soviet ships to prevent them from penetrating naval screens and approaching aircraft carriers and other capital ships, but there was no consistent policy of embarrassing or endangering Soviet naval forces. In contrast, Soviet ships so frequently and needlessly violated the rules as to indicate an established policy of harassing Western naval forces in order to demonstrate aggressiveness and professionalism.

The number of incidents of harassment from 1956 to 1972 is not known, but there appears to have been an increase in both the frequency and the severity of such incidents over the years. In 1967, one encounter resulted in the collision of Soviet and U.S. destroyers in the Pacific. There were several near collisions, and some minor contacts apparently occurred. During the Arab-Israeli War of June 1967, Soviet harassment of the Sixth Fleet in the eastern Mediterranean was particularly severe, and it resulted in several near accidents.

Soviet harassment continued until the United States and the Soviet Union signed the Incidents at Sea Agreement in 1972, despite the fact that international maritime law was adequate to govern U.S.-Soviet naval encounters on the high seas. It was only after the signing of this agreement, in which the United States openly admitted that Soviet operations endangered U.S. naval forces (thereby tacitly admitting that the United States was having difficulty coping with Soviet aggressiveness on the high seas), that the Soviets ceased such tactics. If this use of harassment was indeed a form of psychological warfare, then signing the agreement was an unwarranted U.S. concession. U.S. diplomatic officials, who should have grasped the implications of the agreement, interpreted it as another reflection of the easing of relations through détente. Gorshkov furthered this impression by stressing the relationship between the agreement and détente, and he implied that the agreement could lead to further steps "for eliminating the consequences of the Cold War in the open sea."[15] He did not stipulate, however, what price the Soviet Union would exact from the West in order to eliminate such tension.

Interjection of Soviet Naval Power in Crisis Situations. / Prior to 1967, the Soviet Navy was too weak to be used against Western naval power in crisis situations. However, in that year, the USSR began employing its forces for that purpose, and subsequently, there were several times when Soviet ships were stationed near crisis-stricken areas. Ships were sent to the Mediterranean during the June 1967 and the October 1973 Arab-Israeli Wars and the Lebanese Civil War in 1976. In the Atlantic, combatants were sent to Conakry, Guinea, in 1970 and operated in the Gulf of Guinea during the Angolan Civil War in 1975–1976. In the Indian Ocean, this naval option was exercised during the Indo-Pakistani War of 1971, the Arab-Israeli War of 1973, and the Ethiopian-Somali War in 1977 and 1978. In the Pacific, it was used during the Sino-Vietnamese War of 1979. Generally, combatant ships have been sent to inhibit the activities of Western navies operating in an area. The exceptions to that procedure are the Angolan Civil War, the Ethiopian-Somali War, and the Sino-Vietnamese War, when no countervailing Western naval power was present.

Operations in Foreign Ports

Naval Port Visits. / Soviet leaders have emphasized the importance of port visits to Soviet state interests. Beginning in 1965, Gorshkov described such visits in increasing detail as an important part of naval operations. In that year, he stated that naval ships had visited more than 12 European and Middle Eastern nations and that hundreds of thousands of people from those countries had visited Soviet ships and talked with their crews. In 1972, he claimed with some exaggeration that Soviet warships had visited more foreign ports in more nations than had ships of the U.S. Navy, and he stated that in 1973, Soviet ships made port visits to 36 nations. In 1974 and 1975, he implied that the scope of such visits had expanded to include many African and Asian ports and that the purpose of the visits was not only to take on provisions, but also to foster friendly relations with the nations of the world. Elsewhere he indicated that in 1975, Soviet naval ships visited 82 ports in 50 nations and that 80,000 personnel went ashore.[16]

Measuring the value of those port visits is difficult as their influence on the attitudes of individuals in the host countries has varied. However, certain generalities can be drawn concerning the immediate effects, their duration, and the impact of repetitive port visits. The significance and uniqueness of Soviet visits have been partially attributed to their highly controlled nature. The Soviets stylize and orchestrate their stays in port in order to create a favorable impression.

Soviet port visits have been categorized into three types, most precisely defined as the operational visit, the official visit, and the good will visit.[17] The operational visit serves primarily to support fleet operations—i.e., to replenish stores and water and allow for crew rest. More than 80 percent of all Soviet visits have been for operational purposes, and over half of those visits have been made by minor combatants and auxiliary ships. Other operational visits have been conducted by hydrographic survey and research ships and by space support ships. These operational visits have been made to ports throughout the world, although the Soviets have enjoyed special access to several nations, such as Cuba, Syria, and Yugoslavia, with which the USSR has maintained a close relationship.[18]

The official visit, conducted for diplomatic purposes, involves a formal protocol and a schedule of activities and is intended to influence the political and military leadership of the host country. The groups of ships that make official visits usually include a major combatant, since the Soviets believe there is a relationship between the size and sophistication of the visiting Soviet ships and their influence. Handpicked crews are accompanied by protocol and legal specialists. These visits are so highly orchestrated that last-minute schedule changes are often impossible. Since the political and military leadership of the host nation is the primary target, the local embassy personnel often help schedule receptions and appointments.[19]

A good will visit lacks the presence of dignitaries and the diplomatic fanfare of an official visit. Among the purposes of a good will visit are liberty for ships' crews and logistic support.[20]

One could argue that since Soviet port calls are so regimented and the movement of ships' crews so restricted, Soviet visits are less effective than those by the U.S. Navy. For example, U.S. visits guarantee that a large amount of money will be spent in the host port, which has a significant effect on the poorer nations. The restrictions on Soviet crews could be seen as a demonstration of the lack of freedom in Soviet society. During the 1950s and 1960s, however, the Soviets perfected a port visit pattern that emphasizes the professionalism of their navy. The repetition of this format

A Soviet official port visit to Boston, Massachusetts, in 1975 exhibited the major characteristics of a classic Soviet naval port visit, including close coordination with the Soviet embassy, tours by the ships' crews, and visits by foreign dignitaries. Americans toured the *Kanin* guided missile destroyer *Boykiy* (top left); Admiral Holloway inspected Soviet naval personnel (top right); Vice Admiral Stansfield Turner greeted

Rear Admiral Kalinin, the senior Soviet naval officer (bottom left); and Soviet Ambassador Anatoliy Dobrynin and Soviet naval officers met with Massachusetts Governor Michael Dukakis (bottom right). (U.S. Navy, R. Woods)

Although the movements of Soviet naval personnel are controlled while ashore in foreign ports, there is often extensive contact with foreign nationals. During the 1975 visit to Boston, Soviet sailors visited Harvard University (top left) and Plymouth Village (top right), saw a Red Sox baseball game (bottom left), and had lunch in Boston (bottom right). (U.S. Navy, W. B. Coman, top left and bottom right)

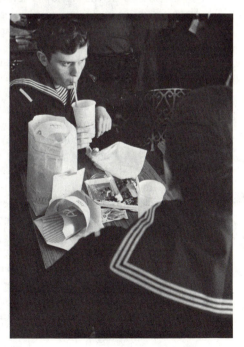

demonstrates their satisfaction with those established techniques, and the expanding scope and success of the program from 1956 through 1980 have attested to its effectiveness.

Naval Access to Port Facilities. / Gorshkov often has pointed out that the Soviet Navy conducts its out-of-area operations without the use of foreign ports. On one occasion, in discussing the value of the naval auxiliary force, he said that Soviet naval operations differed from those of the United States, which rely on a large complex of naval facilities and ports throughout the world. Nonetheless, from 1956 through 1980, the Soviets actively pursued agreements for the use of port facilities and, once acquired, used them with great regularity. At various times during the period, their navy used facilities in Albania, Syria, Egypt, and Yugoslavia in the Mediterranean; Cuba, Sweden, Guinea, and Angola in the Atlantic; Somalia, South Yemen, and Ethiopia in the Indian Ocean; and Vietnam and Singapore in the Pacific.

A general pattern developed. First, the Soviets would visit the ports of several countries in a given area. After assessing the success of these visits, they would focus their attention on one or two nations with the hope of increasing Soviet influence and gaining access to port facilities. That access allowed for support of the fleet, which facilitated but often was not essential to the success of the naval operations. Access also permitted a constant Soviet presence in foreign ports, which provided excellent opportunities to influence a nation's affairs, particularly in the realm of naval operations.[21]

Political Operations. / A political operation is the direct interjection of naval power into an area in order to influence regional events in support of Soviet foreign policy. This seldom requires combat operations; rather, the ships are there to deter actions that would be adverse to Soviet interests. Examples of political operations in the Mediterranean include the frequent presence of ships in Egyptian and Syrian ports in the 1960s and 1970s to prevent Israeli naval operations against those cities. In the Atlantic, the repeated deployment of combatants to the Caribbean may have been intended to inhibit U.S. actions vis-à-vis Cuba and certainly to demonstrate support for Castro's regime. Naval operations in Conakry, Guinea, began in 1970, and the intermittent deployment of *Bear D* reconnaissance aircraft to Conakry probably did much to consolidate the political position of the Guinean government. Naval maneuvers in the Gulf of Guinea in 1976 apparently were designed to guarantee the success of Soviet-sponsored forces in the Angolan Civil War. In the Indian Ocean, naval presence in Somalia, South Yemen, Ethiopia, and Iraq probably aided political operations that were aimed at furthering the USSR's international position. Finally, in the Pacific, the naval presence in Vietnamese ports indicated support for Vietnam in its struggle with China.

In the chapters that follow, the Soviet naval operations in the Atlantic, Pacific, and Indian oceans and the Caribbean and Mediterranean seas are examined in relation to the four principal purposes for which the modern Soviet Navy was created. Particular attention is give to the Soviets' use of their navy as a means of attaining political objectives in areas that would most effectively alter the balance of power by enhancing the Soviet position at the expense of the West—especially the United States. Naval operations in the Mediterranean are emphasized, since it is there that the Soviet Navy has been used for political purposes most often and most aggressively.

Notes

1. Joseph Schiebel, "The USSR in World Affairs: New Tactics, New Strategy," in *The Soviet Union: The Seventies and Beyond,* ed. Bernard Eissenstat (Lexington, Mass.: Lexington Books, 1975), p. 74.

2. Ibid., pp. 74–75. Much of our understanding of the Soviet manipulation of these adversary relationships is the result of the pioneering work of the late Professor Joseph Schiebel. He stated that operationally, the concept meant "the creation of variants of dual power situations or the exploitation where they exist independently, of sets of adversary relationships outside the Soviet Union, which permit the Soviet Union to achieve, in alliance with one party against the other, goals she would either be unable to achieve with her own means, or which could be resisted by the intended victims. In this way, too, whatever goals are pursued or attained are legitimized by the association with an established cause or party" (pp. 74–75).

3. V. I. Lenin, "Speech Delivered at a Meeting of Activists of the Moscow Organization of the RCP(B), December 6, 1920," in *Lenin Collected Works,* vol. 31 (Moscow: Progress Publishers, 1966), pp. 438–439, 442–450. Although Stalin influenced Soviet foreign policy in the 1930s and 1940s, Leninist ideology remains a guiding influence. Lenin's postulations might be viewed as a prism through which the Soviet leadership perceives the international arena.

4. Ibid., pp. 443, 453, and Schiebel, "The USSR in World Affairs," p. 74.

5. Schiebel, "The USSR in World Affairs," pp. 84–88.

6. Ibid., pp. 88–91.

7. A detailed examination of Soviet naval construction is beyond the scope of this work, however, Table 1 presents the naval order of battle as of October 1, 1982.

8. Sergei G. Gorshkov, "On the High Seas and Oceans," *Pravda,* 14 February 1968, p. 3.

9. Sergei G. Gorshkov, "Navies in War and Peace," *Morskoy Sbornik* 12 (1972):19–22.

10. Sergei G. Gorshkov, "On Ocean Watch," *Red Star,* 11 February 1976, p. 2.

11. Sergei G. Gorshkov, "A Most Important Factor of the Navy's Combat Readiness and Combat efficiency," *Tyl i snabzheniye sovetskikh vooruzhennykh sil* 7 (1976):3–9.

12. In January 1978, the U.S. Navy stated that it "is generally considered to have leadership in the areas of carrier aviation, amphibious assault, submarine detection, submarine noise level control, underway replenishment, and nuclear surface ships. The Soviet Navy is generally considered to be leading in: antiship missiles, submarines, small combatant craft, tactical coordination, ocean surveillance, new technology application, shipbuilding initiative, military/naval education, minewarfare, integration of maritime resources and conventional surface ships" (U.S., Department of the Navy, Office of the Chief of Naval Operations, *Understanding Soviet Naval Developments,* 3d ed. [Washington, D.C.: Government Printing Office, 1978], p. 62).

13. Gorshkov, "Navies in War and Peace," 12 (1972):16.

14. Bruce W. Watson and Margurite A. Walton, "Okean-75," *U.S. Naval Institute Proceedings* 102 (July 1976):94, and U.S., Department of the Navy, Office of the Chief of Naval Operations, *Understanding Soviet Naval Developments,* p. 38.

15. Sergei G. Gorshkov, "Ruggedness of Naval Life," *Ogonek* 31 (July 1972):5, and Sergei G. Gorshkov, "For the Security of Navigation on the High Seas," *Izvestiya,* 8 July 1972, p. 4.

16. Sergei G. Gorshkov, "Loyal Sons of the Motherland," *Pravda,* 24 July 1965, p. 2; Gorshkov, "Navies in War and Peace," 12 (1972):21; Sergei G. Gorshkov, "The Maritime Might of the Land of the Soviets," *Pravda,* 28 July 1974, p. 2; Sergei G. Gorshkov, "The Oceanic Guard of the Homeland," *Agitator* 13 (July 1974):32–33; and Sergei G. Gorshkov, Navy Day Speech on Moscow Domestic Television Service, 27 July 1975.

17. Anne M. Kelly, *Port Visits and the "Internationalist Mission" of the Soviet Navy* (Arlington, Va.: Center for Naval Analyses, 1976), pp. 8–19. Kelly defines the three types of visits as business, official good will, and friendly unofficial or courtesy visits. Her classification of the three types of visits is generally accepted and is used in this work. However, the terms *operational, official,* and *good will* are more widely accepted and are used throughout this work.

18. Ibid., pp. 8–9.

19. Ibid., pp. 10–16.

20. Ibid., p. 8.

21. Gorshkov, "A Most Important Factor of the Navy's Combat Readiness and Combat Efficiency," pp. 4–5.

Part 1

The Atlantic Ocean

2

Soviet Naval Operations in the North Atlantic, 1956–1980

The North Atlantic and the Norwegian Sea were the primary operating areas of the Soviet Navy in 1956. That those operations were oriented toward the nation's defense and were only peripherally related to foreign policy objectives demonstrates that defense was the navy's most important mission. Securing the North Atlantic and Norwegian Sea approaches was considered critical to achieving the nation's long-range strategy goals. Without safeguards against U.S. and NATO military strength, all Soviet undertakings in the Third World could be countered by direct attack or the threat of attack on the Soviet Union. Soviet leaders apparently thought of invulnerability from U.S. intervention in terms of security from U.S. maritime and strategic nuclear power, and they consciously developed a twofold response to those threats. First, they built a naval force capable of competing with the West's naval forces. Second, they created a nuclear weapon arsenal as a strategic counterthreat.[1]

Terminology: The Out-of-Area Ship Day

An examination of the Soviet Union's maritime security strategy will more fully define the security problem as the Soviets saw it and the importance of the North Atlantic in this context. However, before discussing this strategy, it is necessary to explain certain terms.

Out-of-area presence, or presence on the high seas, is defined in terms of a basic unit of measurement called the out-of-area ship day. In the case of the USSR, out-of-area encompasses all the world's ocean areas except Soviet inland waterways, coastal waters, and local exercise areas. For example, whenever a Soviet ship travels westward from the North Cape, exits from the Baltic, passes southward through the Turkish straits, leaves the Sea of Japan, or proceeds eastward from the Sea of Okhotsk, the ship is out-of-area. An out-of-area ship day is an entire day or a portion of a day spent by a ship outside local waters.

This basic measurement for computing naval activity on the high seas is valuable for a number of reasons. Analyzing ship-day figures for several consecutive years indicates trends in deployed naval strength. Statistics can be further refined in terms of ship type, geographic area, and nature of activity. Looking at ship days by ship type (surface combatant, amphibious warfare ship, submarine, auxiliary ship) yields a combatant-auxiliary ratio that can provide an insight into the kind and quantity of auxiliary support a navy needs in order to deploy a fleet of combatants. Comparing the surface combatant–submarine ratio is helpful in assessing a nation's motives in a given area. For example, a traditionally high submarine presence in the Atlantic poses both a strategic ballistic missile threat and a significant antishipping threat to the West and is primarily defensive in nature. In contrast, one of several factors accounting for the high surface combatant presence in the Mediterranean is that these ships provide a highly visible manifestation of Soviet power in contrast to the low visibility of submerged submarines. This force composition indicates that the Mediterranean Fleet is assigned a significant political mission in addition to its defense purpose.

The geographical distribution of ship days shows which areas of the world are most important to the Soviet Union at a particular time and, concurrently, the amount of power the navy either is able to deploy or considers necessary in order to fulfill its assigned missions. Computing ship days in terms of ships' activities can help explain the purpose of a given contingent of ships. The major activities of naval ships include transit (movement from one location to another), exercises, patrols and other operations, time at anchor, and port visits.

Soviet Naval Strategy

The keys to the Soviet maritime defensive strategy are the four sea approaches. The first approach—north through the Norwegian Sea, around the North Cape, and south into the Barents Sea—was used for the U.S. and British landings at Archangel and Murmansk in 1918. The second approach is eastward from the North Atlantic into the Baltic. The third is north from the Mediterranean into the Aegean Sea and through the Turkish straits to the Black Sea, a route used by the British in the Crimean War. The final approach is from the Pacific through the Tsushima, Tsugaru, or La Perouse straits and across the Sea of Japan to Soviet ports.

Tables 2 and 3 demonstrate that the Atlantic Ocean has consistently been the scene of much greater out-of-area activity than the Pacific, reflecting the importance of the western approaches. Even the Mediterranean, although it provides access to Black Sea ports and the vital oil fields at Baku, has been considered less vital than the Atlantic approaches, since the maritime threat posed by the Mediterranean-based U.S. Sixth Fleet is not as great a strategic danger to the Soviet Union as the land-based NATO forces. Inversely, Leningrad, Tallinn, Kaliningrad, the other Baltic ports, and the strategic industrial complexes are extremely vulnerable to seaborne attack and thus have received first priority. Also, it is extremely difficult for the navy to sustain operations on the high seas, and it is doubtful whether the Soviets could have amassed a force in the Mediterranean capable of combating the U.S. Sixth Fleet prior to the mid-1960s.

The route through the Norwegian Sea and around North Cape has been important because the primary submarine threat to the United States and NATO has been largely from the Northern Fleet. For these reasons, the initial Soviet operations involving Soviet security were concentrated in the North Atlantic and in the Norwegian and North seas.

The Redistribution of Soviet Naval Power

Positioning the naval forces was the first task in making the maritime approaches to the Soviet Union secure. Map 2.1 shows that the USSR has four geographically suitable locations for the staging areas for the navy's Northern, Baltic, Black Sea, and Pacific Fleets.[2] The Pacific ports are ideal for a fleet that can defend the nation's eastern flank. However, because of the isolation and relatively lesser importance of the East, it initially was assigned a lower priority for naval resources than was the West. The same was true for the Black Sea Fleet.

The Baltic Sea ports are excellent for stationing ships to defend the Soviet coast, as well as Leningrad and other major Soviet ports. The Baltic is not

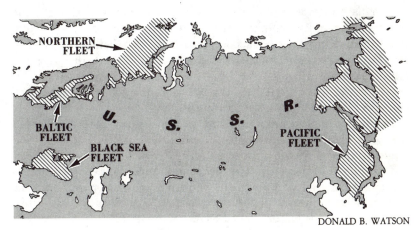

DONALD B. WATSON

MAP 2.1   The four Soviet fleet areas.

well suited as a staging area for deployments to the high seas, however, because Soviet ships exiting to the Atlantic must pass along the potentially hostile German and Danish coasts and through the sea's restricted entrance, where they are extremely vulnerable to detection and attack.

Although the Northern Fleet's coastal waters freeze over during winter, submarines moving from this area to the Atlantic are much less vulnerable to detection than are those leaving the Baltic. As a result, a significant portion of available Soviet sea power has been assigned to the Northern Fleet.

In the early 1950s, most of the navy's surface combatants and submarines were based in the Baltic, a traditional practice during the Lenin and Stalin eras when great importance was attached to Baltic politics and to protecting Leningrad and the western Soviet industrial complexes. However, under Admiral Gorshkov, the Northern Fleet, which previously had had only a few surface ships and about 30 submarines, was reinforced significantly. The Black Sea Fleet was also bolstered, since it was responsible for supporting the Mediterranean operations.[3] The Pacific Fleet has been expanded over the years, and the Baltic Fleet has become primarily a training fleet.

Soviet Naval Operations on the High Seas in the North Atlantic

Ballistic Missile Submarine Deployments

In the 1950s, Soviet ballistic missile submarines posed little strategic threat to the United States. The first were the converted *Zulu* diesel-powered boats, and they were followed by 23 *Golf* submarines in the late 1950s. The diesel-powered *Golfs* have limited underwater endurance and must surface in order to fire their missiles, thus greatly increasing their chances of being detected and destroyed. The *Golfs* carried 3 SS-N-4 *Sark* missiles, which had a range of about 350 nautical miles. In the early 1960s, 8 *Hotel* nuclear-powered ballistic missile submarines were built. Since the *Hotel* was also armed with only 3 SS-N-4s, Soviet submarines remained a limited strategic threat. Mechanical problems further reduced the utility of both the *Golf* and the *Hotel* submarines.

Significant improvements occurred in 1968 when the first *Yankee* nuclear-powered ballistic missile submarine became operational. The *Yankee* carries 16 SS-N-6 missiles, and they can be fired while submerged and have an estimated range of 1,300 nautical miles. The *Yankee* nuclear propulsion plant allows for virtually unlimited underwater endurance. In 1968, *Yankee* submarine patrols began off the U.S. Atlantic coast within missile range of the eastern United States.

Soviet ballistic missile submarine patrols have had their problems. In February 1972, this *Hotel* ballistic missile submarine was disabled while on patrol off New-foundland. A large rescue detachment, including the helicopter cruiser *Leningrad,* escorted the *Hotel* back to the Northern Fleet. (U.S. Navy)

The *Yankee* submarine was a tremendous improvement over the previous classes, but it is vulnerable because it has to cruise in international waters to be within missile range of U.S. targets. This vulnerability was potentially overcome through the construction of the *Delta* submarines, of which 35 were in service in the autumn of 1981. Armed with missiles having an estimated range of more than 4,000 nautical miles, the *Delta* can be within strike range of Boston, New York, Washington, D.C., and other U.S. East Coast and Midwest cities while still in Northern Fleet waters. Admiral Elmo R. Zumwalt, former Chief of U.S. Naval Operations (1970–1974), has observed that the *Delta* is the Soviet equivalent of the U.S. *Trident,* and in deploying it, the Soviets stole an entire construction generation from the United States.[4] Navy spokesmen have described the potential wartime effect of the Soviet ballistic missile submarines.

The Soviet Navy's nuclear-powered *Yankee* ballistic missile submarines began patrolling off the U.S. East Coast in 1968 and off the West Coast in 1971. These patrols were continued throughout the 1970s by the 34 submarines of this class, each designed to carry 16 ballistic missiles. (U.S. Navy)

> From the 1960s onward there has also been a marked increase in submarine activities. These have included both torpedo and cruise missile attack submarines, and strategic missile submarines. The latter has particular significance because of the greatly reduced flight time of submarine-launched ballistic missiles compared to the 30-minute flight time of intercontinental ballistic missiles launched from the Soviet Union, or the several-hour flight time of manned bombers from the Soviet Union if attacking targets in the United States. The Soviet SLBM capability could threaten U.S. bomber bases and Minuteman ICBMs as well as national command centers, possibly destroying bombers and "pinning down" missiles before they could be launched. (SLBMs generally are considered to lack the accuracy to destroy Minuteman ICBMs in underground silos.)[5]

Yankee and *Delta* submarine deployments to the Atlantic have significantly strengthened Soviet maritime security by providing a deterrent to a U.S. nuclear strike and a combat capability that could be employed almost immediately if nuclear war occurred.

The capability of these submarines to defend Soviet territory has been enhanced by surface combatants, attack submarines, hundreds of patrol craft, and numerous amphibious warfare ships, which assure the Soviets use of the Baltic and Norwegian seas while denying those waters to any enemy. A fleet of torpedo-attack submarines totaling approximately 450 units in 1958 could be used to interdict Atlantic shipping lanes in time of war. Submarine forces subsequently have been developed to counter U.S. aircraft carriers and ballistic missile submarines. By 1975, the Soviets had made substantial progress in their ability to challenge the U.S. Navy in the North Atlantic approaches to the Soviet Union.

Naval Presence, Surveillance, and Harassment in the Atlantic

From the end of World War II until 1956, Soviet out-of-area operations consisted of small-scale training exercises, port visits, and infrequent transfers of ships between the Northern and Baltic Fleets. In 1956, the level of out-of-area activity began to increase and included frequent training operations, regular patrols by diesel-powered submarines, and intermittent surveillance of U.S. and NATO naval ships, particularly during exercises. The first deployments of nuclear-powered submarines probably occurred in 1959–1960, and in 1964–1965, Northern Fleet submarines patrolled in the Mediterranean. These early out-of-area operations placed a tremendous burden on the Soviet Navy. Frequent equipment malfunctions required towing disabled ships back to local fleet waters, and several collisions of Soviet naval ships indicated a lack of experience in operations on the high seas.

By 1965, however, the Soviets were operating almost continuously in the Norwegian Sea. Their activities include monitoring all NATO exercises and Western naval ships in the area. An intelligence collection patrol was established off the U.S. East Coast in 1959 to monitor U.S. naval activity, the submarine base at Charleston, and space activity at Cape Kennedy. Patrols were also established in the English Channel, the Norwegian Sea, and later off the *Polaris* submarine facility at Holy Loch, Scotland. A similar patrol off the naval base at Rota, Spain, began to observe U.S. naval movements and all traffic through the Strait of Gibraltar in 1964. These patrols, intermittent at first, gradually have become constant, providing rapid, accurate information on U.S. and allied naval movements.

Table 2 shows that from 1965 until 1971, there was a continuing increase in out-of-area ship days in the Atlantic, rising from 5,400 to 14,800 days. Soviet ships were constantly in the Norwegian Sea, U.S. and allied naval activity was closely monitored, and Soviet actions reflected their increasing influence in the area. Harassment tactics became increasingly common, indicating a growing Soviet aggressiveness.

Naval Exercise Activity

From 1948 until 1956, Soviet out-of-area exercises were infrequent, rarely lasted more than two or three days, and were usually conducted by groups of 2 or 3 surface combatants and submarines. Equipment reliability and crew

Since 1956, the Soviets have become expert in at-sea intelligence collection. The Soviet intelligence collector *Khariton Laptev* (right rear) awaits the test firing of a U.S. *Poseidon* ballistic missile off the coast of Florida in 1970. The USS *Calcaterra* is at left, and the USS *Observation Island* is in the foreground. (U.S. Navy)

competence were low; command and control procedures, unsophisticated. This trend changed in 1957, when the Soviet Navy conducted its first fleet exercise in the Norwegian Sea, with as many as 20 ships participating. Since then, major naval exercises have been more frequent and have involved ships from both the Northern and Baltic Fleets. Generally, these exercises have been held in the spring or autumn and have been oriented toward anti-carrier warfare, with defense of the Soviet Union as the dominant theme. Simulated enemy forces steam northward into the southern Norwegian Sea, where they are intercepted by submarines, aircraft, and surface combatants.

The Okean Exercises. / Soviet exercise activity gradually became more elaborate, culminating in the worldwide *Okean* exercises of 1970 and 1975. Held in the spring of 1970 and 1975 at the end of the Eighth and Ninth Five Year Plans respectively, the exercises demonstrated the navy's progress in each five-year period. They were the most valid indicators of Soviet naval potential in the early and mid-1970s.

Although the exercises were global in scope, the most concentrated exercise play was in the North Atlantic and the Norwegian Sea, so the *Okean* exercises are discussed in this chapter. Because of this concentration and because the exercises are the best indication of the progress the navy made in fulfilling its defense responsibilities, they deserve detailed examination.

Under Gorshkov, who played a major role both in the navy's development and in the evolution of Soviet maritime strategy, the navy was expanded in a deliberate and precise fashion. A prime indicator of this growth, in April 1970, was the Soviet Union's use of more than 200 ships and submarines in an operation, which it called its first worldwide coordinated naval exercise to test and further improve the level of combat skill of the navy and the operations preparedness of the staffs.

The *Okean-70* exercise involved all recently developed weapon systems and ships, including the *Moskva* guided missile helicopter ships, *Kresta* guided missile cruisers, *Kanin* guided missile destroyers, and Il-38/*May* antisubmarine warfare aircraft. Although *Okean-70* was referred to as "coordinated," it was more precisely an effort by the four Soviet fleets to operate separate elements under the control of Moscow. In fact, it was governed by a preplanned exercise scenario.

At the time, *Okean-70* was the largest Soviet naval exercise ever conducted, and it involved antisubmarine and antiaircraft carrier warfare and amphibious landing operations. Soviet Naval Air Force, Air Force, and Long Range Air Force aircraft participated in simultaneous attacks against targets in the Atlantic and the Pacific, demonstrating a Soviet capability to conduct preemptive attacks on U.S. naval forces in both oceans.[6] *Okean-70* also exhibited innovative command and control procedures. U.S. Navy spokesmen said:

> The Soviet Navy has developed advanced conventional communication equipment for the tactical coordination of strike forces. For example, Soviet surface missile ships, missile-armed submarines, and aircraft are able to rapidly exchange targeting information and coordinate strikes against surface ship targets. During the large-scale OKEAN maneuvers of 1970 and 1975, the Soviets were observed to simulate several coordinated attacks against surface ships. In some phases of the multi-ocean exercise, naval bombers simultaneously flew simulated strike missions in both the North Atlantic and western Pacific oceans, with warships in different oceans being attacked at the same moment.

Published Soviet reports describing OKEAN 1970 tell of the Navy Commander-in-Chief being able to communicate with major units anywhere in the world almost instantly, knowing that an order had been executed by a ship in a "matter of minutes," having available in real time the status of air, surface, and underwater situations, including friendly and enemy orders of battle, and being able to monitor "how the [ship] commander conducts a search and judges the effectiveness of his actions."[7]

Following *Okean-70,* the Soviets continued their impressive shipbuilding program. They also concentrated on using space technology, including electronic intelligence and active radar communications satellites, both for more efficient ocean surveillance of enemy forces and for coordinated command of their own naval forces. During the period 1970–1975, the Soviets conducted small exercises that concentrated on one or two themes. Until 1973, these themes centered on antiaircraft carrier warfare and communications; after that date, emphasis inclined toward antisubmarine warfare and ocean surveillance. Each of the exercises combined the most modern ships carrying advanced weapons with innovative tactics, thus enabling the Soviets to test and evaluate new systems and concepts at sea under relatively realistic simulations of combat conditions.

In April 1975, the Soviet Navy conducted another worldwide coordinated exercise. As significant as *Okean-70* had been, it was dwarfed by *Okean-75* in scope, magnitude, and complexity.[8] Scheduling *Okean-75* for the period April 1–27, 1975, probably was related to the end of Ninth Five Year Plan, since in theory the congresses of the Communist Party of the Soviet Union approve the military production cycles on a five-year basis. The Soviet Navy probably was approaching the end of a production cycle and used the exercise to demonstrate how effectively previously allocated funds had been spent.

Approximately 220 ships, submarines, and associated naval units representing all four fleets participated in *Okean-75.* These units were deployed in most of the major oceans and seas and were supported by Soviet aircraft, which flew approximately 700 sorties from bases inside and outside the Soviet Union. As Map 2.2 shows, the major exercise areas included the Norwegian and Barents seas, the North Sea, the northern Atlantic Ocean, the Mediterranean Sea, and the northwestern Pacific Ocean, with the most concentrated activity in the Norwegian Sea and the North Atlantic. The real significance of the exercise was not in the numbers or types of units deployed, but in the missions those units fulfilled.

Okean-75 can be divided into four phases: deployment, reconnaissance, strike, and termination. During the deployment phase, which ran from April 1 to April 14, approximately 100 units were dispatched from all fleet areas to augment the approximately 120 ships and submarines routinely

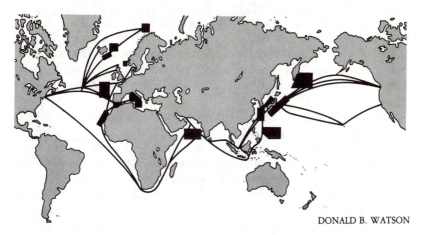

DONALD B. WATSON

MAP 2.2   *Okean-75* exercise areas (black areas) were located across many of the world's major sea lanes of communication. The Soviet Navy demonstrated that it was capable of disrupting commerce on these routes. (Adapted from *U.S. Naval Institute Proceedings.* Copyright 1976, U.S. Naval Institute.)

operating beyond Soviet home waters. The total force eventually formed into 12 groups. In the Atlantic Ocean, Soviet ships were located to the north of the North Cape, northeast of Iceland, in the Greenland-Iceland–United Kingdom gap, southwest of the English Channel, in the North Sea and Baltic Sea approaches, and off the hump of Africa. As the surface and submarine units were maneuvering into exercise positions, Tu-95 *Bear D* long-range reconnaissance aircraft were deployed to Conakry, Guinea, and Havana, Cuba.

The reconnaissance phase, which lasted from April 15 to April 17, involved coordinated reconnaissance by both Soviet reconnaissance and antisubmarine warfare aircraft and Soviet ocean surveillance radar satellites, which were augmented by surface-ship and land-based direction-finding sites. Soviet surveillance aircraft apparently had no prior knowledge of the location of the naval exercise forces, and the surveillance forces were successful in locating and identifying most, if not all, of the "hostile" surface ships before the strike phase began.

The strike phase took place from April 17 to April 19. On April 17–18, coordinated simulated strikes were carried out by both aircraft and antisubmarine warfare combatants, and the enemy's commercial sea lines of communication were interdicted. The prime hostile targets included submarines, carrier task forces, other major surface forces, and convoy formations. After the initial strikes, a simulated rapid escalation of hostilities occurred, apparently culminating in a nuclear warfare exercise on April 19.

The climax of the exercise was on that date, when ballistic missiles were actually launched from submarines in the Barents Sea, witnessed by Admiral Gorshkov and Defense Minister A. A. Grechko. The termination phase, from April 19 until April 27, involved the return of many units to local waters. A Soviet press release on April 27 signaled the formal conclusion of the exercise.

In *Okean-75,* the Soviets demonstrated many innovations. In the past, naval exercises had concentrated on a 1,500 nautical mile "defense perimeter" around the Soviet Union. In *Okean-75,* however, many units operated well beyond that limit. This change apparently denotes an appreciation of changing Western naval capabilities and an understanding that hostile forces must be reduced before they can reach the primary Soviet defense zone. Such tactics significantly increase the potential threat to NATO defensive and convoy operations, thus diminishing the opposition to Soviet land forces in Europe and permitting small concentrations of major Soviet surface units in NATO coastal areas. In this context, developing such craft as the *Nanuchka* missile attack boat and the *Grisha* patrol escort in the 1970s suggests that the Soviets may intend to use these fast, heavily armed, lightweight craft in coastal areas, thus permitting the use of guided missile–equipped destroyers and larger ships in the open seas. Such a development has ominous implications for the navies of the free world.

The ocean surveillance capability demonstrated in *Okean-75* reflects a further refinement of the Soviets' technically advanced systems. Soviet reconnaissance aircraft flew hundreds of missions in the North Atlantic, the Norwegian Sea, and elsewhere. The Soviets also launched several electronic, photographic, and radar reconnaissance satellites before and during the exercise, possibly indicating that aircraft and space reconnaissance activities were coordinated. The two radar satellites were all-weather reconnaissance vehicles and may have been able to detect large surface craft or ships in convoy. When perfected, this system could provide a significant qualitative increase in Soviet surveillance. Although the extent of the surveillance by submarines was undetermined, it can be assumed that they monitored both major U.S. surface units and simulated "hostile" exercise units.

An important capability that became more apparent in *Okean-75* than in *Okean-70* was an ability to coordinate global operational activities, including reconnaissance and surface, submarine, and air attacks. During the strike phase, the Soviets conducted repeated antishipping strikes against simulated task forces in the Atlantic and Pacific oceans and the Norwegian Sea. These strikes were primarily by aircraft, but they probably were supported by, or coordinated with, submarine attacks. The attacks may have been virtually simultaneous in all areas, indicating that the strike forces had excellent locating data and were controlled very effectively.

A higher priority apparently was assigned to coordinated air and submarine attacks on enemy shipping. This shift in emphasis could portend a greater use of Soviet aircraft and submarines against such targets. *Okean-75* proved, at least, that the Soviets have enough aircraft and submarines capable of effective interdiction and that their mission has been expanded to augment an already impressive interdiction capability on the part of the surface combatants.

Since many aircraft equipped to locate and destroy submarines were involved in *Okean-75* — apparently coordinated with surface antisubmarine units — it is clear that a prime area of interest was antisubmarine warfare. This emphasis certainly reflects a Soviet concern with the U.S. ballistic missile submarine threat and probably with Soviet antisubmarine warfare inadequacies.

Protecting Soviet merchant shipping also was emphasized for the first time. In 1975, Soviet sea power included a vast maritime fleet composed of the world's fourth largest merchant marine, the third largest fishing fleet, and the largest ocean research and survey fleet. *Okean-75* included incidents aimed at testing the navy's ability to protect these maritime assets. At least two of the known Soviet task forces had Soviet merchant ships with them, and some of these ships may have sailed from foreign ports to join the Soviet combatants at sea. Also, in the Norwegian Sea, at least seven merchant ships were observed in company with amphibious units, indicating that the Soviets intend to continue using merchant ships as troop carriers and support ships for amphibious operations. Before this exercise, the only merchant ship association with the navy observed beyond home waters had been nonmilitary tanker support of combatants and submarine rescue assistance.

In interdicting the sea lanes of communication between the United States and Europe, the major exercise areas included the eastern North Atlantic, the waters off the hump of Africa, and the Strait of Gibraltar. The purpose of the West Africa operations could have been to simulate a blockade of Mideast oil destined for Western Europe and to intercept U.S. ships arriving to defend that sea route. The Africa patrol could also have represented an attempt to seal the western approaches to Gibraltar.

Exercise units deployed to the Bay of Biscay were in position to deny a convoy resupply of northern Europe through France or England. The Norwegian and North Sea units, although not operating along major sea lines of communication, were well located to cut off the flow of oil from the newly developed fields in those areas. It is particularly significant that, in this era of world dependence on Middle East oil, the Soviets, for the first time, exercised in the primary sea lanes from the Persian Gulf to Europe as well as astride the classic lanes from the United States to Western Europe.

Finally, the Soviet Navy expanded its operating area. The Soviet presence off the west and east coasts of Africa may have had implications other than a denial of the sea lanes of communication to Europe and the United States. The two areas lie generally along an east-west line through North Africa, an area in which there is relatively little U.S. influence and West European influence is declining. The Soviet presence in this area may have been designed to enhance Soviet influence in Africa and to diminish recent inroads by the People's Republic of China, or the Soviets may have decided that their already large and continuously expanding merchant and fishing fleets needed protection in times of both war and peace. This latter explanation also could partially explain Soviet convoy operations in the *Okean-75* exercise area. The Soviets were establishing a firmer presence on the seas in expanding their political and economic base, and the missions of the Soviet Navy may be changing accordingly.

In contrast to *Okean-70, Okean-75* was truly a worldwide exercise in which the capabilities of the most modern ships were tested. Official statements from Soviet leaders indicate that they were pleased with the results of the exercise. Gorshkov, for example, stated:

> Since the XXIV Congress of the CPSU, all our fleets have conducted many and varied exercises. The most complex of these, which took place under the leadership of the Minister of Defense Marshal of the Soviet Union A. Grechko and the Chief of the General Staff General of the Army V. Kulikov, were especially fruitful. They became significant landmarks in raising the level of fleet training. These exercises rightly became the measure of the Navy before the Central Committee of the Communist Party, the Soviet government, and all the people, against which the fleet's readiness and military training are measured. These exercises allowed admirals and officers, and the crews of ships and aircraft, to learn all the complexity and tension, the enormous scope and dynamism, and the multiplicity of forms and methods of modern armed combat at sea. These exercises provided a gauge of our naval tactics. We were able to acquire experience in the direction of forces in a complex combat environment, test the reliability of ships, equipment, means of combat, and show new achievements in the development of naval research.[9]

What can be said of the Soviet Navy based on observation of *Okean-75?* First, it has improved vastly and poses a powerful threat to U.S. naval power. However, the Soviet Navy is not omnipotent. In 1975, the Soviets could bring to bear naval power in one or two areas, but they could not simultaneously control all the world's seas in event of war. They did not have the overwhelming naval superiority that the United States once enjoyed, but they were making impressive progress toward the development of a superior navy.

Okean-75 is significant primarily as an indicator of Soviet naval accomplishments and future trends. Since 1975, the Soviets have produced more sophisticated satellite, air, surface, and submarine detection systems. Two *Kiev* aircraft carriers designed for antisubmarine warfare have been sent to sea. The missions of naval aircraft and submarines have continued to expand and include an increasingly important antishipping mission that could threaten the free and open flow of commerce among the nations of the world. The techniques used to protect Soviet merchant shipping have become more refined with the continued expansion of the Soviet merchant fleet.

In the years after 1975, the Soviet Navy has become more powerful, better directed, and more widely deployed, and it has continued to support Soviet political goals throughout the world and to challenge the navies of the United States and its allies with growing effectiveness.

Naval Port Visits

During the decade from 1956 to 1966, most visits in the Atlantic were to ports of NATO nations (see Tables 4–6 and Map 2.3). Frequently, they were official visits, usually by a few older combatants (see Table 7). The senior officers aboard the ships were usually flag officers, but in some cases they were high-ranking civilians. Norway, Sweden, and the United Kingdom were the nations visited most often. The first visit to France did not occur until 1967. The majority of these visits lasted four to six days, conforming to an established pattern.

The navy's first postwar port calls were to the United Kingdom in 1953. A *Sverdlov* cruiser participated in a review for the coronation of Queen Elizabeth, and another ship called at Portsmouth in the same year. There were no visits to the United Kingdom in 1954, but in 1955, six ships called at Portsmouth. In 1956, the program was expanded to include Denmark, the Netherlands, Norway, and Sweden. Perhaps the most prestigious appearance of 1956 was in May when the cruiser *Ordzhonikidze* and two destroyers with Nikita Khrushchev and Nikolai Bulganin aboard visited Portsmouth. Three ships were at Oslo, Copenhagen, and Gothenberg, and five at Rotterdam.

Thirteen Soviet ships called at Norwegian ports from 1958 through 1966. None appeared in the United Kingdom from 1957 through 1963, but seven ships visited British ports over the next two years. Between 1967 and 1980, France and Ireland were included in the program. Calls to Sweden began in 1954, but most of them were to Gothenberg for ship repair rather than official visits.

In 1973, probably as a reflection of the relaxed Soviet-American atmosphere of détente, Soviet auxiliary ships began calling at U.S. ports.

MAP 2.3   Northern European ports visited by Soviet naval ships from 1953 through 1980.

Baltimore, Philadelphia, and Savannah were visited in 1973 and 1974. In 1975, an exchange of official visits occurred in which two Soviet combatants visited Boston, and U.S. ships sailed to Leningrad. The tightly controlled six-day stay in Boston conformed to the traditional official Soviet pattern.

It appears that particularly in the 1950s, port visits had two aims. The first was a desire to gain recognition. The Soviet Navy was burdened with an extremely modest tradition, having been little more than an adjunct of the

Soviet Army in World War II. The Soviets probably hoped the visits would convey the impression that they had a navy capable of operating on the high seas and of defending the Soviet Union—an appearance that would be of value to Soviet long-range policy. By creating the image of a powerful navy through assertive operations on the high seas and official port visits, the Soviets hoped to gain concessions from the West.

A second likely motivation for the visits was to assuage Western fears concerning the nature of future Soviet naval operations. Since 1917, the Soviet Union sometimes meticulously honored international law but blatantly disregarded the international order at other times, as in the occupation of Eastern Europe after World War II and the suppression of the Hungarian revolution in 1956. Some people in the West felt uneasy about Soviet naval construction in the latter half of the 1950s, and the port visits conveyed the impression that the USSR intended to conduct its naval operations in the traditional manner of maritime nations and with due regard for international law. Intentional or not, this approach proved effective as only a few commentators have questioned whether Soviet naval operations would change if the USSR were permitted to develop a preponderance of power.

Summary

The Soviets first redistributed their naval forces and then used tactical operations such as naval presence, coastal defense, exercises, surveillance, harassment, ballistic missile submarine deployments, and port visits to further the nation's defense by securing the sea approaches in the Baltic and Norwegian seas. Since the Soviet Navy has not been tested under wartime conditions, it is necessary to examine both Western and Soviet naval operations in order to evaluate the USSR's progress in securing its western and northern sea approaches.

Implicit in U.S. naval operations during the 1970s was a de facto concession of Soviet naval hegemony in the White Sea, the Barents Sea, and the Sea of Okhotsk. U.S. naval combatants rarely, if ever, operated in those waters. The U.S. out-of-area ship-day structure also implicitly conceded that the Barents, Baltic, and Black seas and the seas of Okhotsk and Japan were local Soviet exercise areas and that Soviet operations in those areas did not entail an offensive projection of naval power. (The governments of Norway, Sweden, Denmark, West Germany, the United Kingdom, Turkey, Korea, and Japan might take exception to that view.)

In the Baltic, U.S. forces conducted periodic exercises and operations, in part as a demonstration of support for the Baltic NATO nations. However, the U.S. Navy neither operated routinely nor stationed a naval force in the Baltic between 1956 and 1980 in spite of a constantly increasing Soviet naval threat, which effected a shift in the naval balance of power in favor of the USSR.

There were similar trends in U.S. naval operations in the Norwegian Sea. The U.S. Navy operated along the Norwegian coast during NATO exercises, but no U.S. naval force was stationed in the sea, and U.S. naval operations, particularly in the 1970s, implied concessions to Soviet power north of the sea's southern approaches. Admiral Zumwalt, discussing Soviet naval activity in the Norwegian Sea, has noted that the Scandinavian peninsula was behind an advanced naval screen from which the Soviets were working for the "finlandization of Sweden and the swedenization of Norway."[10]

Soviet naval operations, particularly those in *Okean-75*, indicate that short of preemptive nuclear strikes, Soviet defenses of the Northern and Baltic Fleets could be penetrated only with extremely heavy and possibly unacceptable U.S. losses. Thus, in wartime, the West probably would attempt initially to contain Soviet power by interdicting the Baltic approaches and establishing a naval perimeter from Greenland through Iceland and the Shetland Islands to the United Kingdom.

Such operations could lead to a nuclear exchange in which the West would be vulnerable to Soviet *Yankee* and *Delta* ballistic missile submarines, a further guarantee of the security of the Soviet approaches. Indeed, a Western defense perimeter from Greenland to the United Kingdom would be ineffectual against the *Deltas* carrying SS-N-8 and SS-N-18 missiles that could reach U.S. targets from the Norwegian Sea.

From 1956 through 1980, the Soviet Navy made great progress toward guaranteeing the security of the North Atlantic maritime approaches to the Soviet Union. As a result, the USSR has acquired a degree of security that, among other things, has enabled it to conduct foreign policy–oriented operations in the Atlantic region, notably along the West African coast and in the Caribbean Sea.

Notes

1. Schiebel, "The USSR in World Affairs," p. 74, and Sergei G. Gorshkov, "Greeting the Twenty-fifth Congress of the CPSU," *Morskoy Sbornik* 2 (1976):8.

2. The Soviets say that they have four fleets—the Northern, Baltic, Black Sea, and Pacific—and they call their forces in the Indian Ocean and the Mediterranean *eskadras* ("squadrons"). However, because of the size of the Soviet Mediterranean force, the U.S. Navy has referred to it as the Mediterranean Fleet since the early 1970s, and that term is used in this book to refer to that force.

3. Norman Polmar, *Soviet Naval Power: Challenge for the 1970s,* rev. ed. (New York: Crane, Russak and Co., 1974), pp. 64–65.

4. Interview with Admiral Elmo R. Zumwalt, U.S. Navy (Ret.), 22 October 1977, Arlington, Va., and U.S., Department of the Navy, Office of the Chief of Naval Operations, *Understanding Soviet Naval Developments*, p. 17.

5. U.S., Department of the Navy, Office of the Chief of Naval Operations, *Understanding Soviet Naval Developments*, p. 17.

6. Ibid., pp. 21–22.

7. Ibid., p. 39.

8. The *Okean* pattern was broken when, for undetermined reasons, the Soviets failed to conduct the anticipated exercise *Okean-80*. However, the expense of the exercise or Soviet concern for Iran and Afghanistan may have prompted a postponement. In the latter case, it is possible that the Soviets wanted to maintain maximum flexibility in their naval forces by avoiding the training, repair, and upkeep periods that *Okean-80* would have required. Part of this discussion on *Okean-75* previously appeared in Watson and Walton, "Okean-75."

9. Gorshkov, "Greeting the Twenty-fifth Congress of the CPSU," p. 10.

10. Interview with Admiral Zumwalt, 22 October 1977.

3

The Caribbean Sea, 1969–1980

Factors Influencing Soviet Naval Expansion in the Caribbean

As in other ocean areas, the four long-range goals discussed in Chapter 1 have influenced Soviet naval operations in the Caribbean. Indeed, the dual themes of national defense and Communist messianism have prompted all of the Soviet military operations in the area. These endeavors, which began at roughly the same time as those in the Indian Ocean and along the West African coast, are in one respect another manifestation of expanding Soviet naval power on the high seas. In another respect, they are a separate development, owing to three factors: a U.S. strategy that assigns a special value to the Caribbean, an overwhelming U.S. naval superiority in the region, and the Cuban missile crisis of 1962.

U.S. Strategy

In addition to having a navy that can project military power and alliances through which it can influence world affairs, the United States has attached special significance to the Western Hemisphere. Since the declaration of the Monroe Doctrine in 1823, U.S. hegemony in this area has been a basic tenet of U.S. policy. Soviet naval operations in the Caribbean have to be conducted with due consideration for the nature of U.S. military power and strategic concerns.

U.S. Military Power

The power of conventional Soviet naval operations in any given area bears a direct relationship to their distance from the nearest Soviet home fleet. The projection of Soviet naval power into the Caribbean was a formidable task, which, coupled with the proximity of the Caribbean to U.S. East Coast ports and air bases and the U.S. commitment to the Caribbean, dictated several things. Any Soviet naval operations in the area has to have tacit U.S. consent. Also, given the scope and character of Soviet and U.S. naval construction programs, it is reasonable to assume that the U.S. naval hegemony will continue for the next several years, possibly decades. The U.S. ability to defend the Caribbean is recognized, and the fact that the United States is willing to do so was demonstrated in the Cuban missile crisis.

Cuban Missile Crisis

Just as Admiral Gorshkov took over the Soviet Navy in 1956, Fidel Castro began his well-publicized guerrilla war in Cuba, which would open the door of the Western Hemisphere to the Soviets. By early 1961, Castro was in control in Cuba and had aligned his new government with the Communist bloc. In Cuba, the Soviets saw opportunities to advance their long-range strategic goals and offset the power of the United States, which always has threatened to counter Soviet enterprises in the Third World by applying U.S. strategic power directly against the Soviet Union. The unsuccessful U.S.-supported attempt to overthrow Castro in April 1961, in what has become known as the Bay of Pigs operation, probably contributed to the Soviet decision to base medium- and long-range ballistic missiles and *Beagle* strike aircraft in Cuba in 1962. Although the nuclear weapons stored in Cuba gave the Soviets strategic power there, Soviet conventional power was not adequate to defend that strategic outpost. Of the four most likely U.S. reactions—invading Cuba, bombing the missile sites, maintaining a naval blockade, or referring the matter to the United Nations—the United States chose a naval blockade. The Soviets subsequently dismantled and removed the missiles in return for U.S. guarantees not to invade Cuba.

The failure of this initial Soviet intrusion into the Caribbean dictated that when Soviet naval operations were begun in the region in 1969, they would be a part of a cautious and extended program that is aimed at weakening the U.S. position.

Types of Soviet Involvement in the Caribbean Region

The Soviet program in the Caribbean appears to have had two aims. The first—building up Cuba's armed forces to counter a possible U.S. invasion—was fulfilled through arms deliveries and deploying Soviet naval ships and aircraft to the Caribbean. These activities were good propaganda. They showed the Soviets defending a weak and isolated Communist nation from alleged U.S. aggression, and they may have preserved Cuba as a future base of Soviet operations. Support of Castro was linked with the Soviets' second aim: to sufficiently weaken the U.S. resolve, as expressed by President John F. Kennedy, to permit the stationing of Soviet naval power in the Western Hemisphere.

The Soviets used the Cuban port of Mariel to unload strategic missiles and associated equipment in 1962. Notice the missile erector in the lower left corner of the photograph. (U.S. Navy)

Soviet Naval Combatant Deployments to the Caribbean Sea and the Gulf of Mexico

Soviet hydrographic research activity began in the Caribbean in the 1960s and continued throughout the decade, but the results of the Cuban missile crisis, a weak sea projection capability, and other demands on Soviet naval power prevented substantial naval operations in the area for several years. The first Soviet naval deployment to the Caribbean included three surface combatants and three submarines, which remained in the area from July 10 to August 13, 1969 (see Table 9 for a complete summary of Soviet

Once the Soviets agreed to withdraw their offensive missile systems from Cuba, Soviet merchant ships, like the *Vogoles* pictured here, were watched by U.S. ships and aircraft to ensure that the Soviet hardware was returned to the USSR. Note the partially uncovered missile on the foredeck (to facilitate U.S. verification) and the canvas-covered missiles on the afterdeck. (U.S. Navy)

deployments to the Caribbean). This move generated considerable press reaction.[1] There was particular concern over the presence of an *Ugra* submarine tender, which confirmed that submarines were involved in the deployment, which was made with considerable fanfare. Three surface combatants visited Havana from July 20 until July 27. Both Raúl and Fidel Castro boarded the ships while Soviet sailors toured the homes of Ernest Hemingway and José Martí and assisted in cutting sugarcane. Some of the ships also visited Fort-de-France, Martinique (August 5–8), and Bridgetown, Barbados (August 10–12).[2]

A second contingent of combatants was sent to the Caribbean in May–June 1970. Staged in conjunction with the Soviet naval exercise *Okean-70,* the operation involved two surface combatants, three submarines, two logistical ships, and naval aircraft. A pair of Tu-95 *Bear D* aircraft from a Northern Fleet base overflew Soviet ships operating in the Iceland-Faeroes gap and landed in Cuba on April 18. This was the first time Tu-95s had

This *Kresta I* guided missile cruiser, *Admiral Drozd,* operated in the Gulf of Mexico and then visited Cienfuegos and Havana during the second Caribbean deployment in May–June 1970. (U.S. Navy, W. A. Poole)

landed outside the Soviet bloc. Two more *Bear Ds* arrived on April 25, and a third pair on May 13. All the aircraft participated in naval exercises en route to and from Cuba.[3]

Naval combatants were sent again to the Caribbean in September and in November–December 1970. Two aspects of the third deployment suggest that the Soviets were looking toward establishing a more permanent presence in Cuba. First, some of the units remained in the Caribbean until January 1971. Second, the composition of the force was noteworthy. It included a submarine tender capable of supporting submarines for extended periods, a tank landing ship that might have been transporting military equipment, and a tug and several barges that went to Cienfuegos were equipped to handle radioactive material from nuclear-powered submarines.[4]

At the time of these deployments, the United States received information that the Soviets were building a submarine base at Cienfuegos. A four-lane highway between Havana and Cienfuegos, which could have military purposes, was under construction. Also, the *Ugra* submarine tender that arrived in Cienfuegos in September 1970 remained in port after the rest of the surface combatants left, implying that Soviet submarines were still in Cuba. These factors supported the conclusion that the Soviets were building a naval facility so they could stage ballistic missile–equipped nuclear-powered submarines for strategic patrols off the U.S. East Coast. Also substantiating this conclusion was the fact that the extensive construction in Cienfuegos included "barracks, recreational facilities, a water tower, the rehabilitation of

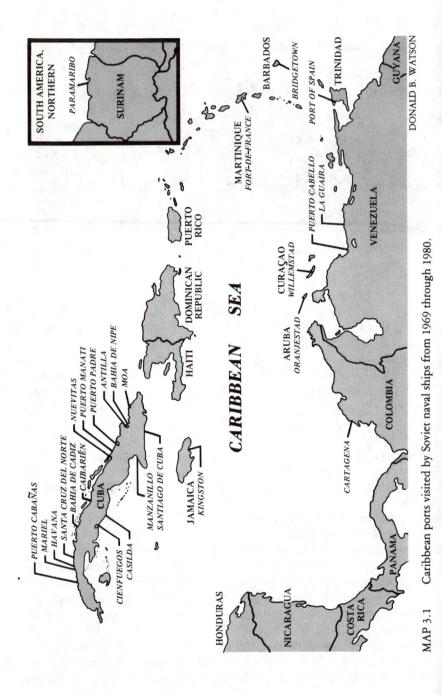

MAP 3.1   Caribbean ports visited by Soviet naval ships from 1969 through 1980.

DONALD B. WATSON

an existing pier, and the laying of moorings for visiting tenders and submarines."[5]

In late September, the United States warned the Soviet Union against building a submarine base, recalling the 1962 understanding that prohibited Soviet strategic arms in Cuba. In November, the U.S. press reported that the Soviets had made an unwritten pledge not to base nuclear submarines, store nuclear weapons, or install naval repair or servicing facilities anywhere in the hemisphere. The first two stipulations worked little hardship on the Soviets, since *Yankee* ballistic missile submarines were now operational and could be staged from the Northern Fleet for patrols off the United States. However, agreeing to the restriction on facilities was a genuine concession, and subsequent Soviet naval activity would be aimed at ameliorating it. For its part, the United States agreed not to invade Cuba and promised not to obstruct periodic Soviet naval visits to the island. This agreement implied de facto U.S. consent to the presence of Soviet naval forces in the Caribbean, a considerable change in the U.S. position within a period of 16 months.[6]

There were more naval deployments to the Caribbean after the tacit understanding with the United States was reached. The time between them varied from approximately 6 weeks to more than 14 months, and time spent in the Caribbean also varied. Generally, two surface combatants and an oiler formed the nucleus of the voyages, while submarines of various classes and assorted auxiliaries participated in many of the operations.

Beginning with the fifth deployment in February 1971 and ending with the eleventh in June 1974, all but one of the forces deployed contained a naval unit that the United States could have interpreted as a Soviet attempt to weaken the effectiveness of the 1970 agreement. In February 1971, the presence of a *November* nuclear-powered attack submarine—a powerful antishipping weapon—evoked little reaction from the United States. The participation of an *Echo* nuclear-powered cruise missile submarine and an *Ugra* submarine tender in May and June 1971 did prompt Senator Strom Thurmond to comment that such naval operations were in violation of the Soviet-U.S. agreement of 1962.[7]

A *Golf* diesel-powered ballistic missile submarine was part of the eighth deployment in the spring of 1972, the first confirmed Soviet strategic weapon system in the Caribbean since the Cuban missile crisis. Two additional forces, both with *Echo II* nuclear-powered cruise missile submarines, operated in the Caribbean during 1972 and 1973 and failed to elicit any strong U.S. reaction. Finally, in May 1974, a *Golf-II* ballistic missile submarine again arrived in Havana, this time as part of the eleventh Soviet combatant group in the Caribbean. The presence of a *Golf* violated the 1962 agreement. Similar action had precipitated the Cuban missile crisis of 1962, but the U.S. reaction in May 1974 is best characterized as one of appeasement; a de facto acceptance of Soviet strategic weapon systems in the Caribbean.

Following this operation, the Soviets curtailed their probing of U.S. defenses, probably in deference to détente. An additional combatant force arrived in 1974, followed by five more in the succeeding three years. The December 1977 deployment of a *Foxtrot* diesel-powered attack submarine, accompanied by two *Krivaks* and an oiler, marked the first time a Soviet submarine had operated in the Caribbean since June 1974. The *Foxtrot,* however, posed less of a threat than the earlier *Golf* and *Echo* submarines. The eighteenth and nineteenth naval deployments to the Caribbean, from March to May 1978 and in the autumn of 1978, respectively, were also relatively unprovocative in composition, although a *Foxtrot* submarine accompanied the latter group. The twentieth deployment, in August 1979 (the last before the end of 1980), lasted only eight days, and the ships did not even visit any Cuban ports. This restraint reflected Soviet concern for the passage of the SALT II treaty, then awaiting Senate action in Washington.

While in the Caribbean, Soviet naval forces have engaged in probing U.S. defenses. For example, several of the forces have penetrated deep into the Gulf of Mexico, sailing westward off the U.S. Gulf Coast before returning to Cuba. Admiral Thomas H. Moorer has expressed concern over the lack of U.S. response to these operations. He feels that such apathy encourages additional, more aggressive Soviet operations. The admiral has noted that a visit by Admiral Gorshkov to Cuba in December 1977 and the extended presence of two *Krivak* guided missile frigates and a *Foxtrot* submarine off the Mississippi Delta in December 1977 and January 1978 both went unreported in the *Washington Post* and the *New York Times*. It was impossible, he said, for the U.S. public to react responsibly if it is not kept informed.[8] The Soviets also have continued to send long-range Tu-95 *Bear D* reconnaissance aircraft to Cuba, and many of them routinely conduct sorties off the southeastern coast of the United States, presumably to monitor U.S. naval and maritime activity.

Two aspects of Soviet activity in the Caribbean are noteworthy. First, the Soviet Navy has challenged traditional U.S. policy in the Caribbean. By varying the composition of the 21 forces sent to that area before mid-1981, the Soviets introduced a wide variety of impressive surface combatants and submarines into the region. *Bear D* operations in the Caribbean have enhanced Soviet reconnaissance and ocean surveillance capabilities, if only intermittently. That these operations have evoked no forceful U.S. opposition supports the conclusion that the Soviets have caused a de facto moderation in traditional U.S. policy.

Second, although the Soviet operations have been assertive, they have been executed conservatively. Except for the deployment of *Golf-II* ballistic missile–equipped submarines in 1972 and 1974, no single Soviet military action was sufficiently blatant to elicit a resolute U.S. response. By moving cautiously and steadily, the Soviets have reduced the U.S. resolve to exclude unfriendly powers from the Western Hemisphere. Admiral Zumwalt expressed a similar sentiment in 1977 when he said: "The purpose of the Soviet naval deployments has been to change the Kennedy-Khrushchev understanding concerning the presence of Soviet nuclear weapons in the Caribbean. Look at the buildup from conventional systems to nuclear propulsion and nuclear weapon systems. Other deployments cover their intentions. They can do now what they want in Cuba; Cuba is a missile base for the Soviets."[9]

Soviet Military Assistance to Cuba

A similar union of caution and assertion has characterized Soviet arms deliveries to Cuba and military construction in that country. Beginning in 1960, the Soviets have supplied Cuba with an impressive list of military equipment, including hundreds of armored fighting vehicles and T-54 and T-55 tanks. Cuba also has received more than 400 helicopters and aircraft, including 250 MiG-15, -17, -19, and -21 fighters and more than 1,200 surface-to-air and surface-to-surface missiles.[10] In 1978, it was reported that the Soviets had delivered MiG-23 *Flogger* aircraft to the Cubans. There is much controversy as to whether they are defensive or offensive variants of the *Flogger* and whether they can carry nuclear weapons. In any event, the aircraft's combat radius enables it to reach many U.S. military facilities, and modifying the aircraft to carry nuclear weapons is relatively simple. Thus, deliveries of the *Flogger* represent a transfer of a potentially offensive strategic system.[11]

Cuba also has received dozens of small combatants and patrol craft, including *Osa* and *Komar* missile-equipped patrol boats, and was the first country to get *Turya* hydrofoil patrol boats.[12] In February 1979, the Soviets delivered a *Foxtrot* diesel-powered attack submarine, then an older *Whiskey* submarine, and several additional *Foxtrots* are scheduled for delivery in the early 1980s.[13] Although a force of five or ten *Foxtrots* would not pose a serious antishipping threat to the United States, the *Foxtrot* and *Flogger* deliveries were a departure from the previous pattern of supplying Cuba with only defensive weapons systems. This deviation could foreshadow additional deliveries of other weapons to enhance the offensive capability of Castro's military forces.

Beyond supplying military hardware, the Soviets have assisted the Cubans in a host of military construction projects, which probably include missile sites, barracks, and port facilities.

Soviet Support of Cuban Operations

Beginning in the early 1970s, Soviet naval combatant forces in the Caribbean occasionally participated in joint Soviet-Cuban naval exercises. This cooperation was expanded in 1975, when Cuba sent forces to fight in the Angolan Civil War. In the ensuing years, the implications of Soviet-Cuban military cooperation in the Third World have become quite evident. Although the Soviets have been unwilling to commit large numbers of their troops to combat in Third World wars, particularly wars of national liberation, they have approved of, supported, and perhaps even prompted Cuban participation in such conflicts. Indeed, it appears that the Cubans have been acting as surrogate forces in support of Soviet foreign policy, thus enabling the Soviets to pursue their goals without facing either accusations of imperialism or direct confrontations with U.S. forces.

Soviet support of the entire Cuban effort in Africa corroborates this view. This support has included arranging for the movement of Cuban troops to Angola in 1975 and 1976, providing an intelligence collection ship off Africa and *Bear D* aircraft over the Atlantic to detect any U.S. reaction to activities in Angola, augmenting a naval force off West Africa to support the Angolan operation, transporting Cuban troops on Soviet passenger ships to Ethiopia for combat in the war between Ethiopia and Somalia, and ordering Soviet General Vasiliy Petrov and Soviet military personnel to Ethiopia to command the Cuban forces.[14] The Soviets have also provided logistic support for the Cuban operations in Africa. Finally, Soviet Air Force personnel were sent to Cuba in 1978, which freed Cuban pilots for duty in Ethiopia.[15] These Soviet operations point up the close military cooperation between the two nations.

The Soviet Military Presence in Cuba

Although Soviet Army matters are beyond the scope of this book, the presence of Soviet Army and Air Force personnel in Cuba cannot be ignored. In addition to Soviet pilots flying air defense missions over Cuba, Soviet Army personnel may have been stationed on the island since the mid-1960s, operating as advisers to the Cuban military. In August 1979, Senator Frank Church of Idaho announced that there was a Soviet brigade of from 2,300 to 3,000 personnel stationed on the island. Subsequent reports have indicated that the troops have been there for at least eight years and that U.S. intelligence has only recently concluded that it was an organized force.[16] Speculation concerning the purpose of the troops has ranged from protecting a Soviet electronic listening facility to training Cuban troops.

The effects of Church's disclosure were far reaching. President Carter's credibility was weakened as he tried to minimize the brigade's effect on SALT II ratification. He failed, since many congressional leaders immediately linked ratification with troop withdrawal. This issue delayed congressional consideration until 1980, when the Soviet invasion of Afghanistan critically weakened remaining U.S. support for the treaty and détente. Also, the issue altered the U.S. position concerning the Monroe Doctrine. The Soviets, in subsequent negotiations, refused to withdraw their troops, and it appears that President Carter modified the traditional U.S. policy by not demanding withdrawal. Finally, although the United States formed the Caribbean Contingency Joint Task Force and conducted amphibious maneuvers in Guantanamo Bay, those basically political maneuvers did nothing to alter the situation.

The Purpose of the Cienfuegos Naval Facility

The Soviet-Cuban relationship has been sufficiently cordial for the Soviets to use the Cienfuegos naval facilities in support of their naval operations in the Caribbean. Whether they intend to use Cienfuegos as a base for extensive naval operations in the area, or whether development of the port is merely another aspect of Soviet military aid, is debatable. There is evidence to support both views.

Factors Supporting the Claim That the Base Is for Soviet Use. / Use of foreign port facilities has become a common characteristic of Soviet naval operations. In 1980, ports in Syria, Yugoslavia, Guinea, Angola, Ethiopia, South Yemen, and Vietnam composed the Soviets' forward naval support structure, and the use of Cienfuegos would be a logical extension of this network.

The Soviets would need a facility if they intend to increase the tempo of their naval operations in the Caribbean. Again, similar requirements in other ocean areas has led to the use of foreign ports for operational support, although in 1980, the Soviets controlled none of those facilities. Port access has been a crucial factor governing the scale of Soviet naval activity in other ocean areas. Indeed, the force level of the Mediterranean Fleet was probably artificially high in the years following the June 1967 Arab-Israeli War because of access to Alexandria, Egypt, and Tartus, Syria. Likewise, the scale of the Indian Ocean Squadron's operations would have been difficult to sustain without access to Berbera, Somalia, and later, South Yemeni and Ethiopian ports. In the Atlantic, the presence along West Africa during the Angolan Civil War might not have been as large if the Soviets had not been able to use Conakry, Guinea, as a port facility.

In the future the messianism of Soviet long-range goals might prompt a more assertive foreign policy aimed at increasing Soviet influence in Latin

America. If traditional patterns prevail, the Soviet Navy could be expected to provide security for such ventures. An adequate naval presence would not be possible without extensive logistic support, so the Soviets probably would rely heavily on indigenous port facilities.

Another factor is that the Soviets have made a tremendous financial investment in Cuba, including economic and military aid, and it is reasonable to expect them to capitalize on those expenditures. Soviet actions in other areas indicate that port access has been considered a reasonable return for investments that were much smaller than those in Cuba. The Soviets could have been expected to use Cuban naval facilities more than they did up to 1981, but other issues, not related to the Soviet-Cuban relationship, may have delayed the expected usage. Those issues probably pertained to U.S. policy in the Caribbean and to Soviet commitments in other parts of the world.

Finally, port visits by Soviet submarines might indicate that they wanted access to Cuban facilities. Ms. Anne Kelly, formerly of the Center for Naval Analyses and an expert on port visits, has demonstrated that the USSR has used submarines as political vehicles. She maintains that their inclusion in port visits is a manifestation of Soviet plans for access to indigenous support facilities. Kelly has noted that the Soviets did achieve port access in 40 percent of the Mediterranean nations that were visited by Soviet submarines from 1965 to 1973.[17] If port access is among their motives, there could be a greater use of Cienfuegos by Soviet submarines.

Factors Supporting the Claim That the Base Is for Cuban Use. / The Cubans were receiving Soviet submarines in the late 1970s but did not have adequate facilities to support them. The new base could be no more than the submarine support element of a comprehensive Soviet military aid project. The Soviets have underwritten military and civilian construction projects of greater magnitude as part of their foreign assistance to other countries, and those endeavors have not been certain indicators of future support for Soviet naval operations. Indeed, on several occasions, the USSR has assisted in building or improving facilities of great potential value to its naval operations and subsequently has not used those installations.

Based on Soviet performance in other areas, it can be concluded that the transfer of submarines to Cuba involved no firm commitment for Soviet access to Cienfuegos. For example, although *Foxtrots* have been exported to Libya and India, neither country has permitted the Soviet Navy to use its naval facilities. Further, the Soviets do not need access to Cuban repair facilities to support their current surface combatant and submarine operations in the Caribbean. The logistic requirements for those relatively low levels of activity are easily handled through standard support procedures. In those instances when unexpected equipment failures might occur, the

Soviets would certainly have access to Cuban ports in order to make repairs, but such random difficulties would not justify the cost of maintaining a large naval base. Finally, and perhaps most significant, an extensive Soviet use of Cuban facilities would be so provocative that it probably would elicit strong U.S. opposition.

Thus, in 1980, two conclusions appeared valid. First, the Soviets do not immediately intend to use Cienfuegos to stage submarines for extensive operations in the Caribbean Sea and the western Atlantic. Such an act would contrast starkly with the cautious approach that has been characteristic of Soviet Caribbean operations. Second, those operations were still evolving in 1980, a reflection of Soviet hopes to play a more influential role in the Western Hemisphere. If circumstances become more favorable to the Soviet Union's Western Hemispheric aspirations, greater naval activity in the Caribbean should be expected in the 1980s. This activity probably would include use of a support facility, possibly Cienfuegos.

Looking into the 1980s, three factors of overriding importance emerge. First, the Caribbean, indeed the Western Hemisphere, is a logical area for future Soviet undertakings. Another factor is that commitments in other regions appear to have retarded the Soviet Caribbean operations. Whether Soviet ventures in Africa either fail or succeed, the Soviets might logically pursue their ideological and defense-related goals in the Western Hemisphere. The final factor is the U.S. resolve to oppose Soviet penetration of the Western Hemisphere. Without access to a naval base, it would be difficult for the Soviet Navy to conduct operations in the Caribbean equal to those it has staged in other ocean areas, and without naval power, Soviet policy would be far less assertive. The U.S. position on Soviet penetration of the Western Hemisphere is defined in the Monroe Doctrine and the Kennedy-Khrushchev understanding of 1962. A continuation of the resolve expressed in those documents could drastically affect the future of all nations in the hemisphere.

Summary

Based on events from 1962 through 1980, it is expected that there will be future Soviet combatant deployments to the Caribbean and the foreign policy goals that have governed Soviet actions in the Caribbean through the 1970s will continue to do so in the early 1980s. Because of the remoteness of Latin America from the Soviet Union, the special significance the United States bestows on outside interference in the Western Hemisphere, and the relative proximity of the Caribbean to the United States and U.S. military power, the Soviets probably will be content to probe U.S. defenses and look for additional concessions. Therefore, it is unlikely that the Soviets will introduce strategic weapon systems in Cuba for several years. Rather, Cienfuegos might be used to stage and support Soviet naval forces that would operate routinely and constantly in the Caribbean and along both coasts of Latin America, which might be how U.S. resolve is to be tested. If the Soviets do not so alarm the United States that the United States demands a cessation of all Soviet naval activity, this naval presence may be gradually accepted as routine. That presence would then guarantee the USSR greater influence in any Latin American affairs in which it wished to participate.

Notes

1. Interview with Admiral Zumwalt, 22 October 1977, and James T. Theberge, *Russia in the Caribbean: Part II, A Special Report* (Washington, D.C.: Center for Strategic and International Studies, Georgetown University, 1973), pp. 100, 103, 106.

2. Theberge, *Russia in the Caribbean*, pp. 99, 106; "Soviet Warships Anchor 75 Miles Off Key West," *New York Times*, 15 July 1969, p. 77; "Seven Soviet Warships Arrive for Week's Visit in Cuba," *New York Times*, 21 July 1969, p. 19; "Showing the Soviet Flag," *New York Times*, 26 July 1969, p. 2; "Castro Says Cuba Is Open to Soviet," *New York Times*, 27 July 1969, p. 19; and "Soviet Fleet Heads for Gulf," *New York Times*, 29 July 1969, p. 74.

3. Theberge, *Russia in the Caribbean*, p. 106.

4. Ibid., pp. 108, 110, 113, and Robert M. Smith, "U.S. Warns Soviet Not to Build Base for Subs in Cuba," *New York Times*, 26 September 1970, pp. 1, 8.

5. Barry M. Blechman and Stephanie E. Levinson, "Soviet Submarine Visits to Cuba," *United States Naval Institute Proceedings* 101:9 (September 1975):33.

6. Ibid.; Robert M. Smith, "U.S. Warns Soviet"; Tad Szulc, "White House Charge on Cuba Puzzles U.S. Officials," *New York Times*, 30 September 1970, p. 2; Neil Sheehan, "U.S. Sees Gain in Nuclear Submarine Operations Off East Coast," *New York Times*, 4 October 1970, p. 23; Benjamin Welles, "U.S. Now Dubious on Cuba Sub Base," *New York Times*, 14 October 1970, pp. 1, 4; "Soviet Reported to Yield on Cuba," *New York Times*, 19 October 1970, p. 9; Benjamin Welles, "Soviet's Removal of Vessel in Cuba Is Awaited by U.S.," *New York Times*, 15 November 1970, pp. 1, 22; Benjamin Welles, "U.S. Officials Say Soviet Has Given Assurances That Nuclear Arms Will Be Kept Out of Hemisphere," *New York Times*, 18 November 1970, p. 11; and "Three Soviet Vessels Begin 17-Day Cuba Visit Tomorrow," *New York Times*, 6 December 1970, p. 5. The panelists of a Georgetown University–sponsored conference in 1971 supported this position concerning Cienfuegos. Noting that "for all essential purposes, Cienfuegos is now a Holy Loch" (p. 25), they observed:

> The operation of Soviet ballistic missile submarines in or from Cuba would not alter the strategic balance in any fundamental way. It would, however, give Moscow certain military advantages that it does not now enjoy such as having more strategic submarines

on station, a shorter warning time in the event of nuclear war, and an approach from the south where U.S. defenses are weakest. But in an era of peaceful coexistence it is not the effect on the strategic balance posed by Soviet ballistic missiles based on Cuba that should be the primary concern of U.S. policymakers.

The strategic balance should not be allowed to mesmerize us and lead us to dismiss a Soviet nuclear presence in the Caribbean as of no real consequence because it does not affect the balance. The United States should resist Soviet efforts to establish a permanent Soviet naval force in the Caribbean or operate strategic submarines in or from Cuba because of the unfavorable political and psychological repercussions this could have. It could have a dangerous impact on U.S. prestige and Soviet perceptions of Washington's determination to oppose encroachments not only in the Caribbean but in other areas as well. [*Russia in the Caribbean: Part I, Panelists' Findings, Recommendations, and Comments* (Washington, D.C.: Center for Strategic and International Studies, Georgetown University, 1973), p. 8.]

7. "Harriman Assails Nixon on Arms Race," *New York Times,* 10 August 1971, p. 21.

8. Interview with Admiral Thomas H. Moorer, U.S. Navy (Ret.), Washington, D.C., 9 January 1978.

9. Interview with Admiral Zumwalt, 22 October 1977.

10. Stockholm International Peace Research Institute, *The Arms Trade Registers: The Arms Trade with the Third World* (Cambridge, Mass.: M.I.T. Press, 1975), pp. 95–96.

11. G. Paul Holman as cited in "Cuban MiG May Be Attack Plane," *Baltimore Sun,* 1 November 1978, p. A2.

12. Stockholm International Peace Research Institute, *The Arms Trade Registers,* p. 96.

13. "Soviets Reported Building Submarine Base in Cuba," *Aerospace Daily,* 3 April 1979, p. 166; "Russian Ships Cross Frigate's Firing Line," *Washington Star,* 13 April 1979, p. A10; and "Russians Give Cuba Its Second Submarine," *Washington Star,* 26 April 1979, p. A7.

14. "More Cubans Reported on Way," *New York Times,* 8 February 1978, p. A5; and Graham Hovey, "Tough Job for Cuba in Eritrea Seen," *New York Times,* 2 April 1978, p. 7.

15. "Sadat Says Soviet Pilots Are Flying for Ethiopia in Fighting with Somalia," *New York Times,* 7 February 1978, p. 4; "More Cubans Reported on Way," p. A5; Graham Hovey, "Soviet Assures U.S. Ethiopians Will Stop at Somalia's Border," *New York Times,* 11 February 1978, pp. 1, 3; "Somalis Abandoning Northern Ogaden," *New York Times,* 9 March 1978, p. A4; "Cubans Said to Fight in Eritrea," *New York Times,* 17 March 1978, p. A7; "Ethiopia Says It Now Holds Entire Ogaden Region," *New York Times,* 25 March 1978, p. 4; and "Somalis Say They Killed 1000 in Ogaden Battles," *New York Times,* 16 April 1978, p. 8.

16. "Senator Church Charges Moscow Has a Brigade of Troops in Cuba," *New York Times,* 31 August 1979, p. A2, and David Binder, "Data Long Implied Soviet Units in Cuba," *New York Times,* 6 September 1979, p. A7.

17. Kelly, *Port Visits,* pp. 23–27.

4

West Africa, 1970–1980

Soviet naval operations on the West Coast of Africa, which began in 1970, were the second component of a two-pronged naval advance along the Atlantic and Indian Ocean coasts of the continent. Beginning with a foothold in Guinea, and six years later in Angola, Soviet influence threatened to expand still further into other nations bordering the Gulf of Guinea.

Influence in West Africa has been of great value to the Soviet Union. From Guinea, they have been able to supply, support, and encourage insurgent movements in other parts of Africa. By the end of 1976, these efforts included protecting convoys of Cuban combat troops en route to Angola. The continued expansion of Soviet influence, primarily through supporting African national liberation movements, increased the likelihood of other nations' creating socialist systems, possibly conforming to the Soviet model. Also the West African ports are near the sea lanes from the Persian Gulf to Europe and the United States and are ideally located for staging antishipping operations along those routes.

From 1971 through 1980, the navy's West African contingent provided security for Soviet political operations in West Africa and ensured the safety of Soviet merchant ships and arms carriers operating along the West African coast. The navy also supported the pro-Soviet Guinean government, conducted port visits along the West African littoral, and assisted Communist insurgent factions during the Angolan Civil War. By staging long-range reconnaissance aircraft from Guinean airfields, the Soviets vastly increased their reconnaissance and intelligence collection capabilities in the Atlantic.

A Chronology of the Soviet Naval Presence in Guinea

The Soviet Union's first opportunity to gain influence in Guinea came in 1958, when the nation became independent of France and Akmed Sékou Touré was declared president. Touré's government attempted sweeping social and political reforms that were intended to move the country toward socialism. From 1958 until 1970, although the USSR and Eastern European countries provided military and economic assistance, Soviet influence was limited. The Soviet-Guinean relationship fluctuated and even resulted in the expulsion of the Soviet ambassador on two occasions, in 1961 and 1969. However, a landmark in Soviet-Guinean affairs occurred in 1970 when an anti-Touré attack on Guinea was staged from Portuguese Guinea. Shortly after this assault, Soviet naval ships arrived at Conakry, presumably at Touré's request.

This naval presence became constant and was an asset to Soviet policy. The force generally included a destroyer or amphibious ship and always an oiler, which provided logistic support to the combatant. The absence of submarines in the force signifies that its purpose was primarily political.

The first ships were sent to Guinea shortly after and presumably in response to the Portuguese-inspired commando raid. Their initial purpose was coastal defense. However, the threat diminished significantly when Portuguese Guinea became the independent nation of Guinea-Bissau. It is therefore noteworthy that the naval deployments to Guinea continued, and the naval presence has assumed an importance to the Soviets that transcends its original purpose. The importance of Guinea to Soviet West African operations is reflected in port visits to Guinea's primary port of Conakry, the most frequently visited Atlantic Ocean port from 1956 through 1980 (see Tables 4–8 for a complete chronology of Soviet visits to Atlantic ports). As time passed, the Soviet presence in West Africa assumed a larger share of Soviet naval operations in the Atlantic. By 1974, if transit times to and from the area are added to the time the ships actually spent on patrol, West African operations accounted for between one-fourth and one-third of all Soviet naval operations in the Atlantic.

The Benefits of the West African Patrol for the Soviet Union

The Soviet naval presence in West Africa provided a foothold for other operations in the region. For instance, the majority of the Soviet naval visits to other ports in the region were staged from Conakry. However, the true significance of this position derives from the strategic value of Africa: the continent's position vis-à-vis the Atlantic sea lanes of communication, its abundant supplies of raw materials, and its largely uneducated masses who were potential converts to communism through national liberation movements.

Location. / Perhaps the most important advantage the Soviets have enjoyed from their strategic position in Conakry is the ability to stage long-range reconnaissance aircraft from Guinean facilities. The concurrent staging of Tu-95 *Bear D* naval aircraft from Conakry, Havana, and Olenegorsk

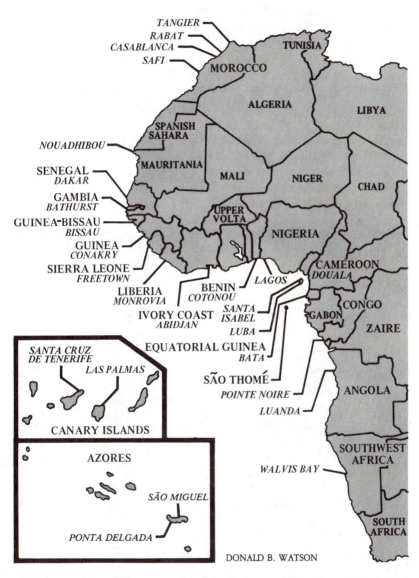

MAP 4.1   West African ports visited by Soviet naval ships from 1958 through 1980.

in the northern Soviet Union has given the Soviets an assured capability. Also, aircraft staged from Conakry can reconnoiter the entire West African littoral. Such a base would prove invaluable in collecting intelligence concerning enemy forces, particularly those of South Africa, in any future African civil wars. Supplying this intelligence to national liberation movements could assure insurgent victories in such conflicts. Thus, access to the airfield at Conakry not only has strategic importance to the Soviet Union in the contexts of defense and its position in the international balance of power, but it also has considerable political value for the execution of Soviet foreign policy.

Finally, access to Conakry has put the Soviets close to the sea lanes leading from the Persian Gulf to Europe and the United States. By the end of 1980, the Soviet Union also had good relations with Benin, Angola, Mozambique, South Yemen, and Ethiopia. All of these nations have radically oriented governments, and all are close to the sea lanes used by ships carrying oil from

Soviet naval air access to Cuban and African bases enables the Soviet Navy to acquire excellent maritime intelligence in the Atlantic. A Soviet Tu-95 *Bear D* reconnaissance aircraft is intercepted by an F-4J *Phantom II* fighter as it approaches the USS *Franklin D. Roosevelt* in the Atlantic in 1973. (U.S. Navy, B. D. Little)

the Persian Gulf to Europe. Not only could Soviet naval forces operating from their ports threaten the Western economies, but the nascent powers of these nations create an additional threat as operations similar to the *Mayaguez* incident could be staged from any of them. Many European nations and possibly the United States would have difficulty stopping such operations if they were supported by a strong Soviet naval force. In 1980, the Western countries showed a lamentable lack of concern for the threat that the Soviet naval force off West Africa poses against their maritime commerce.

National Liberation Movements. / There are abundant examples of Soviet attempts to overthrow existing governments by staging military forces from sanctuaries, which are usually adjacent to the victim nation. Guinea evidently has served as a forward sanctuary from which African insurgent movements could be supplied. In the early 1970s, the Soviets apparently supported insurgent operations in Portuguese Guinea from Conakry. Later, the Soviets used Conakry as the primary staging area for ships sent into the Gulf of Guinea during the Angolan Civil War. There is evidence that the Soviets were attempting to establish a permanent base in Guinea. In 1976, Drew Middleton reported in the *New York Times* that the Soviets had offered to build a naval facility for the Guinean Navy on Tamara Island near Conakry. The proposed agreement stipulated that the USSR could retain a part of the facility for its own use. Middleton noted that Touré was delaying a decision, possibly not wanting a greater Soviet naval presence in Conakry.[1] Although the Soviets were not allowed to establish the base on Tamara Island, they have such free access to Conakry that it has served as a de facto Soviet base. This, in turn, has important foreign policy implications, since it means that Conakry could serve as a foothold for the expansion of Soviet influence in Africa.

The Soviet Role in the Angolan Civil War

Soviet operations related to Angola were expanded in the early 1970s with seaborne deliveries of arms to the Popular Movement for the Liberation of Angola (MPLA). These arms were unloaded in Tanzanian and Congolese ports and then moved overland to the MPLA forces. Later, when the MPLA occupied Angolan coastal ports, the arms were shipped directly to Angola. The tempo of such deliveries increased considerably in late 1975 and involved Soviet, East European, and Cuban merchant ships.[2] In June 1975, Holden Roberto, president of the opposing Angolan National Liberation Front (FNLA), stated that the Soviet Union was supplying the MPLA with tanks, guided missiles, and artillery.[3] These seaborne deliveries were so crucial to the war's outcome that the FNLA attempted to occupy MPLA-held

Soviet passenger ships, like the *Odessa,* were used to transport Cuban troops to Angola and Ethiopia and were elements of extensive Soviet assistance to friendly forces in those two nations. (Photographer unknown)

Angolan coastal cities in order to stop the deliveries. The loss of Lobito by Roberto's forces in August 1975 was a major setback.[4]

Because of these arms deliveries, the intense fighting in Angola, and possibly concern for the safety of the Soviet arms carriers, the USSR strengthened its naval presence in West Africa. The augmented force generally consisted of seven ships—a *Kresta II* guided missile cruiser, a *Kotlin* guided missile destroyer, an *Alligator* tank landing ship, a *Juliett* cruise missile submarine, an intelligence collector, and two oilers. The surface combatants were staged from Conakry into the Gulf of Guinea for operations off the Angolan coast. Beyond patrolling to protect the arms carriers, the navy actively assisted MPLA forces fighting in Angola, thereby demonstrating an assertiveness heretofore unseen in Soviet crisis responses. Specifically, on February 11 and 12, 1976, while Soviet ships were operating off the Angolan coast, the Angolan press reported that Soviet combatants had shelled Holden Roberto's FNLA forces in the ports of Lobito and Benguela. Although these reports were unsubstantiated, there is some evidence to support their validity. The *Kresta II* cruiser, *Admiral Makarov,* was in the vicinity of those cities and, in the absence of any countervailing naval power, could certainly have conducted the operations with minimum risk to the ship and crew.[5]

A similar incident had been reported earlier. On February 10 and 11, three Soviet-supplied landing craft were reported to have shelled the port of Moçâmedes for two days before several hundred Cuban soldiers were landed at or near there. Although the nationality of the crews was uncertain, the MPLA reportedly had not had the craft long enough to be proficient in their use, thus implying that the crews were Soviet.[6] If the Soviets did in fact participate in the attacks, those operations were among the most aggressive and provocative uses of Soviet naval power in defense of a client. It is noteworthy that the Soviet commitment to Angola, which according to President Ford had involved financial expenditures in the neighborhood of $200 million and according to Admiral Moorer had included transporting more than 15,000 Cuban troops to Africa, justified in Soviet eyes the minimal risks of such assertive operations.[7]

In addition to these naval operations, the Soviets conducted a comprehensive reconnaissance program. Tu-95 *Bear D* long-range reconnaissance aircraft operated from bases in Cuba and Conakry and conducted reconnaissance over both the Atlantic Ocean and the Gulf of Guinea, and an intelligence collection ship was stationed in the mid-Atlantic for early warning of any U.S. naval reaction to the war. These reconnaissance operations provided the Soviets with accurate and complete information on both U.S. naval activity and African developments pertaining to the Angolan Civil War.

Although the Soviet force was too weak to confront a U.S. naval response, it was strong enough to ensure control of the sea off West Africa as long as the United States or NATO did not intervene. The Soviet Navy's mission was to support the MPLA and to prevent involvement by moderate or conservative African nations, particularly South Africa. Furthermore, the fact that the West African naval force was augmented after the successful conclusion of the war implies that Angola was not a final goal but merely a step toward more extensive operations in Africa. Ambitious Soviet diplomatic, economic, and cultural programs in Africa, and the continued disinclination of the United States to oppose this offensive, support the belief that the Soviets are making a major attempt to establish themselves as the dominant influence on the continent.

Soviet Naval Activity Along West Africa, 1976–1980

Increasing the size of the West African naval force has allowed the Soviets to continue an active port visit program. However, the most impressive of the visits was not conducted by ships assigned to the continent; rather, it was a visit to Luanda, conducted in 1979, by the aircraft carrier *Minsk* and her escorts. Indeed, the *Minsk*'s operations were so important that they are worth examining in detail.

The Minsk's *West African Operations,*
March–April, 1979

The *Minsk* departed the Black Sea on February 25, 1979, bound for her new home port in the Pacific. Her voyage is an example of the successful integration of operational and political requirements. The group consisted of five of the most modern ships in the Soviet Navy. The *Minsk*, the second of the *Kiev* aircraft carriers, was on her maiden voyage. Capable of carrying both Yak-36 *Forger* aircraft and Ka-25 *Hormone* helicopters, these heavily armed ships are the epitome of Soviet naval surface combatant construction. In addition, two *Kara* guided missile cruisers, the *Petropavlovsk* and the *Tashkent* (also on her maiden voyage), were in the group. Heavily armed and versatile, the *Karas* are extremely impressive combatants. Two additional ships rounded out the task group. Both were on their maiden cruises, and both were transferring from the Baltic to the Pacific Fleet. The first was the landing platform dock (LPD) *Ivan Rogov,* the prototype of her class and the front line of Soviet amphibious warfare technology. The largest amphibious ship ever built in the USSR, the *Ivan Rogov* is approximately three times the size of an *Alligator* tank landing ship. Armed with guns and surface-to-air missiles, she can carry helicopters and has a floodable well deck from which landing craft can be launched. The fifth ship was the *Boris Chilikin* tanker *Boris Butoma.* Like the *Minsk, Tashkent,* and *Ivan Rogov, Boris Butoma* was a new ship, embodying some of the latest Soviet technology.

The *Ivan Rogov,* the Soviet Navy's most modern amphibious warfare ship, transferred with the aircraft carrier *Minsk* to the Pacific Fleet in 1979. (U.S. Navy)

Map 4.2 shows the *Minsk*'s voyage. After an 18-day stay in the Mediterranean, during which time she operated with her sister aircraft carrier the *Kiev*, the *Minsk* entered the Atlantic through the Strait of Gibraltar on March 14. The most interesting aspects of the *Minsk*'s West African operations were her failure to visit Conakry, a port visit to Angola, and operations off South Africa.

The *Minsk* did not visit Guinea because of a recent cooling in the Soviet-Guinean relationship. Although the Soviet presence in Guinea had assured the security of the Touré regime, there is a great deal of evidence to support reports that Touré was becoming increasingly dissatisfied with the USSR. These reservations resulted in a more distant Soviet-Guinean relationship, which worsened as Guinea improved relations with its neighbors. Thus, in March 1979, as the *Minsk* task group steamed southward along the West African coast, the change in this relationship was evident. For example, on January 29, President Touré discussed several trends in an interview. He argued for Guinean cooperation with the capitalist nations, and he defended the Monrovia Conference, noting that reconciliation with Senegal and the Ivory Coast promoted Guinean security. Finally, Touré defended a recent visit to Morocco and a visit with King Hassan II, stating that although the Moroccan government was not socialist, it had made positive social changes.[8] Thus, while the Soviet-Guinean relationship was cooling, Guinean revolutionary fervor was being tempered, affording at least short-term cooperation with the United States, Europe, and the more moderate African

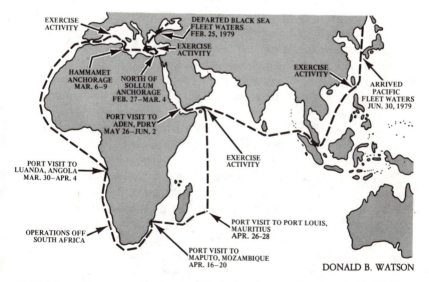

DONALD B. WATSON

MAP 4.2 The route taken by the *Minsk* when she transferred to the Pacific Fleet in 1979.

nations. In this context, a port visit by the *Minsk* group was not appropriate as the Soviets believe that a visit by such a prestigious combatant reflects a particularly warm relationship with any recipient nation.

The Minsk *Group's Visit to Luanda, Angola, March 30–April 4, 1979.* / Interrupting her southbound voyage along the African coast, the *Minsk* began a six-day port visit to Luanda, Angola, on March 30. The targets of the visit were the Angolan government and, as we shall see later, South Africa.

Although the Western press gave the visit relatively little notice, considerable attention was paid to it by Soviet, Angolan, and South African papers. Soviet coverage was limited to descriptive reporting, noting that the ships' crews had visited Luanda, toured the People's Armed Forces of the Liberation of Angola Museum, and met with Luandans and Angolan Navy personnel. Considerable coverage was given to Angolan President Agostino Neto's visit to the *Minsk*. *Krasnaya Zvezda* (Red Star) noted that he was met by V. Loginov, the Soviet ambassador to Angola, that he toured the ship, and that the ship's crew gave a concert for him. It was noted that Neto wrote in the *Minsk* visitor's book that his visit occurred during a period of "strengthening ties between the Angolan and Soviet peoples and in the spirit of the Soviet-Angolan Treaty of Friendship and Cooperation."[9]

The visit occurred during a period of significant economic decline in Angola, and severe economic problems were probably a major cause for Neto's seeking a reconciliation with the West. Many reporters considered that a visit by Senator George McGovern in December 1978 had been a signal of that policy shift. During that visit, McGovern had seen Neto and had been told that Angola wanted to establish relations with the United States but that South African aggression was a major obstacle. McGovern had responded that the continuing presence of Cuban troops in Angola presented a similar problem for the United States. Thus, although problems existed, it was evident that Angola was considering a reconciliation with the West and that negotiations toward that end had been conducted. Further evidence of this effort had been seen in March, when Neto said that he would consider a reduction in Cuban troops in Angola if South Africa would withdraw from South-West Africa.[10]

The visit of the *Minsk* at this juncture was a timely exercise in naval diplomacy. It was part of a concerted Soviet effort, which involved a visit in late March by a Soviet delegation headed by A. K. Vlaslov, an alternate member of the Communist Party's Central Committee, and the appointment of five Soviet-trained Angolan officers as deputy defense ministers on March 31 and April 5. The *Minsk*'s presence was probably an attempt to impress Neto and other high-ranking Angolan leaders with Soviet power. The visit had considerable impact, as was reflected in the Angolan press. Both radio stations and the press gave Neto's tour of the *Minsk* extended coverage, complete with an extensive description of the ship's capabilities.[11] The effects of the *Minsk*'s visit are difficult to assess, but in the aftermath of Neto's death there was no reconciliation with the West, and the Soviet and Cuban presence in Angola did not diminish significantly.

The *Minsk*'s visit also was probably calculated to indicate resolute Soviet support for Angola in its struggle with the South African government. Angola and South Africa had undergone a period of border conflict that threatened to escalate into more widespread hostilities. The visit to Luanda, coupled with the *Minsk* group's presence off the South African coast, conveyed the message that the USSR would honor its commitment to Angola and would not tolerate hostile South African action.

The Minsk *Group's Presence Off South Africa.* / In March 1979, Iran, South Africa's major oil supplier, severed relations with that country and discontinued oil shipments, and the United Nations condemned South Africa for aggression against Angola. Internal riots and increasingly adverse U.S. public opinion concerning South African politics rounded out the country's bleak economic and political situations. Thus, as the *Minsk* group departed Luanda on April 4, it was approaching a nation whose government felt particularly isolated.

The group steamed along the coast of South Africa, en route to the Indian Ocean. The South African government appears to have attempted a news blackout. The press made no mention of the *Minsk* group after its Luanda

The South Africans, who still view themselves as anti-Communist protectors of the Cape shipping route, were obviously concerned about the presence of the Soviet Navy's *Minsk* task group off their coast in April 1979. Here, the South African destroyer *President Steyn* keeps close tabs on the *Minsk*. (South Africa)

port visit until news of the group's presence off the South African coast finally broke on April 11. The *Cape Times* and the *Rand Daily Mail* both quoted Mr. I. J. Adams, captain of the trawler *Lobelia*, who stated that he had seen the Soviet ships off Cape Point. When asked for further details, he replied he had been told that "it was all confidential."[12]

It appears that the South African government viewed the presence of the group as potentially threatening. It is difficult to quantify the effects of the group's presence on South Africa, but, to the extent that that presence stood as a sign of Soviet opposition to South Africa and as a sign of support for Angola and Mozambique, it benefited Soviet foreign policy.

Summary

The Soviet Navy's West African contingent is now constantly present in the area. It conducts an ambitious port visit program and can carry out coastal defense and crisis response operations. Naval aircraft deployed to the region, probably now from bases in Angola as well as from bases in Guinea, are capable of extended reconnaissance, which can provide valuable intelligence concerning U.S. naval and merchant shipping operations in the North Atlantic and activities in Africa. Thus, the contingent is both a regional and a potential international threat. Regionally, it stands as the military force that safeguards Soviet policy initiatives in Africa, and its performances in Guinea and during the Angolan Civil War show that the Soviets are not afraid to use their power. Internationally, the contingent is positioned in areas close to the vulnerable sea lanes leading from the Indian Ocean to Europe and the United States.

The importance of the contingent is linked to Soviet long-range strategy. The Soviets did not reduce their naval presence along the West African coast after the conclusion of the Angolan Civil War. That fact, together with the ambitious Soviet diplomatic, cultural, and economic programs in Africa, indicates that in the early 1980s, the Soviets may attempt to establish themselves as the primary external influence on the continent. A continued failure of the United States and West European countries to oppose this offensive will contribute to Soviet success.

Notes

1. Drew Middleton, "Soviet Foothold Is Worrying NATO," *New York Times*, 19 January 1976, p. 11.

2. Drew Middleton, "New Soviet Role in Africa Alleged," *New York Times*, 10 December 1975, p. 11.

3. *New York Times,* 12 June 1975, p. 14.

4. "Movement Loses Port," *New York Times,* 15 August 1975, p. 5.

5. "Angolan Faction Is Said to Push Deep into South Against Little Resistance," *New York Times,* 15 February 1976, p. 52.

6. Ibid. and "Soviet Ships with Cuban Force Reported 30 Miles Off Angola," *New York Times,* 6 February 1976, p. 2.

7. Bernard Gwertzman, "Soviet Proposes Plan to Resolve Arms Pact Snag," *New York Times,* 24 January 1976, p. 1; David Binder, "Aid to Angolans Ended by House in Rebuff to Ford," *New York Times,* 28 January 1976, pp. 1, 3; and interview with Admiral Moorer, 9 January 1978.

8. "President Ahmed Sékou Touré in Benin," *Horoya,* 7 March 1979, pp. 2, 5, translated in *Joint Publications Research Service: Translations on Sub-Saharan Africa,* 8 June 1979, pp. 20–23.

9. G. Savichev, "Soviet Ships Visit Angola," *Red Star,* 11 April 1979, p. 3.

10. "Cuban Troops Counterbalance to South African Contingents," *Herald* (Salisbury), 29 March 1979, p. 6.

11. "Neto Visits Soviet Ships in Luanda Harbor," *Jornal de Angola,* 6 April 1979, pp. 1, 6, translated in *Joint Publications Research Service: Translations on Sub-Saharan Africa,* 10 May 1979, pp. 19–20, and Report on Luanda Domestic Service, in Portuguese, 3 April 1979, translated in *Foreign Broadcast Information Service: Vol. 8, Southern Africa Daily Report,* 4 April 1979, p. E1.

12. "Red Ships 'Sighted' Off SA's West Coast," *Cape Times,* 11 April 1979, p. 1, and "Soviet Ships Sighted Off SA Coast," *Rand Daily Mail,* 12 April 1979, p. 4.

Part 2

The Mediterranean Sea

5

Soviet Mediterranean Fleet
Operations, 1958–1964

The functions of the Soviet Mediterranean Fleet have been to improve the Soviet Union's international position and to participate in transforming the world's nations into socialist systems subservient to Moscow. As noted in Chapter 1, the fleet's presence in the eastern Mediterranean has contributed to the USSR's national defense by securing from seaborne attack the maritime approach to the Black Sea, the oil complexes, and the entire southwestern sector of the nation. Since the threat of such an attack is considerably less than the threat of an attack by NATO land forces in Europe, the fleet's defense mission probably has been considered to be less important than its foreign policy responsibilities.

The creation of a permanent Mediterranean naval force in 1958 was the USSR's first attempt to exert naval influence on affairs in the Third World. As Tables 2 and 3 demonstrate, the largest deployed naval force from 1967 onward almost always has been the Mediterranean Fleet, testimony of the importance the USSR assigns to that part of the world.

The function of the fleet as an instrument of Soviet policy in the Middle East is a reflection of Lenin's postulations concerning the antagonism between industrialized nations and the Third World (seen most clearly in emerging Arab nationalism) and of the Soviet conviction that the United States is a major force against which Soviet strategy must operate. The USSR cannot become the dominant world power until the United States is reduced to secondary status. Soviet policy toward the Third World was designed ultimately to undermine the U.S. position, even in instances of U.S.-Soviet cooperation. Thus the de facto temporary U.S.-Soviet alliance that created Israel in 1948 led to the Arab-Israeli adversary relationship, Egypt's subsequent reliance on the Soviet Union, and a greater Soviet influence on Egyptian affairs than might otherwise have been permitted. The Soviets' aim was to increase their influence over the Suez Canal, which would further their international and strategic positions and adversely affect the United States.[1]

The U.S.-Soviet adversary relationship of the 1960s and 1970s was sharply delineated by the Mediterranean naval rivalry. The Soviet Mediterranean Fleet was established to neutralize the influence of Western sea power in the Mediterranean, particularly that of the U.S. Sixth Fleet, and to enable the Soviets to wield a preponderance of power in the region. Stated another way, the Soviet Union has aimed at attaining the strategic position in the Mediterranean that the United States enjoyed at least through 1958 — one of absolute strategic control through the deployment of naval power.

The Suez Canal

A major reason for Soviet emphasis on the region is the Suez Canal. Approximately 107 miles long, this waterway, which was opened in 1869, is an important factor in the Soviet-Western balance of power. For Europe, the canal has both military and commercial importance. Militarily, it permits rapid movement of naval power into the Indian Ocean, which could be vital to the protection of Western interests in East Africa, the Persian Gulf, and South Asia. The canal also divides the Arab Middle Eastern nations, and its control means increased influence over emerging Arab nationalism. If the Soviet Union could deny use of the canal to the West, it could threaten Western interests along the periphery of the Indian Ocean, while using the canal to rapidly deploy its own naval power.

Commercially, the canal is vitally important to the West. The European industrial complexes rely on Persian Gulf oil and the trade with South Asia and the Far East, which pass through the waterway. The canal drastically reduces the distance (and time) from Europe to South Asia. For example, compared with the detour around Africa, the canal means a difference of approximately 5,000 nautical miles from London to the Persian Gulf and about 3,700 nautical miles from London to Singapore. If ships travel at the speed of 10 knots, the canal reduces transit time by approximately 21 days and 15 days, respectively, from London to the Persian Gulf and from London to the Singapore Strait. If the Soviet Union could deny Europe the use of the canal, it would drastically affect the European economies. More or larger ships would be required for the longer distance around Africa, thereby increasing the transportation costs of goods and materials coming from the Persian Gulf, South Asia, and the Far East. Soviet control of the canal would also adversely affect the West's defense posture.

The canal also has value for the Soviets, both militarily and commercially. The Soviets perceived the U.S.-Soviet rivalry and the emerging Third World as the major themes of the postwar period and intended to play a major role in Africa and Asia in the 1960s. That involvement would include arms deliveries, which would be guaranteed through Soviet military power. Given the isolation of those regions from the USSR, a naval force in the Indian Ocean would be needed to provide that military power.[2] The crucial question was where to home port such a force and how to support it. A canal open to Soviet naval ships would make it possible to home port most forces earmarked for Indian Ocean operations in the Black Sea. Therefore, Soviet naval use of the canal would be most valuable, and its denial would adversely affect the Soviet Union's ability to rapidly project its naval power into the Indian Ocean.

Commercially, the canal's importance is even more dramatic. For example, the distances from Odessa on the Black Sea via the canal and around Africa to the Persian Gulf are approximately 4,300 nautical miles and 12,200 nautical miles, respectively; to Singapore, the distances are approximately 6,200 nautical miles and 12,800 nautical miles, respectively. At an average speed of 10 knots, use of the canal shortens voyages from Odessa to the Persian Gulf by approximately 33 days and to the Strait of Malacca by approximately 28 days.

For these reasons, controlling the canal was probably an early goal of Soviet policy, and stationing a fleet of ships in the Mediterranean was the first step toward establishing influence over the waterway. Significant operations began in 1956 and subsequently included naval presence, port visits, establishing port facilities, surge deployments during crisis situations, and political operations by some naval ships.

Naval Operations in the Mediterranean Before 1956

Stationing a continuous naval force in the Mediterranean began in 1958, but Soviet naval operations in the area predate that event by many decades. However, the ships employed in those earlier operations posed almost no strategic threat. The Soviet Navy was then viewed as little more than an adjunct of the army, and the USSR was unable to project substantial naval power beyond its coastal areas. It could not muster naval responses to attacks on its merchant ships, such as one that occurred during the Spanish Civil War. However, those earlier naval operations were significant as harbingers of Soviet intentions to use sea power for purposes other than national defense. Since the Soviet Union had little ability to project sea power, operations prior to 1958 consisted primarily of exploiting those port visits that the navy was granted. The Soviets have long realized the potential of the port visit as a means of furthering their influence. As far back as September 1928, for example, the training ship *Vega* visited Algiers and over the years, visiting arrangements became markedly more sophisticated. Senior naval officers were assigned as ranking officers on ships during those port visits that had high political value.[3]

Soviet port visit activity gained momentum in the 1950s. The first naval visit in the Mediterranean since the 1930s occurred from May 31 to June 4, 1954, when the cruiser *Admiral Nakhimov* and two destroyers visited Albania. The senior officer was the commander of the Black Sea Fleet, then Vice Admiral Sergei Gorshkov.[4] The lack of a strong sea power projection capability became an increasing liability for the Soviet Union in the 1950s as it attempted to extend its influence to areas that were not contiguous to its borders. This liability was recognized before 1956 and resulted in the selection of Gorshkov as head of the navy. However, the Soviet Union suffered three major setbacks from 1956 through 1962 because it still lacked adequate naval power. The Mediterranean was the scene of the first two, the Suez crisis and the Lebanon crisis. The third was the Cuban missile crisis.

The Suez Crisis

The Soviets had assessed that there would be a potential adversary relationship in the Middle East between Israel, backed by Europe and the United States, and the Arab world, supported by the Soviet Union, and, hence, they supported the creation of Israel in 1948. The intensifying Arab-Israeli animosity gave the Soviet Union an opportunity to make inroads into the Arab world, with Egypt as the key. However, lacking adequate sea power, the Soviet Union was less able than the United States to influence the events of the 1956 Suez crisis.

The United States used its naval power skillfully during that crisis. One analyst noted that the United States had three aims: to be prepared in case the crisis expanded into a major conflict; to protect and, if necessary, evacuate U.S. citizens in the Middle East; and to attempt to restrain the adversaries. U.S. naval power around the world had to be shifted to accomplish the first objective. Ships were deployed from the West Coast to the central Pacific, those in Hawaii were moved westward, and Seventh Fleet ships were ordered southward into the South China Sea. From there, some Seventh Fleet ships, including amphibious forces, were dispatched to the Arabian Sea, which is within striking range of the Red Sea and the Persian Gulf. Concurrently, ships were deployed from the U.S. East Coast to an area south of the Azores, and ships from the Sixth Fleet were moved eastward in the Mediterranean. In effect, there was a general convergence of U.S. naval power on the Suez. The second and third aims, the evacuation of U.S. citizens and restraining the adversaries, were accomplished primarily by the Sixth Fleet, which operated in an area southeast of Crete. All of these redeployments helped stabilize the situation as the contending nations ceased hostilities. U.S. amphibious forces evacuated some 2,000 Americans

U.S. naval power was unchallenged during the Middle East crisis of 1956. U.S. naval landing craft evacuated U.S. citizens from Alexandria, Egypt, without incident. (U.S. Navy)

from Alexandria, and other ships and aircraft evacuated about the same number of people from Israel and other nations.[5]

Although Egypt was soon to be a client of the Soviet Union, the USSR was unable to come to Egyptian President Nasser's defense, because it did not have the capacity to send adequate naval power into the Mediterranean. Even if the Soviet Union had had such power, it lacked the strategic strength to confront the United States. Thus, the Soviet role was limited to defending Egypt in U.N. debates and warning France and Great Britain to comply with a U.N. resolution calling for a withdrawal of troops behind armistice lines.

The Aftermath of Suez

Although the Soviet Union was unable to control the crisis, the canal's proprietorship was transferred to Egypt, which was susceptible to Soviet overtures. Thus, after the crisis, Soviet diplomatic and cultural activities, military and economic aid, and naval activity focused on Egypt.

Military Aid

The U.S.-Soviet arms race had left large quantities of obsolete equipment in the defense inventories of both nations, and the Soviet Union had a ready market for its less advanced equipment in the Arab nations. Arms contracts with liberal credit became the basis for increased Soviet influence in Egypt and other Middle Eastern nations, and Soviet training missions created a further Arab military dependence on the Soviet Union. Finally, Egypt had to turn continually to the USSR for newer equipment, which resulted in a long-term Egyptian economic dependence on the Soviet Union.

Although data on the quantity of arms supplied are sporadic, deliveries to Egypt began with the Czechoslovakian arms agreement in 1955, which included 2 *Skoryy* destroyers, 5 *Whiskey* and 1 *MV* submarines, 4 T-43 fleet minesweepers, and at least 12 P-6 motor torpedo boats.[6] In November 1956, Great Britain estimated that Egypt had received $420,000,000 worth of Soviet arms. Syria purchased $100,000,000 worth prior to its union with Egypt on February 1, 1958. The United Arab Republic later borrowed an additional $500,000,000 for Soviet arms. In 1959, the Egyptian armored forces were operating T-54 and T-55 tanks, and in January 1959, 3 additional *Whiskey* submarines were delivered.[7] Deliveries of naval equipment in 1962 included 2 *Skoryy* destroyers, 2 *Whiskey* submarines, and 3 *Komar* guided missile patrol boats. In 1963, Egypt and the USSR concluded an arms agreement for the purchase of 2 submarines, 2 destroyers, more than 30 *Osa* and *Komar* guided missile patrol boats, and various other ships. In 1966, naval deliveries included 5 *Romeo* diesel attack submarines, 10 to 12 *Osas*, 4 or 5 *Komars, Polnocny* rocket assault ships, and several *MP-SMB1* amphibious utility craft.[8] These and other arms sales increased the capabilities of the Egyptian military; the sales were not limited to conventional weapons but included chemical warfare agents as well. Egypt used *Ilyushin* aircraft to drop napalm and nerve gas on Yemeni villages on several occasions in the 1960s.[9]

Naval Activity

Following the Suez crisis, there was a dramatic increase in Soviet naval activity in the Mediterranean (Table 2 shows a 500 percent increase in Mediterranean ship days from 1956 to 1957). Although the number of out-of-area ship days in the Atlantic also increased in 1957, the rate of increase in the Mediterranean far exceeded that in other ocean areas. For the first time, the Soviets were conducting significant foreign policy–motivated naval operations. These operations reflected the importance attached to the Mediterranean and to the Suez Canal. It is significant that this type of operation began ten years before the Soviet Navy was capable of fulfilling its defense mission, which means that Soviet foreign policy excursions could be countered easily by the threatened use of U.S. Atlantic- and Pacific-based naval power against the Soviet homeland. Thus, there were limits to the utility of the Soviet Navy as a foreign policy vehicle.

The reasons for beginning foreign policy–oriented naval operations were twofold. First, increased naval activity in all geographic areas reflected the decision made before the Twentieth Party Congress to develop a navy that could counter the restraining influence of U.S. military power. Second, those operations marked the beginning of the Soviet offensive in the Third World and indicated the importance the Soviets attached to the Mediterranean in that offensive. The events of 1956, which resulted in a change in the proprietorship of the Suez Canal and the consolidation of Khrushchev's political power, prompted expanded involvement in the Mediterranean. In part, this involvement was associated with arms deliveries to Arab clients. The arms would be delivered by Soviet merchant ships (a seaborne extension of the Soviet enclave tactic by supplying "progressive" forces from Soviet sanctuaries), and those ships had to be protected from interference by unfriendly nations. Stationing naval combatants in the Mediterranean was the best method of providing effective military power.

In 1957, the Soviets maintained an intermittent naval presence in the Mediterranean as a prelude to more extensive naval operations. The majority of the operations during this period were port visits. In addition to continuing port visits to Albania and Yugoslavia, visits to Egypt and Syria were begun in 1957. The first visit to Syria was made to Latakia on September 21, 1957, by the destroyer *Svobodniy* accompanying the *Sverdlov* cruiser *Zhdanov*, with Vice Admiral V. F. Kotov, first deputy commander in chief of the Baltic Fleet, aboard.[10]

More active naval operations in the Mediterranean required assured logistic support. Since the Soviet Navy had few auxiliary ships, access to a Mediterranean port facility was essential. Albania had such facilities, and from 1956 until 1958, the Soviets apparently negotiated arrangements to use them. Ships visiting Albania jumped from no more than five in any of the previous years to eight in 1957, and the number of days spent in Albanian ports rose to an unprecedented 38, more than double the number of 1956. There was an even greater increase in 1958, when submarines operated out of Valona, and the Soviets established a constant presence in the Mediterranean. Prior to the establishment of this presence, however, another crisis occurred—this time in Lebanon.

The Lebanon Crisis, 1958

Although the Soviets had not responded militarily to the Suez crisis of 1956, the Arabs considered Soviet naval power a potential counterforce to the Western naval forces in the eastern Mediterranean. That assumption was prevalent in Egypt and was probably reinforced by the Soviets' anti-Turkish stand during a period of Syrian-Turkish discord in 1957. That belief could partially explain Egypt's assertive behavior before the U.S. landing in Lebanon in 1958, which played a part in making the crisis detrimental to Soviet policy interests in the Mediterranean and the Middle East.

The crisis deepened when riots began in Beirut in May 1958. The Egyptian participation consisted of supplying weapons, military training, and financial assistance to the Lebanese opposition forces and conducting a propaganda campaign against the Lebanese government on Radio Cairo.[11] When the riots broke out in Beirut, the Egyptian news media mirrored national confidence that Soviet power would restrain the U.S. Sixth Fleet. However, such confidence declined in the following months as it became evident that the United States might soon intervene. Responding to a request from Lebanese President Camille Chamoun, the United States landed Marines in Lebanon on July 15 and later brought in U.S. Army units from Europe to restore national stability.[12] President Nasser immediately flew to Moscow for meetings with Premier Khrushchev. Khrushchev agreed to announce that the Soviet Union was conducting maneuvers along its southern borders, but he would not agree to a more significant response. The Soviet leader told Nasser, "to be frank, the Soviet Union is not ready for a clash with the West, the result of which would be uncertain."[13]

The Soviet naval response was minimal: The Black Sea Fleet conducted regularly scheduled naval exercises with an exceptional degree of fanfare. From the Soviet point of view, this restraint was wise. In view of the inferiority of Soviet naval power relative to that of the United States in 1958, the most rational course was to pursue an option other than direct military confrontation. However, the Egyptians, faced with Western naval power that threatened to thwart Arab nationalism in Lebanon, needed and expected the Soviet Union to commit enough naval strength to the Mediterranean to negate the power of the West. The Egyptians interpreted the Soviet failure to do so as an unwillingness to confront the West militarily. The failure of the Soviet Union to adequately convey its military weakness to Egypt before the crisis resulted in loss of Soviet credibility in Egypt, and it was under this stigma that the Soviets operated in the early 1960s.[14]

Soviet Mediterranean Fleet Operations, 1958–1964

From 1958 until 1961, the Soviets attempted to establish a permanent naval presence in the Mediterranean for the first time. Their operations included naval presence, exercises, port visits, and maintaining port facilities in Valona, Albania. Access to Valona was vital, despite the fact that the eastern Mediterranean is close to Soviet Black Sea ports, because Soviet naval ships face both geographic and diplomatic restrictions on their passage from the Black Sea through the narrow and easily interdicted Turkish straits into the Mediterranean. Also, the Montreux Convention, governing traffic using the Turkish straits, imposed diplomatic restrictions on the passage of Soviet combatants. The Turkish government required eight days' notice of the transit of Soviet naval ships, with the exception of liquid carriers (oilers and distilling ships). The convention also stated that submarines could pass from the Black Sea through the straits only en route to other ports for repairs. Thus, there were significant limitations on the rapid deployment of Soviet combatants in response to Mediterranean crises, and short of abrogating the treaty, stationing submarines in the Black Sea was not feasible. As a result, all Soviet submarines operating in the Mediterranean had to come from the Baltic or Northern Fleets, and the existing naval auxiliary force simply could not support such operations. The acquisition of Albanian support facilities enabled the beginning of expanded and continuous Mediterranean operations in 1958.

The fact that these operations started in 1958 might imply that they were a reaction to the Lebanon crisis. However, the preparations probably required several months, and although the crisis may have accelerated the start of the operations, they were probably planned before the crisis. Soviet *Whiskey* submarines were at Valona shortly after the Lebanon crisis and remained there until June 1961. In 1958, an initial force estimated at 8 submarines arrived. That force soon was increased to about 10 and then approximately 12, and support ships were also deployed throughout the period.

Tables 2 and 3 provide a clear picture of the burgeoning Mediterranean operations. Out-of-area ship days in the Mediterranean grew by 66 percent in 1958 over 1957, and there were additional increases of 310 percent and 37 percent in 1959 and 1960. Ship days rocketed from 600 in 1957 to 5,600 in 1960. In the context of all of the out-of-area Soviet naval presence, that in the Mediterranean increased from 26 percent to 72 percent from 1957 to 1960. Thus in 1960, almost three out of every four Soviet naval ship days spent on the high seas were in the Mediterranean, primarily in support of long-range foreign policy goals rather than for defense.

Soviet ships spent 11,283 days in Albanian ports from 1953 through 1980, making Albania the third most heavily visited nation during that period (see Table 25). This access permitted the Soviets to maintain a submarine force in the Mediterranean for almost three years, and it enabled them to gain experience in force projection and in operations on the high seas. Exercises such as the one in September 1960 in the Aegean Sea, which involved ten surface ships and ten submarines, were invaluable in developing the modern navy.[15]

Access to Valona ended abruptly in June 1961 as a result of a deterioration of Soviet-Albanian relations. The Albanians expelled the Soviets and seized two submarines when the countries severed diplomatic relations. From the time of this expulsion until 1964, the Soviet naval presence in the Mediterranean was almost nonexistent. Without forward support facilities, the navy simply was unable to maintain a constant presence.

Summary

The Soviet fleet's Mediterranean operations from 1956 to 1964 constituted the first clear-cut Soviet attempt to use naval power in support of foreign policy. The operations met with mixed success. Although the preponderance of U.S. naval and strategic power diminished the Soviet fleet's effect, the operations were still significant. A traditionally sparse presence yielded to more extensive operations in 1956, and a significant intermittent naval presence was maintained in the Mediterranean from 1956 to 1958. With access to Albanian port facilities, the Soviet presence was continuous from 1958 until June 1961, which provided great political and propaganda returns. There also was progress in the conduct of port visits as visit routines became more sophisticated, and port visits increased both in number and in the number of countries visited.

The expulsion from Albania in June 1961 brought this phase of Soviet Mediterranean naval operations to a close. However, the experience gained in exercise and surveillance activities and port visits was a positive factor in the successful operations conducted from 1964 through 1980, and thus, those earlier operations had great relevance for the future.

Notes

1. Lenin, "Speech Delivered at a Meeting of Activists," p. 453, and Schiebel, "The USSR in World Affairs," pp. 91–92.

2. The use of Soviet naval power is implicit in Gorshkov's discussion of the application of Western naval power in "local wars of imperialism" (see Sergei G. Gorshkov, *Morskaya moshch gosudarstva [Sea Power of the State]* [Moscow: Voyennoye Izdatel'stvo, 1976], pp. 257–263, 266–270, 275–276, 278–279, 344–345, 380–386, 407, and Bruce W. Watson, "Comments on Gorshkov's *Sea Power of the State*," *U.S. Naval Institute Proceedings* 103 (April 1977):44.

3. George S. Dragnich, *The Soviet Union's Quest for Access to Naval Facilities in Egypt Prior to the June War of 1967* (Arlington, Va.: Center for Naval Analyses, 1974), p. 3.

4. Ibid., p. 5.

5. J. C. Wylie, "The Sixth Fleet and American Diplomacy," in *Soviet-American*

Rivalry in the Middle East, ed. J. C. Hurewitz (New York: Frederick A. Praeger, 1969), pp. 55–56.

6. Dragnich, *The Soviet Union's Quest for Access,* p. 6. See also Franklyn D. Holzman, "Soviet Trade and Aid Policies," in *Soviet-American Rivalry in the Middle East,* ed. J. C. Hurewitz (New York: Frederick A. Praeger, 1969), p. 111.

7. H. L. Hoskins, *Soviet Economic Penetration in the Middle East* (Washington, D. C.: Government Printing Office, 1959), p. 9; Harry B. Ellis, *Challenge in the Middle East* (New York: Ronald Press Company, 1960), p. 164; and Dragnich, *The Soviet Union's Quest for Access,* p. 17.

8. Dragnich, *The Soviet Union's Quest for Access,* pp. 23, 25, 43.

9. United Nations, Security Council, "Exchange of Communications with the Deputy Permanent Representative of Saudi Arabia to the United Nations," (S/7842), 6 April 1967, pp. 1–18.

10. Dragnich, *The Soviet Union's Quest for Access,* pp. 10–12.

11. Ibid., pp. 13–16.

12. Wylie, "The Sixth Fleet and American Diplomacy," pp. 56–57.

13. Dragnich, *The Soviet Union's Quest for Access,* p. 15.

14. Ibid., pp. 15–16.

15. Ibid., pp. 17–18, 20, and Polmar, *Soviet Naval Power,* p. 65.

6
Soviet Mediterranean Fleet Operations, 1964–1973

Substantial Soviet naval operations in the Mediterranean were resumed in mid-1964 when Soviet naval ships moved southward through the Turkish straits to begin the second phase of the Soviet Mediterranean operations. The navy was becoming a formidable force as it was equipped with new surface combatants, submarines, and auxiliaries, products of the construction program approved by the Twentieth Party Congress in 1956. The increasing size of the Mediterranean Fleet created a growing threat to the U.S. Sixth Fleet. This increased threat was particularly evident in periods of intense exercise activity, during the 1967 and 1973 Arab-Israeli Wars, and in the Jordanian crisis of 1970. As a product of the heightened activity, the number of ports visited by Soviet ships increased during this period.

The Soviet Drive for Access to Egyptian Ports

The Soviets made overtures to Egypt for use of port facilities shortly after their expulsion from Albania in 1961, but the campaign was not successful until 1967, when Egypt, gravely weakened by its defeat in the Six-Day War, traded access to its facilities for large quantities of military assistance. Senior Soviet leaders made a series of trips to Egypt. These included one by Khrushchev in May 1964; one by Grechko in December 1965; and four by Gorshkov in December 1961, March 1965, May 1966 (as a member of a delegation headed by Kosygin), and January 1967. These contacts produced some progress toward the Soviets' goal. For example, in April 1966, the *New York Times* reported that Soviet naval ships had been operating in the Gulf of Sollum and that their crews had been allowed to go ashore.[1] (The Gulf of Sollum, strategically located due south of North of Sollum Anchorage — see Map 6.2 — was to become a major Soviet naval anchorage in the 1960s and 1970s.) There was no constant naval presence in Egyptian ports prior to June 1967, however.

DONALD B. WATSON

MAP 6.1   Mediterranean ports visited by Soviet naval ships from 1954 through 1980.

Soviet Naval Operations, 1964–1967

A Soviet cruiser and two destroyers moved southward through the Turkish straits in the summer of 1964 when Turkish-U.S. relations were at a low point. Norman Polmar recognized the political aspect of this deployment when he observed that it occurred at a time when President Johnson was critical of the Turks for their activities on Cyprus. Polmar implied that the Soviets took advantage of this strained situation to induce Turkey to ease its restrictions on the passage of naval ships through the Turkish straits.[2] It is worth recalling that the Soviets have continued to exploit periodic friction among the allies.

In 1964, the daily force level of the Mediterranean Fleet averaged 5 ships. Tables 2 and 3 show the dimensions of the Soviet presence in the Mediterranean from 1964 to 1966. In 1964, deployments came to 1,800 ship days, 20 percent of the total out-of-area presence. The deployments more than doubled to 3,700 ship days in 1965 and accounted for 32 percent of all Soviet ship days on the high seas in that year. In 1966, the figure rose to 5,400 ship days, almost equal to that of 1960, the previous peak year of Soviet naval activity in the Mediterranean, and there was a daily average of 15 Soviet ships in the area.

Port Visits, 1964–1966

Map 6.1 shows the Mediterranean ports visited by Soviet naval ships from 1954 through 1980. No ships visited Albania after 1961, and eight visited Yugoslavia in the period 1964–1966 (see Table 10). From 1963 to June 1967, however, the scope of the visits was broadened to include Algeria, Egypt, France, Gibraltar, and Italy. Calls at Gibraltar and Italy were for replenishment and crew rest. The visits to Marseille and Toulon averaged six days (see Table 12) and were a part of the surge of Soviet port visits to NATO countries discussed in Chapter 2.

Visits to Algeria began in 1966 when nine ships called at Algiers and eight at Oran. These Algerian visits occurred yearly through 1980 and may indicate that the Soviets hope for permanent access to Algerian ports. Several visits to Alexandria and Port Said reflected continuing attempts to gain unrestricted access to Egyptian facilities.

The Six-Day War, June 1967

The 1967 Arab-Israeli War was a turning point in Soviet naval operations as it was the first time Soviet naval power was used extensively in a military crisis. This war tested both the Soviet Mediterranean Fleet's crisis management capability and its value as an instrument for achieving the long-range goal of furthering the Soviet Union's international position.

Soviet and U.S. Naval Activity During the War

Unlike their position before the Lebanon crisis of 1958, the Soviets had operated continuously in the Mediterranean for almost three years prior to June 1967. Their Mediterranean Fleet was composed of modern surface combatants and submarines equipped with impressive fire power and complex electronic systems. Soviet operating techniques and command and control procedures had improved tremendously. When war broke out in June 1967, the U.S. Sixth Fleet confronted the greatest fleet assembled by any nation potentially hostile to the United States since World War II.

But this armada was not omnipotent. It was a fleet untested in combat, and many of its senior officers probably remembered too clearly the unimpressive performance of their navy in World War II. Realizing their strengths, they should also have realized their weaknesses, particularly their vulnerability to the U.S. aircraft carriers. June 1967 was to be a crucial test. The presence of the Soviet fleet meant that the Soviets no longer intended to stand by and allow the West in general and the United States in particular to enjoy complete strategic control of the Mediterranean.

For several reasons, U.S. naval power was less decisive in June 1967 than it had been during the crises of 1956 and 1958. It is true that because Israel won the war rapidly, extensive U.S. involvement was unnecessary, but restrictions on Sixth Fleet operations may have been the first indications of a yielding to both Soviet and Third World pressures. Scheduled Mediterranean port visits were not curtailed. Amphibious ships carrying 2,000 marines remained in Malta throughout the war, almost 1,000 miles from the conflict. Although some Sixth Fleet forces were moved eastward in the Mediterranean, they did not proceed to the Egyptian or Israeli coasts, but remained in the vicinity of Crete, more than 300 miles from the Suez.[3]

In early June, in anticipation of the impending crisis, the USSR bolstered its fleet by sending 10 additional ships from the Black Sea. The Mediterranean Fleet eventually numbered more than 70 ships, including 2 cruisers, 15 destroyers, and 10 submarines. During the war, Soviet ships often attempted to penetrate the screens of the escort ships accompanying the U.S. aircraft carriers *Saratoga* and *America* by using harassment tactics that endangered both U.S. and Soviet lives.[4]

Results of the War

The success of the Soviet naval reaction in June 1967 can be judged by the results of the war and the fleet's postwar operations. On the negative side,

A *Kashin* guided missile destroyer passed close to the USS *Franklin D. Roosevelt* in September 1967. Although particularly severe in the June 1967 war, Soviet harassment of U.S. Sixth Fleet ships was commonplace in the 1960s. (U.S. Navy)

closing the Suez Canal disrupted the Soviet resupply of North Vietnam from Black Sea ports. In 1966, an average of almost three Soviet merchant ships had used the canal each day, many of them delivering arms to North Vietnam. With the canal closed, the arms carriers had to travel around Africa, an additional 6,600 nautical miles or approximately 28 more days per trip, traveling at a speed of 10 knots. The number of merchant ships supplying North Vietnam had to be increased, thus curtailing Soviet participation in the world maritime trade during the late 1960s and early 1970s.

Closing the canal may also have inhibited subsequent operations of the Soviet Indian Ocean Squadron, which began in 1968, because the Indian Ocean operations had to be staged from the Pacific Fleet rather than from the Black Sea, thereby increasing the naval supply problem and probably resulting in a smaller and less active presence than otherwise would have been the case.

On the positive side, the Soviets were permitted to use Egyptian naval facilities after the war and until 1976. Thus, the USSR was able to maintain a much larger naval force in the Mediterranean. The fleet's performance during the war had great propaganda value and probably was used to justify the Soviet claim that the USSR had supported its Arab clients. The Soviets' strong support of the Arab cause after June 1967 allowed them to station additional ships in the Mediterranean without accusations of imperialism from Third World nations.

On balance, the Soviet naval operations during the war were successful. The Mediterranean Fleet was limited to a naval show of force, which it performed efficiently. Assigned missions never exceeded fleet capabilities. Thus, the use of Soviet sea power in the Six-Day War was a prelude to future, more assertive crisis reactions.

Soviet Mediterranean Fleet Operations, 1967–1973

Soviet Mediterranean Fleet operations matured after the war. The fleet was kept at a quantitatively higher level than before the war, which permitted the development of more complex naval operating patterns, patrols, exercises, command and control procedures, and surveillance. The scope of the port visits was expanded to include previously unvisited Mediterranean nations, the number of port visits increased accordingly, and the port visit procedures were refined. Finally, facilities in Egypt were used extensively during this period, further exploiting the political value of the fleet.

The Force Level

In 1967, 8,800 naval ship days were logged in the Mediterranean by the Soviet fleet, an increase of 3,400 days over the previous year. Table 2 shows that this trend continued, with the number of ship days rising to 18,700 in 1971. The total decreased slightly in 1972 to 17,700 and then jumped to an all-time high of 20,600 days in 1973. This pattern indicates that in 1971, when the Soviet Union claimed it had reached strategic parity with the United States, the USSR finally was able to support what it considered to be an adequate naval force in the Mediterranean, a force with a daily average of 51 ships.

In relation to other worldwide out-of-area deployments, the number of days spent in the Mediterranean declined rather consistently during this same period, however. This fact does not signal that the Mediterranean had lost importance, but that the USSR was expanding its naval commitments. Table 3 shows that the Indian Ocean and Caribbean Sea operations, which began in 1968 and 1969, respectively, accounted for an increasing fraction of the total out-of-area presence, ranging from 5 percent in 1968 to 22 percent in 1972.

The availability of the port facilities in Alexandria allowed for an increase in the size of the Soviet Mediterranean Fleet, which averaged between 43 and 61 ships daily and was composed of:

8 to 10 torpedo attack submarines

2 to 3 cruise missile attack submarines

2 to 4 cruisers, some or all armed with guided missiles; periodically, 1 helicopter missile cruiser of the *Moskva* class.

9 to 12 destroyers and escort ships, some armed with guided missiles

1 to 3 minesweepers

1 to 3 amphibious ships

15 to 20 auxiliary ships

5 to 6 survey, oceanographic research, and intelligence collection ships[5]

An examination of the types of ships sent to the Mediterranean during this period demonstrates the importance of the fleet (and the area) to the Soviet Union. With the exception of the nuclear-powered ballistic missile submarines that operated in the Atlantic and Pacific oceans, the Mediterranean Fleet consistently included the lion's share of the most modern naval combatants. Many of these ships were based with the Black Sea Fleet and were dispatched almost solely to the Mediterranean for their out-of-area operations. From 1967 to 1976, almost all deployments of the two *Moskva* guided missile helicopter ships were to the Mediterranean, as well as an overwhelming majority of the deployments of *Kara, Kresta,* and *Kynda* guided missile cruisers; *Kashin, Kotlin,* and *Krupnyy* guided missile destroyers; *Foxtrot* diesel-powered attack submarines; and *Charlie* nuclear-powered cruise missile submarines.

The success of Soviet naval operations in the Mediterranean resulted from the resolution of several critical problems. The development of ships equipped with surface-to-air missiles provided air cover for the Mediterranean Fleet, and during the years 1967 to 1972, additional air cover was provided by aircraft operating from Egyptian and Libyan bases. When Egyptian air bases were closed to the Soviets in 1972, the Soviet reconnaissance capability in the Mediterranean decreased. However, in wartime, it is almost certain that the Soviets would use fighter and bomber aircraft based in the southwestern part of the Soviet Union for strike operations against both U.S. Sixth Fleet and NATO targets.

Restrictions on the use of the Turkish straits imposed by the Montreux Convention and the confines of the straits themselves became less burdensome. Although the majority of Mediterranean Fleet surface combatants and auxiliaries were home ported in the Black Sea, a standing force of 43 to 61 ships was constantly in the Mediterranean to counter the threat of the fleet's being bottled up in the Black Sea by a closing of the straits. Also, part of the Mediterranean surface combatant force was drawn from the Northern Fleet. In the late 1960s and early 1970s, submarines from the Northern Fleet were rotated to the Mediterranean in groups on a roughly semiannual basis.

Surge deployments, which are mandatory for a rapid augmentation of the standing Mediterranean force in times of crisis, were made possible through a circumvention of the Montreux Convention, which was accomplished by constantly submitting to the Turkish government contingency declarations that would be honored only in times of crisis. In this manner, the Soviets could rapidly detail ships to the Mediterranean without openly violating the convention.

The Geographic Disposition

During this period, the Soviets maintained a heavy presence in the eastern Mediterranean (east of the Ionian Sea), a moderate presence in the central Mediterranean (from the area east of the eastern border of Algeria to the eastern coast of the Ionian Sea), and a token presence in the western Mediterranean (the waters from the Strait of Gibraltar to the eastern coast of Algeria). There were several reasons why the heaviest presence was in the eastern Mediterranean, the most important being national defense and fleet defense requirements, Soviet emphasis on the Suez Canal, and Soviet relationships with the Arab nations. By concentrating ships in the area east of the Ionian Sea, the Soviets increased the threat to U.S. attack aircraft carriers operating in those waters. In wartime, the United States would have to commit carrier task forces to the eastern Mediterranean in order to reach desired targets efficiently or to conduct other missions, such as amphibious operations, in the Middle East. In addition, it is important to maintain a constant U.S. naval presence in the eastern Mediterranean, since a dominant Soviet naval presence in the area could invite adventurism by both the Soviet Union and its clients.

The Operations of the Fleet

The Soviet Mediterranean Fleet's operating patterns differed considerably from those of the U.S. Sixth Fleet during this period. Sixth Fleet surface combatants usually spent the majority of their time making calls at southern European ports or at sea participating in operational and exercise activities. Soviet surface combatants, on the other hand, spent well over half their time at anchor in one or more of the several Mediterranean anchorages. There were relatively few Soviet combatant port visits, and those that were conducted tended to be highly stylized and aimed at furthering Soviet prestige and influence. The majority of the surface combatants were from the Black Sea Fleet and normally were in the Mediterranean four to six months. They usually proceeded to a Mediterranean anchorage and remained there for an extended period. Occasionally, groups of combatants would participate in exercises, only to return to their anchorages when the exercises were concluded.

Soviet amphibious ships were perhaps the least active in the day-to-day operations. These units usually went immediately from the Black Sea to an

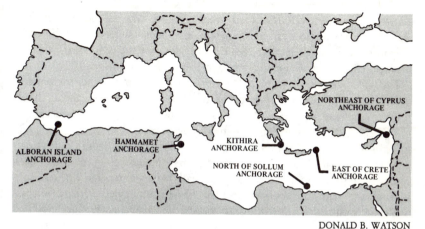

NORTHEAST OF CYPRUS
ANCHORAGE

ALBORAN ISLAND
ANCHORAGE

HAMMAMET
ANCHORAGE

KITHIRA
ANCHORAGE

NORTH OF SOLLUM
ANCHORAGE

EAST OF CRETE
ANCHORAGE

DONALD B. WATSON

MAP 6.2   The anchorages most often used by the Soviet Mediterranean Fleet.

eastern Mediterranean anchorage or port and rarely moved to one of the other anchorages. Minesweepers appeared to have greater freedom of movement than did amphibious ships, but even they were not particularly active. There is less information about the operations of Soviet submarines. The majority of their time was spent on patrol or in anchorage, and port visits by submarines were infrequent.

Logistic support was provided primarily by the Black Sea Fleet. Naval oilers and merchant tankers went from anchorage to anchorage and then to friendly ports for water and provisions, periodically returning to the Black Sea for additional fuel. The naval oiler force was augmented by Soviet merchant tankers to a greater extent in the Mediterranean than in any of the other ocean areas where the navy operated. (This augmentation by merchant tankers demonstrates the control and coordination of the merchant ships by the Soviet Navy.) Other logistic ships, such as stores ships and water tenders, followed patterns similar to that of the oilers. Repair ships spent the majority of their time in Mediterranean ports, primarily in Alexandria where the Soviets had access to a repair facility.

Reporting Activities of the Fleet. / Fleet operations required the manning of several anchorages and patrols in order to accomplish early warning and surveillance duties. An anchorage in the vicinity of Alboran Island, about 150 nautical miles east of Gibraltar, enabled the Soviets to monitor maritime traffic through the Strait of Gibraltar and to keep accurate tabs on Sixth Fleet operations in the western Mediterranean. Normally, at least one combatant and an auxiliary ship for logistic support were at anchor in the Alboran Basin. In the central Mediterranean, one or two combatants and some logistic ships usually were present in the Gulf of Hammamet, just south of the Strait of Sicily. This station enabled the Soviets to monitor maritime activity in the restricted waters of that strait, a choke point between the eastern and western Mediterranean. Soviet ships leaving the Gulf of Hammamet were often the first units to monitor the movement of U.S. attack aircraft carriers eastward through the strait.

The anchorages in the eastern Mediterranean most often used by the fleet were Kithira, an anchorage just east of Crete, one north of the Gulf of Sollum, and one northeast of Cyprus. Kithira anchorage was used extensively because it is convenient for ships moving to and from the Black Sea and it is ideally located to monitor and intercept any ship sailing northward into the Aegean Sea. Several combatants, including guided missile-equipped cruisers and destroyers, normally were at anchor in Kithira. Sollum anchorage, also used extensively by the fleet, gave the Soviets a location close to the Suez Canal. By stationing ships in both Kithira and Sollum anchorages, the fleet was in position to monitor and intercept ships proceeding further east in the Mediterranean. Stationing ships at the anchorage east of Crete enabled the Soviets to observe many of the ships going to and from the Suez Canal and to monitor maritime activity in the Aegean Sea. With ships at both Kithira and east-of-Crete anchorages, the Soviets could keep track of virtually all traffic in the southern approaches to the Aegean. Thus, those two anchorages were important for the strategic defense of the Soviet Union. Finally, the ships stationed northeast of Cyprus maintained a presence near the Syrian, Lebanese, and Israeli coasts.

Intelligence Collection Activity. / In addition to monitoring maritime activity from the Mediterranean anchorages, the Soviets also used intelligence collectors for active intelligence gathering. These collectors were auxiliary ships that had been specially equipped with electronics devices, and they were used on patrols off the U.S. *Polaris* submarine base at Rota, Spain, and off the Syrian and Lebanese coasts in the eastern Mediterranean. The Rota patrol monitored both U.S. naval activity at Rota and the passage of ships through the Strait of Gibraltar. The ship on patrol off Lebanon watched activity in Israel and the Middle East. Whenever a U.S. carrier operated in the eastern Mediterranean, it generally was under close surveillance by at least one Soviet ship.

Exercise Activity. / The Soviet Mediterranean Fleet conducted several naval exercises each year, but an exercise that lasted longer than a week was rare. The exercises were almost exclusively in the eastern Mediterranean, with only a few in the central Mediterranean. The recurrent themes were antisubmarine and anticarrier warfare. Antisubmarine warfare exercises were conducted by cruisers and destroyers using conventional search and attack procedures. An analysis of these exercises indicates impressive Soviet proficiency. Surface combatants and probably cruise missile–equipped submarines were engaged in the anticarrier exercises. Generally, a simulated U.S. aircraft carrier, played by a Soviet cruiser or a *Moskva* guided missile–

Soviet intelligence collectors constantly monitor U.S. carrier movements and the U.S. base at Rota, Spain. Here, a Soviet intelligence collector takes station astern of the USS *Franklin D. Roosevelt* in the Mediterranean Sea in April 1975. (U.S. Navy)

equipped helicopter cruiser, would be the target. A second combatant, often a *Kashin* guided missile destroyer, would act as the surveillant or "tattletale," and a cruise missile–equipped cruiser, such as a *Kynda,* would act as the attacking ship. Since nuclear-powered cruise missile submarines, such as the *Charlie,* operated in the Mediterranean, submarines probably also participated in the exercises.[6]

Soviet Port Visit Activity, 1967–1973. / The June 1967 war had a decided impact on Soviet visits to Egyptian ports. From 1967 through 1973, the Soviets maintained an almost constant naval presence in Port Said, Alexandria, Matrûh, and the Gulf of Sollum, with the most intense activity in Alexandria. A significant number of port visits were made to Syria. Tables 10 and 11 show that visits to southern European countries were less frequent during this period, but they were generally more formalized than those to Egypt. Visits to Greece and Spain began in 1972, but none were made to Israel during the entire period, reflecting the generally consistent anti-Israeli policy of the Soviet Union. Visits to Algeria, however, continued regularly, attesting to continued Soviet interest in that country, and visits to Tunisia and Libya began in 1968 and 1969, respectively.

Soviet Use of Egyptian Port Facilities. / In July 1967, Egypt, drastically weakened by the war that had just ended, considered that foreign assistance was essential to its security. Since the United States was closely linked with Israel and since the notion of supporting Egypt, a nation closely identified with Soviet initiatives in the Middle East, was not popular in either the United States or Europe, the Egyptians had but one course of action: to depend more heavily on the Soviet Union. The USSR responded with both military and economic aid and received several concessions in return, among them the use of Egyptian naval facilities (Tables 13–14 and Table 25 show that Egyptian ports were the most used by Soviet naval ships from 1953 through 1980, even though the Soviets did not use them after 1976).

Soviet naval personnel were present in Egypt's major Mediterranean ports almost constantly from 1967 to 1976, and they could thus report on and possibly take an active part in Egypt's naval and maritime affairs along the Mediterranean coast. Considering the coordination between the navy and other Soviet government organs in executing port calls and the fact that Soviet economic, political, and military involvement in Egypt was extensive during the period, the Soviet Navy's role in Egypt was considerable. Specifically, the naval presence was part of a coordinated network that secured for the Soviets a significant role in Egyptian internal affairs. That role gave the USSR an opportunity to realize in Egypt one of the USSR's basic long-range goals—transformation of non-Communist governments into socialist systems based on the Soviet model. This goal was not achieved in Egypt, largely because of Nasser's death, the orientation of his successor (Sadat), and the failure of an aggressive Soviet policy in the early 1970s—a policy that may have involved an attempted coup d'etat against Sadat.

Throughout the period from 1967 through 1973 and continuing into 1976, a Soviet naval presence was amicably maintained. A testament to the special naval relationship between the Soviet Union and Egypt is that the Soviet Navy was allowed to use Egyptian facilities until 1976, even though other Soviet military and civilian personnel were expelled from Egypt during the early 1970s.

The naval presence in Egypt also demonstrated Soviet support for the Arab cause vis-à-vis Israel. Since Soviet ships were present in all the major Egyptian Mediterranean ports, Israel may have been discouraged from conducting naval or air strikes against those ports, lest they hit Soviet ships and possibly prompt a Soviet counterstrike. The effect of the Soviet naval presence may be reflected in the fact that Egyptian coastal commerce suffered no serious disruption from Israel during the period between the 1967 and 1973 wars. Soviet naval ships stationed in Tartus and Latakia afforded similar protection to those Syrian ports.

Operations carried out against Israel also protected Egyptian airfields. Soviet naval reconnaissance aircraft operated from Egyptian bases from 1967 to 1972. Before the 1967 war, the Soviet air presence in the Middle East was restricted because Soviet aircraft could not fly over Third World countries without prior consent. However, the airlift of arms to Egypt via Yugoslavia in the summer of 1967 set a new precedent; the route was again used in December 1967 for "demonstration flights" by Soviet bombers. These and other squadrons of Soviet aircraft are known to have moved from one Arab base to another during "good will' visits. Furthermore, it is reported that Soviet pilots flew reconnaissance missions from Egyptian bases in Soviet-made aircraft with Egyptian markings as early as the spring of 1968, and they flew unchallenged over the borders of nations normally allied to the West. The Soviets also flew "defensive missions," particularly Egyptian air patrols over Cairo and reconnaissance missions over the U.S. Sixth Fleet.[7]

The use of Egyptian ports coincided with a radical increase in the size of the Mediterranean Fleet. Extrapolations from Tables 10–12 indicate that the Soviets maintained an average naval presence of 5 to 12 ships in Alexandria from 1969 to 1976 and that the length of the visits far exceeded the normal four-to-six-day pattern followed elsewhere. The fact that many of the ships were oilers and cargo ships implies that Alexandria served a logistic purpose in support of the fleet. It is probable that auxiliary ships were able to get water and provisions in Alexandria, and given the duration and intensity of the Soviet use of the port, it is likely that the Soviets had established some type of logistic facility there. Alexandria also provided the Soviets with ship repair facilities.

The presence of Soviet naval aircraft at Egyptian bases bolstered the Mediterranean Fleet's power by augmenting that force's reconnaissance capability, which could have compensated for the lack of seaborne aircraft. U.S. Navy spokesmen have stated:

> The air bases in Egypt used by the Soviets from 1967 until 1972 permitted Soviet land-based naval reconnaissance and ASW aircraft to operate over the eastern Mediterranean without overflying Greece or Turkey. The loss of Egyptian air bases to the Soviets in 1972 unquestionably reduced Soviet military capabilities in the eastern Mediterranean. However, the Soviet naval position in 1972 after the loss of the air bases was still far superior to that of a decade earlier.[8]

The Soviet Navy's Role in the Jordanian Crisis, September 1970

The Jordanian crisis, which occurred approximately midway between the Arab-Israeli conflicts of 1967 and 1973, was an interim test of the Soviet Navy's ability to successfully oppose the Sixth Fleet. The crisis was the result of a long period of Middle East tension. In June, the kidnapping of a U.S. diplomat and an attempted assassination of King Hussein had led to four days of hostilities between Palestinian and Jordanian forces. A truce lasted into late August, when hostilities again erupted, and on September 2, there was a second attempt on the king's life. Continuous conflict between Jordanian and Palestinian forces followed, and on September 7, Palestinian guerrillas tried to hijack four commercial airliners. Three of the attempts were successful; one of the hijacked planes was destroyed in Cairo, and the other two were landed in the desert approximately 25 miles from Amman, Jordan.

On September 8, 1 of the 2 Sixth Fleet aircraft carrier task groups was ordered into the eastern Mediterranean. The Soviet Mediterranean Fleet numbered 47 ships, including 9 submarines and 18 surface combatants. On September 10, Palestinian commandos captured another commercial aircraft and landed it next to the two planes in the desert near Amman. On September 13, the three aircraft were destroyed. Intense fighting then occurred, and by September 16, Jordanian forces had inflicted heavy losses on the fedayeen. On September 17, the *Kennedy* carrier task group was ordered to enter the Mediterranean, and a second amphibious task force proceeded eastward in the sea. The Soviet Mediterranean Fleet had been augmented slightly and, on September 17, totaled 49 ships, including 10 submarines and 16 surface combatants. After invading Jordan on September 20, Syrian forces were defeated after three days of intense combat. The crisis then subsided as the Jordanians consolidated their control.[9]

A superficial analysis might indicate that the incident was no more than another Mediterranean conflict, which the United States responded to with a show of force. Admiral Zumwalt, however, offers a different insight into the mood of the Joint Chiefs of Staff (JCS) during the incident. Citing statements made at the time by Admiral Moorer, General Bruce Palmer, Assistant Secretary of Defense David Packard, and in official JCS papers, Zumwalt has declared that the JCS believed that U.S. naval power was so overcommitted that it could not respond adequately if it were challenged by the Soviet Mediterranean Fleet.[10] In retrospect, it appears that the Soviet Union did not augment its fleet sufficiently to confront the Sixth Fleet and that the crisis was resolved by effective Jordanian military action. Admiral Zumwalt concludes:

> In a geo-political sense, the Syrian invasion was a test by a Soviet client state as to whether the massive Soviet strategic and maritime building program had sufficiently shifted the "correlation of forces"—a phrase the Soviets use to cover the political-economic-military relationships between nations—to make it possible for the Soviet Union to conduct an aggressive foreign policy in a part of the world where the U.S. writ used to run. The Soviet conclusion must have been "not yet, but soon." They learned that . . . though the United States was

deeply concerned with what happened in the Middle East, it was stretched very thin there in a military sense. The terrible danger of that last state of affairs is, of course, that in a major crisis—which the Jordanian trouble was not—the alternatives became backing down (abandoning old principles and old friends) or escalation (risking total war).[11]

Summary

For the world, "soon" meant October 1973, when such a crisis did occur and the Sixth Fleet was put to a severe test. The advantages gained from access to Egyptian and Syrian port facilities, coupled with a continuing construction program, enabled the Soviets to stage a most complex and assertive naval reaction in 1973.

Notes

1. Dragnich, *The Soviet Union's Quest for Access,* pp. 21–22, 25–26, 28–36, 39–47, and Hedrick Smith, "Soviet Navy Said to Increase Use of UAR Ports," *New York Times,* 5 April 1966, p. 10.

2. Polmar, *Soviet Naval Power,* pp. 65–66.

3. Wylie, "The Sixth Fleet and American Diplomacy," pp. 57–60.

4. Based upon personal observation. See also Neil Sheehan, "Admiral Says Soviet Shadowing Often Imperils Ships in Sixth Fleet," *New York Times,* 1 June 1967, p. 18.

5. U.S., Department of the Navy, Office of the Chief of Naval Operations, *Understanding Soviet Naval Developments,* p. 13.

6. Watson and Walton, "Okean-75," p. 93.

7. J. C. Hurewitz, *Middle East Politics: The Military Dimension* (New York: Frederick A. Praeger, 1969), pp. 99–100.

8. U.S. Department of the Navy, Office of the Chief of Naval Operations, *Understanding Soviet Naval Developments,* pp. 13–14.

9. Elmo R. Zumwalt, Jr., *On Watch: A Memoir* (New York: Quadrangle/New York Times Book Company, Inc., 1976), pp. 293–301.

10. Ibid., pp. 293–296.

11. Ibid., p. 301.

7

Role of the Soviet Mediterranean Fleet in the October 1973 Arab-Israeli War

The Arab-Israeli War of October 1973, or the Yom Kippur War, was one of the most significant events to shape the international maritime scene in the post–World War II period. It marked a shift in the U.S.-Soviet strategic and maritime balances of power and focused the world's attention on the importance of the Middle East.

For a variety of reasons, including the inability of the United States to maintain clear-cut strategic and military superiority over the USSR, the United States and the Soviet Union developed a détente relationship in the early 1970s and attempted to limit their strategic weapons inventories through the Strategic Arms Limitation Talks. During the 1973 Middle East conflict, however, détente did not prevent the Soviet Union from almost doubling the size of its Mediterranean Fleet, denying the United States control of the seas in the eastern Mediterranean, and conducting a policy of brinkmanship that created one of the most severe international crises of the post–World War II era.

The Background of the October 1973 War

Egypt's perception of its defeat in 1967, the resulting national disgrace, and the economic chaos that emanated from the war made a future conflict with Israel likely. The Israeli intransigence to Arab positions made such a war inevitable. Although grateful for the Soviet assistance that assured Egypt's national survival in the period immediately following the 1967 war, Egypt became increasingly impatient with the Soviets' unwillingness to provide the military equipment and training that Egypt felt was necessary for a future military victory. Soviet-Egyptian relations also became strained by the actions of Soviet personnel serving in Egypt. After 1967, Soviet involvement was substantial in the military, cultural, and economic sectors of Egypt. That involvement, coupled with reports and rumors of the heavy-handedness and frugality of Soviet personnel in Egypt and the revulsion many of the more politically moderate or religiously conservative Egyptian leaders felt toward communism, hastened the Egyptians' disillusionment with their Soviet benefactors.

After Nasser's death in 1970, one commentator noted that the Soviets aimed at maintaining an atmosphere of "no war, no peace" in the Middle East and became "directly involved militarily during the Egyptian-Israeli war of attrition in 1970."[1] Such a policy was beneficial to Soviet long-range goals because it guaranteed the Arab requirement for Soviet assistance, thus assuring the continuation of Soviet influence in the Middle East. The policy also prevented the creation of a situation that could lead to a U.S.-Soviet confrontation, which might adversely affect the lucrative concessions granted the Soviets as a result of détente. In this manner, the Soviets strengthened their inroads into the Middle East while containing U.S. reaction, thus synthesizing the Soviets' regional aims with their aims in the U.S.-Soviet dialogue.

The Soviet unwillingness to supply the more potent equipment, presumably MiG-23 *Flogger* aircraft and *Scud* missiles, that Egypt believed it needed to successfully engage Israel in combat, led to Sadat's further dissatisfaction. Large-scale attempts to extend Soviet influence in Egypt also drew criticism from Sadat, and the Soviets may have decided at this time that his removal was necessary. Thus, according to Sadat, they assisted Ali Sabry in an attempted coup d'etat in May 1971.

That act and continued Soviet refusals to supply Egypt with more sophisticated weapons led to the expulsion of approximately 20,000 Soviets from Egypt in July 1972. For Egypt, the departure of those personnel and Soviet aircraft meant a loss of security. However, the expulsion also freed Egypt to prepare for war without Soviet restraints. For the Soviets, the expulsion meant a loss of airfields that had supported a significant reconnaissance capability over the eastern Mediterranean. However, the move did extricate the Soviet Union from future hostilities that could have triggered a U.S.-Soviet or a Soviet-Israeli confrontation. Sadat did not completely close the door on a Soviet-Egyptian reconciliation since he allowed the Soviet Navy continued access to the port facilities at Alexandria, facilities that were necessary if the Soviet Mediterranean Fleet activities were to continue on the scale of the 1971 operations.[2]

The Soviet Naval Response to the War

At noon on October 6, 1973, the Egyptian Army crossed the Suez Canal and assaulted Israeli positions on the east bank. The offensive, carefully and secretly prepared, was brilliantly executed. Although the Soviet Union had not supplied Egypt with the most modern Soviet weapons, those arms the Soviet Union had provided were sufficiently abundant and effective when coupled with excellent training and preparations. Egypt made substantial gains against Israel on the battlefield during the first days of the war.[3]

Because of the eastern Mediterranean's proximity to the Black Sea, deep Soviet policy commitments to Egypt, and the tremendous naval power inherent in the U.S. Sixth Fleet, the Soviets, in October 1973, staged their most assertive naval reaction of the 1970s. On October 4, 1970, the Soviet Mediterranean Fleet had numbered 52 ships. Among them were 11 submarines, probably including 2 cruise missile or nuclear attack submarines and several *Foxtrot* diesel attack boats; 3 cruisers (2 guided missile equipped); 6 guided missile and conventional destroyers; 5 frigates; 2 minesweepers; and 2 amphibious ships. However, the Soviets normally relieved their Mediterranean-deployed submarines en masse on roughly a semiannual basis, and such a turnover was considerably overdue in early October. Thus, a guided missile destroyer, 4 submarines, and an auxiliary ship arrived in the Mediterranean on October 5, fortuitously bolstering the Soviet fleet. That the arrival of the turnover group had been delayed may indicate that the Soviets had foreknowledge of Egyptian intentions to attack Israel.[4]

The Sixth Fleet, which was considerably above its normal level of 48 ships as a result of a recently conducted amphibious exercise, included 2 attack aircraft carrier task groups: the USS *Independence* group, which was at Athens, Greece, and the USS *Roosevelt* group, which was in the western Mediterranean. U.S. amphibious forces were in the vicinity of Soudha Bay, Crete.

On October 5, the Soviets began to reposition their forces. Their naval ships departed Alexandria and Port Said, and the flagship of the commander of the Soviet Mediterranean Fleet, which was passing through the central Mediterranean to meet the new submarine group in the western Mediterranean, reversed course and proceeded to a rendezvous with other Soviet naval forces in an area south of Crete. Surveillance of the principal U.S. naval ships, including the USS *Independence,* the Sixth Fleet flagship USS *Little Rock,* and the amphibious contingent, was reinforced. That surveillance provided both the Soviet fleet commander and Moscow with rapid and accurate intelligence on the U.S. naval operations.

From October 5 through October 10, the Soviets delayed the departure of those submarines that were due to return home, which gave them a submarine force in the Mediterranean of 16 units by October 9, including 4 cruise missile or nuclear-powered attack submarines — a most potent threat to the U.S. naval forces. In addition, expansion of the fleet's surface combatant force level was begun on October 9, so that the following day there were

The Soviet Navy maintained close surveillance of all U.S. ships in the eastern Mediterranean during the October 1973 Arab-Israeli War. This *Kotlin* destroyer monitored the movements of the USS *Independence*. (U.S. Navy)

21 surface combatants in the Mediterranean, including 3 cruisers, 9 destroyers, and 2 amphibious ships. Many were missile equipped. Operations in this period included evacuating Soviet citizens from Arab ports and positioning combatants near Sixth Fleet ships in the eastern Mediterranean. The submarines that were scheduled to return home were held in the western Mediterranean and moved eastward after the U.S. airlift to Israel began.

The initial U.S. response was indecisive, probably reflecting existing foreign policy vis-à-vis the USSR and possibly reflecting concern for the inadequacy of available U.S. sea power. The U.S. government did not permit any provocative naval movements. Admiral Zumwalt has strongly criticized this tactic, implying that the movement of the Sixth Fleet ships was controlled by the White House, which resulted in an extremely undesirable positioning of the fleet and adversely affected its ability to carry out its missions.[5] Admiral Daniel Murphy, then commander of the U.S. Sixth Fleet, also supported this view:

> The initial guidance advised that the United States would maintain a low key, even-handed approach toward the hostilities. To project this attitude, the Sixth Fleet was directed to continue routine, scheduled operations and to avoid overt moves which might be construed as indicating the United States was preparing to take an active part in the conflict. . . . There was one exception to this low-key approach: Carrier Task Group 60.1 (the *Independence*'s group) conducted a short notice sortie from Athens to join the Sixth Fleet flagship in a holding area south of Crete to provide a significant, but conservatively placed U.S. naval presence in the eastern Mediterranean.[6]

Admiral Zumwalt concluded:

> "Conservatively placed" is right. It is hard to imagine a less forthcoming response to the plight of a friend who has just become the victim of a bloody surprise attack than the one Dan Murphy thus described. Moreover, the orders were extraordinarily rigid. They specified latitudes and longitudes and gave Dan little or no room for tactical maneuvers aimed at making his missions easier to carry out or his forces easier to protect or, optimally, both. Several times during the next few days Dan asked permission of the JCS—for in situations of this kind the CNO [Chief of Naval Operations] has control over the operations of the Navy only in his capacity as one of five members of the Joint Chiefs—to move these ships or those toward the east in order to make his surveillance of the battle scene more effective and evacuation of Americans from the Middle East, if it came to that, more rapid. Each request was turned down by Admiral Moorer, acting, he told me, on instructions from the White House, which almost certainly meant Henry Kissinger.[7]

Thus, by delaying the departure of the relieved submarines and reinforcing the fleet with several combatants from the Black Sea, and because of the poor positioning of U.S. naval forces, the Soviet Navy was well on its way to denying the United States sea control of the eastern Mediterranean after the first five days of the war.[8] On October 14, the Soviet Mediterranean Fleet was further increased to the unprecedented level of 69 ships. Continued augmentation brought the number to 80 by October 24.

Among the Soviet objectives was a desire to sustain the Soviet image as the champion of the Arab cause. This objective was achieved by resupplying depleted Arab arms inventories, conducting diplomatic and propaganda activities in support of Egyptian and Syrian aims, and creating a naval presence sufficiently strong to discourage U.S. military action in the Middle East. The Soviet Fleet surpassed its performance of June 1967, when it had merely maintained a heightened presence. Since the fleet's performance in 1973 was the most ambitious use of the Soviet Navy for political purposes up to that time, it is instructive to examine each of its functions.

The Soviet Resupply Effort

The tremendous equipment losses suffered by Syria, Egypt, and Israel dictated that hostilities could not continue without outside assistance. On October 9, the Soviet Union began to resupply its Arab clients by both sea and air. The sealift was conducted by Soviet and East European merchant ships and by Soviet Navy amphibious ships. The airlift, conducted by Soviet military transports augmented by Aeroflot aircraft, initially involved from 10 to 30 flights a day, but that number soon was increased. When the airlift ended on November 8, approximately 1,100 flights had delivered an estimated 20,000 tons of equipment.[9] Statistics for the sealift are even more impressive. By November 10, more than 100 Soviet and East European ships had delivered at least 1,300,000 deadweight tons of equipment.

Until the Soviet resupply of the Arabs began on October 9, superpower involvement was similar to that of 1967: The U.S.-Soviet naval confrontation in the Mediterranean paralleled but remained divorced from the Arab-Israeli conflict. However, when the resupply began and since the United States delayed in replacing Israel's losses of equipment at the Golan Heights and in the Sinai, the Soviet resupply of the Arabs could have drastically altered the outcome of the war.

Israel's survival depended on persuading the United States to replace the Israeli losses of equipment and consumables, perhaps even by independent action against the Soviet supply line, which would threaten to precipitate a major clash between the United States and the Soviet Union. Whether that was the Israeli intent on the night of October 11–12 is still shrouded in controversy. At any rate, Israeli missile boats hit the Soviet merchant ship *Ilya Mechnikov* during an attack on the port of Tartus. The Soviet response was to station guided missile destroyers between Cyprus and Syria, where they could react to any further attacks on merchant ships.

Sea Denial Operations by the Fleet

Between October 14 and 24, the Soviet Mediterranean Fleet was increased from 69 to 80 ships. The force included 47 combatants, 16 of which were submarines and 4 of which were nuclear-powered or cruise missile boats, which posed a powerful threat to aircraft carriers and shipping. The 31 surface combatants included 3 cruisers and 19 destroyers or frigates, many of them missile equipped. There was a heavy emphasis on surface-to-surface missile-equipped ships, including the initial deployment of a *Mod Kildin* destroyer. That destroyer and the other missile ships posed a strong threat to U.S. carriers. Several surface-to-air missile-equipped ships, particularly *Kashin* destroyers, were deployed for antiair warfare because of the threat of the U.S. aircraft carriers. However, in actual combat, the Soviets would not have had air superiority.

The main body of the Soviet surface combatant force was located south of Crete, close to the USS *Little Rock* and the USS *Independence*. The *Kashin* destroyers and the other surface-to-air missile-equipped ships performed "tattletale" duties against the *Independence* and other major ships, while the surface-to-surface missile-equipped ships and, presumably, the submarines remained close by, prepared to execute missile strikes against those targets.

In response to the increased tension in the Middle East and in preparation for the U.S. airlift, the USS *Kennedy,* three escorts, and an oiler proceeded from the North Sea to the Gulf of Cádiz, but were held out of the Mediterranean. Zumwalt concluded:

> Thus Admiral Murphy, who once the airlift began had to take on the additional missions of providing it with surveillance, warning, and sea-air rescue services, was required to operate with his Fleet widely dispersed and vulnerable. He was denied the help of *JFK's* group outside the Straits of Gibraltar. He was denied permission to bring *Franklin D. Roosevelt's* group eastward to join *Independence's* group in what would have been a sound defensive deployment. He was ordered to keep his amphibious forces in the vulnerable anchorage at Soudha Bay in Crete.[10]

Admiral Murphy supported Admiral Zumwalt's account:

> SovMedFlt was in a normal peacetime disposition during the first phase of the crisis (from the start of the war to the start of the American airlift). The scheduled turnover of Foxtrot (Soviet attack) submarines was in progress and, as a result, the turnover force of at least five conventional attack boats became augmentees. Almost all the Foxtrot submarines were located in the western Mediterranean during Phase I. Soviet units in the vicinity of the Task Group holding area south of Crete during this period neither represented a severe threat nor gave indications of an increased state of readiness. One conventional attack and two cruise missile firing submarines were in the general area but coordination with Soviet surface units was infrequent and sporadic. Therefore, ComSixthFlt did not perceive SovMedFlt a threat to successful completion of any of the perceived missions during Phase I. . . .
>
> Normally one ship trails a U.S. carrier task force in the Mediterranean. The trailer usually is a destroyer, seldom a cruiser. The Soviet fleet commander almost never appears on the scene but works out of anchorages. Since 9 October a cruiser and a submarine tender have remained near Task Group 60.1. Another cruiser and a guided-missile destroyer arrived from Kithira, after navigating the eastern end of Crete, early this morning. There are two admirals and two other command authorities on the Soviet ships. The object of this presence may simply be to let us know that they are aware of our activities and to make us aware of theirs.[11]

Admiral Moorer also believed that the situation in the Mediterranean was uncertain. He stated: "Victory in the Mediterranean encounter in 1973 would have depended on which navy struck first and a variety of other factors. Victory would have depended on the type of scenario which occurred."[12] The U.S. public and many sectors of the U.S. government would not fully realize the implications of the U.S.-Soviet balance of power in the Mediterranean until October 24.

Among the 80 Soviet ships in the Mediterranean on October 23 were 7 amphibious ships (2 *Alligator* tank landing ships and 5 *Polnocny* medium landing ships). This force was capable of transporting more than 2,000 troops and their equipment. A good part of the amphibious force was sent to provide logistic support for the Arab belligerents. Two of the *Alligators* and 3 of the *Polnocnys* probably were involved in resupplying Syria. These ships could have ferried equipment, including tanks, from the Black Sea to the Middle East, and their amphibious landing capability made unloading at established, and possibly congested, ports unnecessary. Since some of these ships were in the Mediterranean longer than the time required to deliver equipment and return home, they may have been used in direct support of the Arabs, by transporting troops or equipment to areas near the front lines.

Brinkmanship—The U.S.-Soviet Naval Confrontation, October 24–30, 1973

A turning point on the Egyptian front occurred when an Israeli offensive was begun on October 14. The tank battles that followed rank among the largest in history, and an estimated 250 Egyptian and 150 Israeli tanks were destroyed. On October 16, Israeli forces under General Ariel Sharon crossed the Suez Canal to join other Israeli units on the west bank of the Suez. From there, the Israeli forces moved northward and southward along the west bank. The situation became increasingly adverse for the Egyptians, and they agreed to accept a cease-fire on October 22.

That cease-fire was broken almost immediately as the Egyptian Third Army attempted to break through the Israeli encirclement. The Israeli forces then advanced on the city of Suez. The initial Soviet reaction to the failure of the cease-fire was contained in a message from Secretary Brezhnev to President Nixon, which stated that Israel had violated the cease-fire and that Brezhnev "hoped that immediate and decisive measures would be taken to prevent further violations."[13]

The Israeli forces continued their advance, trying to capture the city of Suez before another cease-fire went into effect. They had reached the city by the morning of October 24, and according to Vice Admiral Vince DuPoix, then director of the Defense Intelligence Agency, they had also occupied the Egyptian naval base at Atavia. Tank battles had occurred on the west bank of the Suez, and during the evening hours, President Sadat requested a UN Security Council meeting, asking that Soviet and U.S. troops be sent to enforce a cease-fire.[14]

The failure to achieve a lasting cease-fire prompted the Soviet Union to contact Washington. Admiral Zumwalt described Secretary Brezhnev's note:

> Ominously, given the elaborate diplomatic courtesy normally used in brusque exchanges, it started "Mr. President" rather than "Dear Mr. President." It said, the Secretary of Defense and Chairman reported, "that the Israelis had deliberately violated the understanding reached by the U.S. and the USSR and were embarked on the path of their own destruction." It suggested that the U.S. and the USSR send troops in to man the cease-fire lines. It said, they reported, "Let me be quite blunt. In the event that the U.S. rejects this proposal, we should have to consider unilateral actions of our own."[15]

It was shortly after the receipt of this note that the White House ordered an alert, the most comprehensive setting of Defense Condition Three (DEFCON 3) since the Cuban missile crisis. Defense conditions are the various states of readiness of the U.S. military: DEFCON 5 is the normal state of readiness, and decreasing numbers indicate progression to a state of maximum readiness for war. DEFCONs may be set worldwide or for certain regions of the world—as, for example, in the Far East during the Vietnam War. DEFCON 3 was an important signal to the Soviet Union.

A controversy arose almost immediately as to the necessity for DEFCON 3. Nixon opponents claimed that the president, deeply embroiled in the Watergate scandal, had ordered the alert to maintain the crisis at an artificially high level in order to bolster support for his administration. Such an argument assumes that the act was merely another political maneuver by the president and that there was insufficient Soviet provocation for DEFCON 3. If the Soviet threat was not sufficient to require DEFCON 3, then the available U.S. military power, i.e., the Sixth Fleet, was capable of countering Soviet actions in the Middle East.

Admiral Moorer believed that the press played a major role in promoting the Watergate theory. He stated: "The suggestion that the JCS would support such a move is a gross insult. This is a prime example of poor press coverage. The press tends to frighten people. They would have people believe that there are two buttons by the President's bed, one to alert the steward to bring the coffee and the other to start World War III."[16]

A host of additional facts contradict the Watergate theory. Admiral Zumwalt has stated that President Nixon was so deeply involved in Watergate that it was Secretary of State Kissinger, not the president, who was formulating U.S. policy toward the Middle East during the war. In addition, DEFCON 3 was set shortly after Kissinger's meeting with Secretary of Defense James Schlesinger; director of the Central Intelligence Agency, William Colby; chairman of the Joint Chiefs of Staff, Admiral Thomas

Moorer; and the White House Chief of Staff General Alexander Haig. The indication is that the decision to set DEFCON 3 was made at that meeting.[17]

Admiral Moorer provided additional insight into the motives for declaring DEFCON 3 and into the conduct of the meeting. He stated:

> Dr. Kissinger had been in Moscow and it was agreed that we would go with a cease-fire. However, there was momentum—a ground action in the canal area. Israel had sent raiding parties across the canal to destroy the missile sites. A battalion of Israelis reported that they were going to return to the Israeli side. General Sharon told them to stay and that he was joining them. In addition, Israel was attempting to cut off Egyptian forces in the South and was conducting a northward enveloping action which would terminate at Port Said. Israel agreed to the cease-fire, but the Israeli forces continued to move in order to consolidate their positions. In addition, there were indications that the Soviets intended to move into the Middle East. They had positioned matériel, including tanks and trucks, in Alexandria and Latakia. There was a standdown in the Soviet airlift. The Soviet airborne troops had been alerted. Finally, a message from Brezhnev had reached the White House a few hours before I was called.
>
> Secretaries Kissinger, Schlesinger, Colby, and I were the principals at the meeting when it was decided to declare DEFCON 3. President Nixon was present at the beginning and the end of the meeting, and also, Dr. Kissinger went upstairs to brief him from time to time. It was almost midnight in Washington which meant that it was almost daylight in the Middle East. We felt that if the Soviets were going into the Middle East, then they would arrive early in the day. This would allow them time to organize before sundown. We felt that there was not time to consult with our allies. Many people have said that DEFCON 3 was unnecessary. My answer is, "Prove that the Soviets would not have gone into the Middle East if we didn't set the condition." If the Russians had gone in then they would still be there.
>
> Actually, the setting of the condition was not that significant. However, the press had exploited it, made it look like an act of war. The point was to get the word to the Russians. We had been at DEFCON 3 in the Far East for much of the Vietnam War, for example. Drs. Kissinger and Schlesinger did not think that the American public should know about the alert and were upset when word was leaked.
>
> The Soviet policy is one which attempts to fill a vacuum. They do not press us and will generally back off. Cuba and Yom Kippur are examples of this.[18]

In addition to Secretary Brezhnev's letter of October 24 stating that the Soviet Union would act unilaterally if the United States refused to agree to a bilateral effort to achieve a cease-fire, there is further evidence to indicate that the Soviets intended to send troops to the Middle East.

1. The Soviet naval force in the Mediterranean at the time was the largest

ever to be assembled in that area. On October 24, the Mediterranean Fleet included 80 ships, and an additional cruiser and 6 destroyers were expected to arrive from the Black Sea in the next few days. Ultimately, the fleet peaked at 95 ships on October 31. That force was composed of

23 submarines
    6 cruise missile–equipped or nuclear attack submarines
   17 diesel-powered attack submarines, mostly *Foxtrot* boats
40 surface combatants
    5 cruisers, including 1 *Kresta II* and 2 *Kynda* guided missile cruisers
   15 destroyers, including 6 *Kashin* and 4 other guided missile destroyers
    6 frigates and light frigates
    8 amphibious ships: 4 *Alligator* tank landing ships and 4 *Polnocny* medium landing ships
    4 fleet minesweepers
    2 *Nanuchka* guided missile patrol boats
  4 Intelligence collectors
28 Auxiliary ships

There were also many cruisers, destroyers, and other surface combatants—many of them missile equipped—available for deployment from the Black Sea Fleet if the Soviet Mediterranean Fleet had needed additional augmentation.

2. Soviet airborne troops had been placed on alert. Golan has stated that the alert involved "seven Soviet airborne divisions consisting of 50,000 front line troops and nearly 100,000 support and rear contingents."[19] Such a force would have outnumbered the U.S. Marine contingent in the Mediterranean. Additional evidence indicates that four of the airborne divisions were put on alert only after the cease-fire had failed and that an airborne command post was set up in the southern Soviet Union at this time, implying that the Soviets were, indeed, about to deploy troops to the Middle East. The Soviets could justify such a move, since President Sadat had requested assistance from the Soviet Union and the United States.[20]

3. The Soviet airlift to the Middle East had ceased. This fact indicated that the An-12 *Cub* and An-22 *Cock* transports, designed for use by airborne troops, were being freed from their supply duties in order to ferry the airborne divisions into the Middle East.[21]

4. There were reports that Yugoslav forces had been placed on alert, possibly in response to a Soviet request to overfly Yugoslav territory.[22]

5. Two additional amphibious ships were expected to be sent from the Black Sea. Those ships could carry 1,000 Soviet marines, fully equipped and

All was quiet at Kithira anchorage on November 8, 1973. But the two *Nanuchka* guided missile patrol boats (left rear and left foreground), which arrived in the Mediterranean during the 1973 Arab-Israeli War, posed a potent threat to U.S. aircraft carriers during the crisis. (U.S. Navy)

ready for combat. The over-the-beach landing capability of the ships could have provided a versatile augmentation capability if Soviet airborne troops had been dispatched to the Middle East. The marines could have been used to establish beachheads along the Israeli coasts or could have been landed in Egypt to reinforce the Soviet forces there.[23]

6. Five additional Soviet submarines were en route to the Mediterranean. The arrival of those submarines would increase the submarine force to 28, thereby intensifying the Soviet threat to U.S. carriers.[24]

7. Soviet pilots were reportedly flying MiG-25 *Foxtrot* reconnaissance aircraft over the battlefield from bases in Egypt. If the Soviets were about to deploy troops to Egypt, it would have been logical for them to have wanted to accomplish their own reconnaissance.[25]

8. The Soviets had much to gain from sending troops to the Middle East. The Soviets had lost most of their influence in Egypt after their personnel were expelled in 1972. The USSR was seeking a means of regaining influence, and Sadat's request for assistance provided such an opportunity. If Soviet troops had been sent to Egypt, the result could have been tantamount to a Soviet occupation of the nation. Once there, the force would have been difficult to remove. It could have facilitated the overthrow of President Sadat and the transformation of the Egyptian political system.

It seems that the Soviets fully intended to put a substantial military force in Egypt. Whether this threat was enough to warrant the declaration of

DEFCON 3 and whether the U.S. Sixth Fleet was capable of countering the Soviets in the Middle East are still being argued. In this respect, the Joint Chiefs of Staff had warned of the weakness of U.S. sea power as early as 1970. During the Jordanian crisis of that year, Admiral Moorer had advised that "U.S. forces would have very little staying power in the Middle East" and cautioned that the United States "should make every effort not to become involved in large-scale military action."[26] Admiral Zumwalt had been even more emphatic.

> General Chapman and I were the only Chiefs who were willing to go the whole non-LeMay route and say outside the executive branch what all of us said so emphatically so often to each other inside: that American military capability had reached the point in several parts of the world at which the odds were that the U.S. would lose a conventional war with Russia and that there were risks, therefore, in taking a strong diplomatic line with the Russians in those places.[27]

Concerning the Mediterranean war, he wrote:

> I gave my view that the Soviets might very well seek to limit it to the Mediterranean because they knew as well as we that with the Greek and Turkish airfields closed to the U.S. Air Force, the Sixth Fleet was the only U.S. force that could engage the Soviets rapidly, and that the Sixth Fleet could not be sure of handling a Soviet "squadron" of more than fifty ships, including more than twelve submarines, plus Soviet naval and long-range air, alone.[28]

Further evidence of the weakness of the U.S. forces is found in a naval analysis completed in July 1970. It concluded:

> 1. Given current and prospective force levels, in a declared confrontation situation such as that posed by the "Cuban missile crisis," the Soviet Union could place the President of the United States in a position similar to that experienced by Khrushchev in 1962.
> 2. a. The current most likely area of confrontation would be in the eastern Mediterranean arising from the Arab-Israeli conflict.
>   b. Should the Soviets announce that they would militarily oppose any U.S. support to Israel, the USSR would pose a significant challenge to the U.S.
>   c. The achievement of relative nuclear parity by the Soviet Union removes one of the major edges the U.S. held over the USSR in 1962. The relative balance of general purpose forces has also shifted significantly since that period, and proposed cutbacks due to budgetary constraints could result in a decisive change in the military options available to the President.
>   d. If the decision to deny the U.S. the opportunity to support Israel were timed to coincide with a large-scale exercise, such as exercise OKEAN, a formidable Mediterranean squadron would exist.

e. Past studies examining sustained carrier operations against the combined air forces of Syria/Iraq and the UAR (assuming that aircraft in these countries were maintained and operated effectively) indicate that at least four CVAs (carriers) would be needed to gain air superiority. The added capability of the Soviet forces would gravely increase the threat to U.S. forces, and would place the U.S. at a disadvantage.[29]

In the years between 1970 and 1973, this position had not changed. At a State Department briefing in 1971, Zumwalt had stated:

The main point I want to leave with you is that the nature of the threat the United States faces is changing . . . Soviet seapower represents a substantially new dimension in world affairs . . . that is already beginning to trigger a quite different strategic environment for the U.S. than that to which we have become accustomed since World War II. We are accustomed to think of the USSR as only a land power. Now they are also a sea power. They threaten to "outflank" us from the sea not only in NATO but in other areas where our influence has been enhanced because our principal adversary could not operate there. We must begin to think of the Soviet presence in global terms—Soviet naval and maritime power make it possible for the Soviets to move beyond revolutionary rhetoric to direct involvement and support of factions anywhere in the world.[30]

During the October 1973 war, Admirals Moorer and Zumwalt both cautioned against expecting too much from the Sixth Fleet. At the Schlesinger-Kissinger-Moorer-Colby-Haig meeting, when it was decided to establish DEFCON 3, Admiral Zumwalt tells us that "Admiral Moorer made the point . . . that we would lose our ass in the eastern Med under these circumstances."[31]

Soviet ship movements shortly after Brezhnev's note was sent indicated that they expected the United States to respond with its Sixth Fleet. Those movements included detailing a *Kynda* cruiser and a destroyer to surveil the *Independence* during the early morning hours of October 25, relieving the less powerful ships of their surveillance duties. The *Kynda* group was one of the units that participated in an anticarrier warfare exercise that began on October 26. It appears from that augmentation and those operations that the Soviets were more actively attempting to restrict the options available to the U.S. Sixth Fleet.

Some people did not share the belief that the Sixth Fleet was inadequate, but the nation's chief naval advisers, Admirals Moorer and Zumwalt, consistently had stated for several years that the United States did not have enough naval power in the Mediterranean to deter Soviet military moves. Thus, the defense condition was set as a clear signal that the United States would oppose militarily the deployment of Soviet troops to the Middle East.

The alert was, in the minds of the nation's leaders, the only means of credibly presenting a threat to the Soviets, since it was believed that the Sixth Fleet alone could no longer restrain Moscow from deploying Soviet troops.

Late on October 24, the United States persuaded Israel to allow the resupply of the besieged Egyptian Third Army. On October 25, the Soviet Union agreed to the stationing of a UN force — one that did not include the superpowers — in the Middle East to man the cease-fire lines. That agreement signified the end to the strategic confrontation; however, once started, the U.S.-Soviet naval confrontation in the Mediterranean continued until the U.S. naval forces began moving westward into the central Mediterranean on October 30.

An *Alligator* tank landing ship that had recently entered the Mediterranean was sighted with Soviet naval infantry on deck. Because Soviet naval infantry is rarely seen on amphibious ships, their confirmed presence was a clear indication that the Soviets were bolstering their posture in the Mediterranean. Elsewhere, a cruise missile submarine was sighted on the surface en route to the Mediterranean. Since Soviet submarines almost always cruise submerged, it seems that the Soviets again were signaling the United States that a further augmentation of their fleet would occur. For its part, the United States made similar moves. On October 25, the attack carrier *John F. Kennedy* and her escorts were ordered to enter the Mediterranean and rendezvous with the U.S. forces south of Crete. At the same time, the attack carrier *Franklin D. Roosevelt,* her escorts, and additional amphibious forces were ordered to move eastward to the holding area south of Crete. U.S. destroyers in the Baltic Sea were ordered to the Mediterranean. Since the beginning of the war, the Sixth Fleet had been strengthened to approximately 65 ships, considerably above its normal level of 48.[32]

Admiral Murphy summarized the Soviet naval threat when he stated:

> SovMedFlt strength stood at eighty naval units in the Mediterranean on 24 October. That total included 26 surface combatants and 16 submarines, possessing a first launch capability of 40 SSMs (surface-to-surface or cruise missiles), 250 torpedos and 28 SAMs (surface-to-air missiles). The activities of Soviet surface combatants had been largely confined to maintaining one of three tattletales on each carrier task group and the amphibious units. Other combatants had remained primarily in port or at the anchorages. At least five conventional attack submarines had also been detached in the eastern Mediterranean on 24 October. Large changes in both the numbers of Soviet ships in the Mediterranean and their actions began on 24–25 October.[33]

One of the most difficult situations for Sixth Fleet forces to deal with is a Soviet anticarrier warfare exercise. When a U.S. ship is used as the simulated target, Soviet ships maneuver so realistically that it is virtually impossible to distinguish between exercise activity and a real attack on a carrier. In these exercises, Soviet forces are in position, and weapons are aimed at the target. All that is needed to transform the exercise into a shooting war is the order to fire. Just such an exercise was begun on October 26. Admiral Murphy summarized the situation.

> On 25 October a Soviet surface action group (SAG) composed of a Kynda (cruiser) and a Kashin (destroyer) joined the Soviet units monitoring TG 60.1. As other U.S. forces joined in the holding area, each task group was covered by a separate Soviet SAG which included an SSM and SAM capability. On 26 October, the Soviets began large-scale anti-carrier warfare (ACW) (exercises) against TF 60 with SSG and SSGN (guided missile submarines, diesel and nuclear) participation; this activity was conducted continously for six days following 27 October. A large-scale, rapid buildup in Soviet forces was also evident. By 31 October, SovMedFlt strength had increased to 96 units, including 34 surface combatants and 23 submarines, possessing a first launch capability of 88 SSMs, 348 torpedos, 46 SAMs. The U.S. Sixth Fleet and the Soviet Mediterranean Fleet were, in effect, sitting in a pond in close proximity and the stage for the hitherto unlikely "war at sea" scenario was set. This situation prevailed for several days. Both fleets were obviously in a high readiness posture for whatever might come next, although it appeared that neither fleet knew exactly what to expect.[34]

The Sixth Fleet and the Soviet Mediterranean Fleet were evenly enough matched so that in a war, the side that attacked first would probably have won. The Soviets, lacking air superiority and having a weak antisubmarine warfare capability, would have suffered significant damage from U.S. air and submarine strikes. However, the cruise missiles launched by Soviet surface combatants and submarines would have taken their toll of U.S. forces. Thus, should the Soviets have attacked preemptively, some, if not all, of the three U.S. attack aircraft carriers, the USS *Little Rock,* and other combatants could well have been damaged, if not sunk. Further, the Soviet forces were so positioned that only the firing order was needed for such an attack to occur. The U.S. forces were also on the alert, their ships were prepositioned, and their aircraft were airborne so Soviet losses would have been heavy. However, it seems that the U.S. forces could have suffered losses so severe that a further augmentation of the Sixth Fleet would have been required to assure U.S. supremacy in the Mediterranean. Thus, for the first time in the post–World War II era, the U.S. Navy had been effectively denied complete control of the seas. Throughout the entire period from 1957 through 1980, the Soviet Navy never posed a greater threat against U.S. naval forces operating on the high seas, nor was the navy's effect ever more relevant in the U.S.-Soviet nonstrategic balance of power.

Summary

During the October 1973 war, the Soviets used unprecedented political, diplomatic, and military power, and their naval, merchant and air transport, and airborne military forces projected a grave military threat in the Middle East. The employment of this power had several effects on the war, not the least of which, it affected the outcome of the war to the detriment of Israel. It has often been postulated that Secretary of State Kissinger's view of détente was one that pictured the United States as failing to have the fortitude to withstand a Soviet offensive. As a result, Kissinger felt that détente was the best means of coming to terms with the expanding Soviet power. This psychology affected the U.S. relationship with Israel to the extent that the United States required a modification of the intransigent Israeli position.

Among the primary effects that détente had on the war was Kissinger's demand that Israel not begin hostilities. This restriction and considerable Israeli overconfidence led to the initial Egyptian military success and an ensuing conflict, which Israel found extremely costly. The effect of Soviet military power continued throughout the war, precipitating the setting of DEFCON 3 and U.S. pressure on Israel to accept a cease-fire. As a result, Israel held only a portion of the east bank of the canal when the cease-fire went into effect, and in the postwar negotiations, Egypt recovered territory that allowed for the reopening of the canal under Egyptian auspices. What is significant is not whether U.S. actions were in the United States' best interest; indeed, in retrospect, restraining Israel and the improvement in U.S.-Egyptian relations have benefited U.S. policy at the expense of Soviet influence. The true significance is that Soviet military power had a very real effect on U.S. decision making and that because of the changed U.S.-Soviet balance of power, the United States may have been forced to act as it did regardless of whether its actions benefited U.S. interests.

The United States learned other lessons during the war. Chief among them were the fragility of U.S.-European relations in connection with crises beyond the borders of NATO and the potency of the Arab oil weapon. For a host of reasons, including a shift in the balance of power that was adverse to the United States, the majority of the NATO nations did not support the U.S. efforts on behalf of Israel. Only Portugal and the Netherlands actively supported U.S. policy. Many nations refused to allow U.S. military equipment stored in Europe to be sent to the Middle East, and Turkey acted directly against U.S. and Israeli interests by allowing Soviet transport aircraft to overfly Turkish territory. This disparity in U.S. and European views concerning Israel colored U.S.-European relations in the mid-1970s.

The war hastened the Arabs' realization of the power of oil as an economic weapon. During the war and in the immediate postwar period, the traditional Arab nations assisted the Arab belligerents in their conflict with Israel by starting an oil boycott. This affected the European and Japanese economies so significantly that it placed strains on U.S. relations with those nations. It also probably hastened the postwar negotiations in the Middle East and affected U.S. relations with the oil producing nations, particularly Saudi Arabia, the United Arab Emirates, and Iran. U.S. dependence on Arab oil, an overriding theme in the early 1980s, could influence U.S. attempts to develop stability in the Persian Gulf in the wake of the Irani revolution, the taking of the U.S. hostages in Teheran, and the Iran-Iraq War.

Finally, although the degree of Soviet involvement in the crisis was unprecedented, the Soviet Union emerged from the Yom Kippur War with less influence in the Middle East than it had enjoyed previously. The involvement of the Soviet Navy was so extensive and impressive that it should have earned the USSR greater benefits than actually accrued. The question is, What went wrong? The answer appears to be that the Soviets failed to gain significant concessions from Egypt in return for Soviet military assistance and support. Thus, although Egypt lost the war, it emerged as an independent nation with renewed prestige, which it refused to share with the Soviet Union. In the final analysis, the Yom Kippur War demonstrates that there are limits to the effect of military power and that such power is most productive when used in conjunction with equally strong political and economic factors.

Notes

1. Galia Golan, *Yom Kippur and After: The Soviet Union and the Middle East Crisis* (Cambridge: Cambridge University Press, 1977), pp. 21–23.

2. A. J. Baker, *The Yom Kippur War* (New York: Random House, Inc., 1974), pp. 23, 25.

3. Concerning these arms, in the interwar period alone, the Soviet Union had supplied Egypt with 1,046 aircraft, 2,769 missiles, 25 naval units, approximately 2,500 tanks, and hundreds of armored vehicles (see Stockholm International Peace Research Institute, *The Arms Trade Registers,* pp. 44–46).

4. Zumwalt, *On Watch,* p. 437.

5. Ibid., pp. 435–436.

6. Ibid., p. 435.

7. Ibid., pp. 435–436.

8. There is a distinction between denying the United States sea control, which is to prevent the United States from exercising all of its options on the seas, and sea control, which is complete Soviet control of the seas. Sea control requires significantly greater sea power than does denying the United States control.

9. Zumwalt, *On Watch*, pp. 432–433; and Golan, *Yom Kippur and After,* pp. 85–89. Once the U.S. airlift of supplies to Israel was begun, it soon outstripped the Soviet effort in terms of both distance covered and tonnage delivered. According to Admiral Zumwalt, the U.S. resupply effort was delayed because Secretary of State Kissinger wished to soften up Israel, thus facilitating the postwar negotiations. Zumwalt stated that the Israeli ambassador to the United States requested assistance a full week before the airlift was begun, that during the week Israel had to curtail its offensive operations against Egypt on the Sinai, and that Israel was thus robbed of the chance of scoring a decisive victory in the first week of the war (see Zumwalt, p. 433).

10. Zumwalt, *On Watch*, p. 436.

11. Ibid., p. 437.

12. Interview with Admiral Moorer, 9 January 1978.

13. Zumwalt, *On Watch*, p. 438.

14. Ibid., pp. 439, 444.

15. Ibid., p. 445.

16. Interview with Admiral Moorer, 9 January 1978.

17. Zumwalt, *On Watch*, pp. 435, 445. In his book, Zumwalt stated that he believed that DEFCON 3 was justified, and he made it quite clear that he was no friend of Richard Nixon. His credibility as a source is thus heightened in light of the fact that if DEFCON 3 were a political ruse, then Zumwalt would have been most willing to identify it as such.

18. Interview with Admiral Moorer, 9 January 1978.

19. Golan, *Yom Kippur and After,* p. 122.

20. Zumwalt, *On Watch*, p. 439.

21. Golan, *Yom Kippur and After,* p. 122.

22. Ibid.

23. Ibid., pp. 122–123.

24. Zumwalt, *On Watch*, p. 439.

25. Ibid.

26. Ibid., p. 294.

27. Ibid., pp. 294–295.

28. Ibid., p. 297.

29. Ibid., pp. 444–445.

30. Ibid., p. 331.

31. Ibid., p. 446.

32. Ibid., p. 447, and Golan, *Yom Kippur and After,* p. 125.

33. Zumwalt, *On Watch*, p. 447.

34. Ibid. The disparity in force level figures (for example, 95 or 96 ships on October 31) occurred because some observers, including Admiral Murphy, counted the ship on patrol off Rota in their 96 ships. Official figures do not include that ship and therefore state that the fleet peaked at 95 ships.

8

Soviet Mediterranean Fleet Operations, 1973–1980

After the October 1973 war, the Soviet Mediterranean Fleet force declined from a high of 20,600 ship days in 1973 to 16,600 in 1980. The majority of the fleet's time was spent at anchorages, and exercise activity followed established patterns. During this period, the fleet reacted to two Mediterranean crises, the Cyprus crisis of July 1974 and the Lebanese Civil War in the spring and summer of 1976. There was no great change in Soviet naval port visit patterns, although some additional ports were visited. The period also witnessed the expulsion of the Soviet Navy from Alexandria and the subsequent Soviet quest for alternative naval support facilities in the Mediterranean Sea.

Soviet Naval Exercise Activity, 1973–1980

The area south of Crete remained the primary exercise area of the Soviet Navy, reflecting the belief that this area is the most likely scene for an initial U.S.-Soviet engagement should hostilities occur in the Mediterranean. The dual themes of antisubmarine and anticarrier warfare continued to dominate the exercises, again demonstrating the Soviet belief that U.S. submarines and aircraft carriers are the two most powerful threats. The Soviet Navy conducted a rather large-scale exercise in June 1976, which was witnessed by Admiral Gorshkov. Because the exercise entailed a series of highly stylized maneuvers, it is possible that its purpose was to allow Admiral Gorshkov to demonstrate the navy's ability to other high-ranking officials. The fleet's combatant force was increased significantly during the exercise, reaching 45 ships on June 8, which was the highest level since the October 1973 war. The exercise involved approximately 30 surface combatants, including a *Moskva* helicopter cruiser, 7 cruisers, and at least 5 submarines, including guided missile–equipped units.

Similar exercises, although smaller in scope, were held in the following years, the most impressive being a series of operations conducted in March

The Soviet Navy demonstrated its growing competence during 1979 Mediterranean operations. While under way, the aircraft carrier *Kiev* and a *Kresta II* guided missile cruiser conducted alongside underway replenishment from the Soviet Navy's new oiler, the *Berezina*, pictured here, and the two *Kiev* carriers conducted joint operations. (U.S. Navy)

1979 (the location of these exercises is shown on Map 4.2). For the first time, the two *Kiev* aircraft carriers worked together. The first joint operation, conducted in the usual operating area south of Crete in early March, followed the traditional two-phased antisubmarine-anticarrier warfare scenario. At least eight combatants worked with the two *Kiev*s. Operations were highlighted by the carriers' Yak-36 *Forger* aircraft and *Hormone* helicopters and by RBU-6000 rocket firings.

The second phase of the exercise occurred in mid-March in the central and western Mediterranean. The exercise participants formed two groups. The first group, consisting of the *Kiev*, a *Kresta II* guided missile cruiser, the landing platform dock *Ivan Rogov*, and three destroyers and submarines, operated between Sardinia and the Balearic Islands. The second group, which included the carrier *Minsk* and two *Kara* guided missile cruisers, operated in the Tyrrhenian Sea between Sardinia and Italy. Although primarily oriented toward antisubmarine warfare, the presence of the *Ivan Rogov*, the navy's most advanced amphibious warfare ship, suggests that the exercise scenario also involved amphibious operations. The positioning of the two carriers on a west-to-east axis in the central Mediterranean and the dual flight operations by the *Minsk* and the *Kiev* indicate that the Soviets were conducting antisubmarine barrier patrols to exercise their capability to intercept U.S. and NATO submarines in time of crisis. Activity of that caliber in the central and western Mediterranean was noteworthy because the Soviet naval presence is traditionally light in that area.

Crisis Management Operations, 1974–1980

The Reaction to the Cyprus Crisis, 1974

The Cyprus crisis of 1974, initiated by hostilities between Cypriots of Greek and Turkish descent, involved both Greece and Turkey. Related Soviet naval actions reached a climax in July, when the Soviets apparently decided the hostilities endangered Soviet citizens. Although the fleet had been decreased in size, some ships were moved into the eastern Mediterranean and conducted surveillance of the Sixth Fleet attack carrier task groups. This situation continued as the United States evacuated its citizens from Cyprus by sea on July 23. Subsequently, Soviet forces evacuated their nationals from Larnaca. Both Soviet and U.S. naval forces later withdrew without incident.

The Reaction to the Lebanese Civil War, 1976

The Soviets responded more significantly during the Lebanese Civil War in June 1976. The U.S.-Soviet encounter that was related to that war had been building for months. It had begun in March, when the USS *America* and her escorts first entered a holding area southeast of Crete, and an amphibious task force had taken up position in the vicinity of that island. Soviet surveillance had been almost continuous throughout the spring as U.S. forces operated in the vicinity of Crete. Tension increased when the *America* task group was moved to the holding area again on June 10, and the amphibious task force steamed eastward on June 11. Large numbers of Soviet ships, many deployed for a major naval exercise, were ideally positioned to intercept the U.S. ships. Recalling the U.S. response to the Lebanon crisis of 1958, it is possible that the Soviets believed the United States was planning an amphibious landing in Lebanon. When the USS *Spiegel Grove* headed toward the Lebanese coast on June 20, a *Kara* guided missile cruiser tagged along. Even when it became obvious that the *Spiegel Grove*'s mission was limited to dispatching her small boats to evacuate U.S. citizens from Beirut, the *Kara* remained in the vicinity.[1] Meanwhile, when the Sixth Fleet flagship *Little Rock* arrived off the Lebanese coast, she too attracted Soviet attention, and a *Kashin* guided missile destroyer was assigned to keep track of her. Although the *Spiegel Grove* proceeded to Athens with the evacuees, the tension continued until the *America* and the amphibious task group moved westward on June 23.

Whether the Soviets actually feared a U.S. landing in Lebanon is not known. Nevertheless, they mustered considerable fire power in response to the U.S. ships' movements, although whether this power could have prevented a U.S. landing is problematic. Nevertheless, the Soviet threat contrasted vividly with the situation in Lebanon in 1958.

Soviet Naval Port Visit Activity, 1973–1980

Tables 10–12 demonstrate that the port visit program continued previous trends. Although visits to Egypt ceased after the Soviet expulsion from Alexandria in 1976 and there were none to Libya during this period, Syrian and Yugoslav ports were visited with increasing frequency as the Soviets sought alternatives to Egyptian facilities. Soviet ships visited several new Yugoslav and Tunisian ports in the period 1974–1980, and the first Soviet naval visit to Malta was in 1978. Finally, there was an increase in visits to all NATO countries along the Mediterranean coast, and the first visits to many Greek, Turkish, Spanish, and Italian ports occurred in this period. The visits to the two latter countries were made for logistic purposes, and they eased the Soviet supply problems considerably after the expulsion from Alexandria. The length of the visits to Ermoúpolis, Greece (see Table 12), probably indicate that the Soviets are repairing auxiliary ships there.

Expulsion of the Soviet Fleet from Egypt

The Arab-Israeli War of October 1973 drastically altered the Egyptian-Soviet relationship. Egypt emerged from the war with renewed prestige and with a good chance of regaining control of the Suez Canal through negotiation. What was required was a tempering of Egypt's position and its acceptance of the United States as the primary arbiter in the Arab-Israeli dispute. Those adjustments were in Egypt's best interests, since negotiations with Israel through the United States appeared to promise greater benefits than did renewal of relations with the USSR. Thus, Egypt's more moderate policies pertained more to the Egyptian-Soviet relationship than to the Egyptian-Israeli relationship. This situation reflected the U.S. aims of achieving peace and reducing Soviet influence in the Middle East. Thus, a prerequisite that the United States implicitly placed on Egypt was that Egypt reduce Soviet influence in its country. The United States, in turn, modified its strongly pro-Israeli stance to permit substantive negotiations in which, it was hoped, both Egypt and Israel would make concessions.

Egyptian moderation did occur, and the Egyptian-Soviet relationship continued to deteriorate through 1974 and 1975. Finally, on March 14, 1976, Cairo announced that it might abrogate its 1971 Treaty of Friendship and Cooperation with the Soviet Union. Three days later, Egypt stated that the Soviets would be denied access to the naval facilities at Alexandria after April 15, and the Soviets withdrew by that deadline.[2]

Soviet hopes of reestablishing access to Egypt were discouraged further in the autumn of 1977, when President Sadat announced that he would visit Israel in an attempt to begin a dialogue that he hoped would yield a lasting peace in the Middle East. U.S.-sponsored Israeli-Egyptian negotiations and the subsequent understanding further dimmed Soviet hopes of regaining a foothold in Egypt.

The potential effects of an ultimate regional understanding could be devastating for the Soviets. Conceivably, Jordan and other Arab nations might join in a more comprehensive and lasting peace agreement if the Palestinian problem can be resolved. In that case, the long-term regional instability, which has been caused by the Arab-Israeli adversary relationship and which has been so beneficial to Soviet policy, might be moderated. A U.S.-sponsored amelioration of the political situation in the Middle East would almost certainly be adverse to Soviet interests. At the close of 1980, any significant improvement either in Soviet-Egyptian relations or in Soviet prestige elsewhere in the northern tier of the Middle East appeared unlikely as long as President Sadat remained in power.[3]

The Search for Alternative Naval Support Facilities

Following its expulsion from Alexandria, the Soviet Navy has made greater use of the Syrian facilities. Those ports, located in the far eastern Mediterranean, are extremely congested and are not well suited for Soviet naval support. As a result, the Soviets have sought access to alternative ports. A prolonged visit to Yugoslavia by Admiral Gorshkov in the summer of 1976, apparently associated with the fleet's support requirements, failed to produce substantial concessions, and Soviet use of Yugoslav ports did not increase notably in the following years. The restricted waters leading to Yugoslavia also reduce the attractiveness of that country's ports.

Port visits to Tunisia and Algeria in 1976 and 1977 probably reflect attempts to gain increased access to those countries' ports. Many of those ports, located on the African coast in the central Mediterranean, have adequate facilities for logistic purposes. Tables 10–12 show that the Soviets have met with some success in Tunisia. There were port visits to Sfax and Sousse in 1976, and visits to Menzel-Bourguiba began in 1977. From 1977 through 1980, the average duration of the calls to Menzel-Bourguiba exceeded the normal 4-to-6-day limit, indicating that the Soviets had some use of that port's facilities. As is shown in Table 11, the Soviet presence there jumped from 161 days in 1977 to 392 days in 1978. The fact that there were slight decreases in 1979 and 1980 suggests that the Tunisians have not granted the Soviets unlimited access.

Soviet ships apparently undergo repair and yard work during their calls to Menzel-Bourguiba (see Tables 13 and 25). The port ranked as the ninth most used Mediterranean port by the Soviet Navy through 1980, with a total of 1,210 days, and Tunisia ranked as the sixth most visited Mediterranean nation (see Table 14) and the fifteenth most visited of all nations. Yet it does not appear that the Soviets have acquired a replacement for the facilities they once had in Alexandria. It also seems that they do not intend to rely again on the port facilities of only one country, however. Since 1976, the Soviet Navy has used Yugoslav, Syrian, and Tunisian ports for repair and has increased its logistic use of Spanish and Italian ports.

Problems Confronting Future Soviet Mediterranean Fleet Operations

From 1958 through 1980, the Soviet Union, through its naval power, its diplomatic, economic, and cultural activities in the Middle East, and its military assistance, greatly diminished U.S. influence in the Mediterranean. As the decade of the eighties began, it appeared that the Soviets would continue to attach great significance to their naval presence in the Mediterranean. Yet, in December 1980, the Soviet Union was confronted with problems that could affect the Mediterranean Fleet's effectiveness in defending the USSR and achieving Soviet foreign policy goals. Of those problems, the following seem paramount.[4]

First, the ultimate goal, control of the Suez Canal, has continued to elude the Soviet Union. Although the June 1967 war had enabled the Soviet Union to exert great influence over Egypt's affairs, closing the canal had negated Soviet influence over the waterway. From 1971 through 1973, the Soviet position in Egypt had declined. After the October 1973 war, however, the canal was reopened under Egyptian auspices. Therefore, the Soviet-Egyptian relationship of 1980 was similar to that of 1966 to the extent that the Soviet Union wanted to control the canal and an independent Egypt wanted to limit Soviet impact on its internal affairs. But other factors were different in 1980.

For example, Soviet influence over the Arab-Israeli relationship had decreased. Soviet policy in the Middle East had focused on exploiting the Arab-Israeli hostility, and until 1973, Soviet success in Egypt was directly related to Egypt's losses in the war with Israel and its alienation from the West. Egyptian success in the October 1973 war, coupled with the beneficial effects of continued peace on that nation's economy, had done much to moderate the Egyptian position vis-à-vis Israel. In January 1981, direct Egyptian-Israeli negotiations offered hope of further reducing the Arab-Israeli animosity. The U.S. role as the principal arbitrator between Egypt and Israel greatly diminished Soviet influence in Arab-Israeli affairs. Thus, although the Soviet's ultimate aim of controlling the Suez Canal remains unchanged, the immediate goal of gaining a foothold in Egypt has been frustrated by changes in Israeli-Egyptian relations. The Soviet Union's future in Egypt remains dim as long as Egypt's political stability and economy do not deteriorate dramatically.

The second problem is that the Soviet Union does not dominate any of the exits from the Mediterranean. The Turkish straits, the Suez Canal, and the Strait of Gibraltar continue to be controlled by nations that are potentially hostile to the Soviet Union. Therefore, Soviet naval power in wartime could be restricted by the loss of access to any one of those exits.

The Turkish straits, easily interdicted in time of war and diplomatically restricted in time of peace, pose a very great strategic problem for the Soviets. To avoid having their ships bottled up in the Black Sea, the Soviets have maintained an inflated Mediterranean Fleet. That fact, coupled with the continued use of contingency or false declarations for transits of the Turkish straits, has eased the threat posed by the waterway, but developing adequate alternative support facilities outside the Black Sea is the only completely acceptable long-range solution. Bases along the Indian Ocean littoral and in the Mediterranean would further guarantee that adequate naval power could be stationed in those two areas.

The state of Soviet-Egyptian relations has had a decided effect on Soviet naval operating patterns. Soviet combatants seldom used the Suez Canal between 1975 and 1980. Before the navy can augment the Indian Ocean Squadron with ships from the Black Sea Fleet on a regular basis, the Soviets have to be sure that the use of that waterway by Soviet combatants is reasonably secure. The minimum requirements for such security would probably be enough Soviet influence over Egypt to ensure the relatively free use of the canal and a worsening of the Israeli military position to the extent that Israel would be militarily incapable of closing the canal. Since those minimum requirements have not been met, the Soviet Indian Ocean operations in 1980 still required stationing major surface combatants in the Pacific, where they are so geographically isolated that they cannot be quickly available for crisis management operations in the West. Thus, Soviet policy in the early 1980s will be directed toward guaranteeing the security of Soviet warships using the canal.

Although Soviet harassment of U.S. naval ships had virtually ended by 1973, Soviet surveillance of U.S. naval operations brings the two navies together. In May 1977, a Soviet *Echo II* submarine suffered damage to her bow and sail when she collided with the USS *Voge* in the Ionian Sea. (U.S. Navy)

The Strait of Gibraltar is also a potential barrier to the Soviet Union. Passage through the strait could be controlled by the British from their self-governing colony of Gibraltar or by Spain or Portugal. The importance of Gibraltar is certain to increase in the future as the Soviet Union continues to expand its presence along the West African coast. Ships operating off Africa have been staged from the Black Sea, Baltic, and Northern Fleets. However, if the Soviet West African presence increases as is expected, their use of the Strait of Gibraltar could become crucial. Thus, both an increase in the Soviet naval presence in the western Mediterranean and diplomatic overtures toward Morocco, on the strait's southern shore, and Great Britain (or Spain if the proprietorship of Gibraltar were to revert to the Spanish) could be expected in order to assure continued Soviet naval use of the strait.

The third major problem centers around the presence of the Sixth Fleet. Although there has been a relative shift in the U.S.-Soviet naval balance of power in the Mediterranean, the Sixth Fleet continues to pose a powerful threat to the Soviet Union. From the eastern Mediterranean, the U.S. fleet is ideally positioned to launch strikes against Soviet forces with response times that would be much more rapid than those by any other type of U.S. military power. The U.S. fleet is also of inestimable value in a variety of other situations. As Admiral Zumwalt has demonstrated, in the years since World War II, the "relevant power" in a crisis has been the navy in almost all cases. He further believes that naval power will continue to be the relevant power, except for those situations involving a nuclear attack on the United States.[5] Admiral Horacio Rivero, commander in chief of allied forces, southern Europe, from 1968 to 1972 and ambassador to Spain from 1972 to 1974, has maintained that the Sixth Fleet has to be "counted as an essential component of NATO defense of the land" and that a reduction of the fleet's aircraft carrier strength in peacetime would "have disastrous consequences for the wartime scheme of defense in the southeastern sector."[6] The fleet also provides the only relevant power in the Middle Eastern conflict situations, as the periodic Arab-Israeli Wars have demonstrated.

As of January 1981, the Soviet Mediterranean Fleet was not strong enough to prevent U.S. operations in the Mediterranean, and U.S. commitments to NATO and Israel necessitate continued Sixth Fleet operations in the area for the next several decades. The Soviet response to that commitment appears to be both military and diplomatic in nature. Militarily, although the force level of the Soviet Mediterranean Fleet has declined since 1973, it is still the Soviet Union's most concentrated presence on the high seas and continues to be composed of the most modern surface combatants. This force concentration is expected to continue in the 1980s, although the trend of a slightly declining force level also will probably continue.

Fourth, in January 1981, the political value of the Soviet fleet was underutilized. The political value of the Soviet Navy was most significant from 1967 to 1972, when the fleet had access to Egyptian ports and Soviet naval aircraft were staged from Egyptian airfields. After that period, the political use of the navy declined and was further curtailed in 1976 when it was expelled from Alexandria. In 1980, political employment of the Mediterranean Fleet was limited to maintaining a presence in the eastern Mediterranean and to conducting a moderate port visit program. The navy exerts important political influence only in Syria, Yugoslavia, and possibly Tunisia. Given the political mission of the fleet and the inherent messianism of Soviet communism, it seems certain that the Soviets will continue to make overtures that are aimed at exerting a greater influence over selected Mediterranean littoral nations. Gaining access to indigenous port facilities appears to be the ideal means of achieving such an influence, and Algeria and Tunisia seem to be the most likely targets. Success in those two countries could lead to a marked extension of Soviet influence in the internal affairs of the region.

Summary

In no other area has the Soviet challenge to U.S. naval forces been as severe as in the Mediterranean. The intensity and dimensions of Soviet operations reflect the importance the Soviets attach to the Mediterranean and that region's relevance toward achieving the long-range goals. The operations signify that the Soviets intend to use their navy as a political instrument. The Mediterranean operations foretell what should be expected in the 1980s and 1990s if the Soviets develop the ability to station naval forces in other ocean areas on a scale equal to that of their Mediterranean Fleet.

Notes

1. James M. Markham, "U.S. Evacuates 263 from Beirut on Naval Vessel," *New York Times,* 21 June 1976, pp. 1, 14.

2. Henry Tanner, "Sadat Acts to End Pact with Soviets Cairo Signed in 1971," *New York Times,* 15 March 1976, pp. 1, 5, and Drew Middleton, "Egypt Begins a Hurried Search to Add to Sources of Weapons," *New York Times,* 28 March 1976, pp. 1, 8.

3. President Sadat's assassination in October 1981 was advantageous for Soviet policy, because it weakened Egypt's ties with the West and because it ushered in a period of uncertainty for that nation. In the months following Sadat's death, his successor, President Mohammed Hosni Mubarak would have to confront two difficult problems, disaffection in the Egyptian military and the resurgence of Islamic fundamentalism in Egypt. Both forces would exert an effect on Egypt's relations with Israel and the West, and both could be manipulated for Soviet purposes.

However, Soviet success is by no means assured. The USSR has been denied significant influence in Egypt since the early 1970s and has since supported Libya, Egypt's enemy. Attempting to manipulate either the military or the fundamentalists is fraught with difficulty, since both have histories of unpredictability. Furthermore, if the USSR succeeds in regaining its prestige in Egypt, it might find itself in a situation similar to its fiasco with Ethiopia and Somalia in 1977, when it supported two conflicting nations. In short then, although Sadat's death has created new opportunities for the Soviets, it does not mean that Soviet success is certain. The situation depends on the success Mubarak has in dealing with Egypt's internal problems and on the skill with which the Soviet leadership handles Egypt.

4. Some of the following ideas have previously appeared in Bruce W. Watson, "Maritime Problems in the Mediterranean Sea As We Approach the Twenty-First Century," in *Problems of Sea Power As We Approach the Twenty-First Century,* ed. James L. George (Washington, D.C.: American Enterprise Institute for Public Policy Research, 1978), pp. 97–122.

5. Zumwalt, *On Watch,* pp. 344–346, 526–527.

6. Horacio Rivero, "Why a U.S. Fleet in the Mediterranean?" *U.S. Naval Institute Proceedings* 103 (May 1977):66–89.

Part 3

The Pacific and Indian Oceans

9

The Pacific Ocean, 1956–1980

Soviet Naval Strategy

The Soviet Pacific Fleet began as a defensive force, but it has grown in size and in strategic capability so that by 1981, it was fully capable of projecting its power for crisis response and for operations in the Indian Ocean.

As is noted in Chapter 2, the Soviet Union's postwar naval strategy was to first secure the nation's four maritime approaches. Of the four, the Northern, Baltic, and Black Sea routes were given precedence over the Pacific. Detailing naval forces to the Pacific isolated them from defending the more important western areas, since the movement of ships from the Pacific to the west involves either an extended voyage through the Pacific and Indian oceans, the Red Sea, Suez Canal, Mediterranean Sea, and Atlantic Ocean or along the northern sea route, which is navigable only during the peak summer months. Also, the Pacific ports often are icebound during the winter months, further reducing the utility of the fleet on the USSR's Pacific flank. As a result, in terms of out-of-area ship days, naval activity has been significantly greater in the Atlantic Ocean than in the Pacific (see Tables 2–3).

In the late 1960s, surface combatants were still being transferred from the west to the Pacific only when the ships could be spared from the western fleets. However, toward the end of that decade, the Soviets began to transfer some newer surface combatants and submarines to bolster the Pacific Fleet. The immediate reason for this change was probably that fleet's regular deployment of ships to the Indian Ocean. However, Soviet security and regional goals in the Pacific also played a role.

In 1971, *Yankee* nuclear-powered ballistic missile submarine patrols were begun in the Pacific, three years after they started in the Atlantic. This was a tremendous boost for Soviet security because the Pacific patrols brought all of the major U.S. mainland cities as well as Hawaii and parts of Alaska within submarine-launched missile range. The subsequent deployment of *Delta* submarines to the Pacific has further increased this security. The range of the *Deltas'* missiles puts them within firing range of Seattle, Portland, San Francisco, Los Angeles, Hawaii, and Alaska shortly after the *Deltas* depart their home port, Petropavlovsk. For the United States to locate and destroy the *Deltas* in wartime would require penetrating the Soviet Pacific Fleet's waters, possibly with heavy losses.

The fleet's strategic capability has been reinforced with impressive numbers of major surface combatants, attack and cruise missile submarines, and a strong naval air force. Coastal defense, mine warfare, and amphibious forces provide further security. With this navy, the Soviets have enhanced the defense of their Pacific coast against seaborne attack and have established control over portions of the Sea of Japan.

Pacific Fleet Naval Operations

Naval Presence, Surveillance, and Harassment

The evolution of the Soviet naval operations in the Pacific paralleled operations in the Atlantic but on a much smaller scale. The initial operations involved training in local fleet exercise areas and movement between the several Soviet Pacific ports. From 1956 to 1966, the number of out-of-area ship days burgeoned from 200 to 2,800, an increase of 1,300 percent. Equipment malfunctions and mishaps similar to those in the Atlantic occurred in the Pacific, and equipment and training problems were probably even more severe, given the lower priority assigned to the Pacific Fleet. As more ships were transferred to the Pacific, the out-of-area operations increased. Pacific Fleet ships logged 3,600 out-of-area days in 1967 and reached a peak of 11,800 days in 1980, 1,400 more than in 1979. Part of this increase was due to operations off Vietnam.

The majority of the Soviet operations have involved exercise and surveillance activities and movements to and from the Indian Ocean. The Soviets apparently do not feel it is essential to maintain a constant surface combatant presence in the Pacific, although the fleet was capable of such operations by the late 1960s. Rather, they have opted for constant Indian Ocean operations and periodic Pacific naval voyages, sometimes as far as the Hawaiian Islands. Meanwhile, they have increased their influence in the Sea of Japan and have established choke point patrols, and U.S. naval ships operating in that area have come under increasing Soviet surveillance. By the early 1970s, periodic U.S.–South Korean naval exercises in the southern Sea of Japan were monitored by Soviet naval units, and Soviet actions grew increasingly assertive. Harassment of U.S. naval units became commonplace. On May 10, 1967, a Soviet combatant even collided with a U.S. Navy ship in the Sea of Japan.

Again, as in the Atlantic, intelligence collection patrols are a vital part of Soviet naval operations in the Pacific. Patrols off Japan began in the late

The Soviet Navy's Pacific Fleet has focused its out-of-area operations on the Indian Ocean. Nevertheless, some impressive Soviet naval operations have been staged near U.S. territory. Two Soviet destroyers, a *Foxtrot* submarine, and an oiler are pictured here, at anchor 25 miles south of Honolulu in 1971. (U.S. Navy)

In the 1960s, the Soviet Pacific Fleet, like the Soviet western fleets, harassed U.S. naval ships. This picture, taken on May 10, 1967, shows the *Kotlin* destroyer *Bessledniy* colliding with the USS *Walker*. Neither ship was seriously damaged in the incident, which was nicknamed "Sea Chicken." (U.S. Navy)

1950s, and by the mid-1960s, intelligence collectors were conducting operations off the U.S. *Polaris* submarine base on Guam Island. Subsequently, patrols were established in the vicinity of the Marshall Islands, and in the mid-1970s, off the U.S. West Coast and the coast of the People's Republic of China.

Pacific Fleet Exercise Activity

Exercises usually are held in the spring and autumn months with national defense the dominant theme. Simulated enemy forces group in the East China Sea and proceed northward. These forces are intercepted by surface combatants and submarines as they attempt to enter the Sea of Japan through the Tsushima Strait. In recent years, coordinated air strikes have also been staged by the Pacific Fleet Naval Air Force.

Okean-75, conducted in April 1975, was one of the most impressive exercises conducted in the Pacific (Map 2.2 shows the *Okean-75* exercise operating areas). Groups of combatants operated east of Japan, in the Philippine and East China seas, and east of the Kamchatka Peninsula. Initially, naval forces were deployed to locate the simulated enemy forces. In subsequent phases of the exercise, the Pacific Fleet carried out a variety of tactics. The groups in the Philippine and East China seas probably participated in interdicting the sea lanes that run through those areas. Both offensive and defensive convoy activities were practiced in an area east of Japan. Finally, the Soviets staged strike operations conducted primarily by aircraft, but probably supported by or coordinated with submarine attacks. These strikes occurred almost simultaneously with others in the Atlantic Ocean and the Norwegian Sea.

The Pacific Fleet's Port Visit Program

Tables 15–19 show that from 1956 through 1980, the Pacific Fleet visited only 31 ports in 22 Pacific nations. This low number reflects the relatively low priority the Soviets have assigned to the Pacific. In the later 1950s, naval ships made port visits to only 2 countries, the People's Republic of China and Indonesia. In the 1960s, there were no further calls at those countries, but visits were made to Cambodia, Canada, Chile, Japan, Mexico, Singapore, and the United States. Those to Canada, Chile, and Mexico reflect the expansion of operations to include the eastern Pacific and were for crew rest and recreation rather than for political purposes. In 1966, Soviet auxiliary ships began visits to Japanese ports. The 1 ship to visit San Francisco in 1967 was also for routine purposes.

An exception to the Pacific Fleet's low-key approach to port visits was its use of Singapore. Brief visits were begun in 1969, and the number increased in 1970 and 1971, but the length of most was 3 to 5 days. The purpose was

MAP 9.1   Western Pacific Ocean ports visited by Soviet naval ships from 1956 through 1980.

possibly to accustom the local inhabitants to seeing Soviet ships as a prelude to more extensive activity from 1972 to 1980. Table 17 shows that the average length of such visits jumped from 3 days in 1971 to 11 days in 1972 to 17 days in 1973, far exceeding the normal 4-to-6-day pattern and indicating that the Soviets were doing minor repair work on their ships while in port.

By 1974, the Soviets were using the Singapore shipyards for extensive repairs. The use of Singapore continued into 1980, both to supplement the inadequate Soviet repair facilities in the Pacific and to contain the growing Chinese influence in Singapore. In the early 1970s, the port was used to export greater and greater quantities of linens, rugs, and other Chinese-produced goods, and through that economic activity, the Chinese were becoming influential politically and socially. The Soviets lost their access to the Singapore repair facilities in 1980, as is evidenced by the relatively low number of ship days spent in Singapore that year. The loss of access may have been as a result of the invasion of Afghanistan, and at least temporarily, it could be a blow to the Pacific Fleet, since its own repair facilities are believed to be overburdened.

Elsewhere in the Pacific, a continuation of previous trends has been evident in most port calls. Those to Australia in 1972 and 1974 and New Zealand in 1971 and 1973 were related to Soviet Antarctic expeditions and were for crew rest and replenishment. The visits to Canada included an official visit in 1976. A visit to Valparaiso, Chile, in 1973 may have been a show of support for the Allende government, but the failure to make any additional visits to Chile indicates that the Soviets intended to make no naval response to either the election of Allende or his death. Visits to Ecuador were probably for replenishment and crew rest. Several visits to Peru are more suspect, since during the time they were made, the Soviets were negotiating with Peru for the sale of military equipment and Su-17 *Fitter* aircraft on very favorable credit terms. The visits to the Fiji Islands, Samoa, and Tahiti are also suspect as they may reflect Soviet desires to gain access to facilities in that area. However, if that was the Soviet objective, it had not been achieved by 1980. Visits by auxiliaries to U.S. West Coast ports signaled both a greater Soviet presence in the eastern Pacific and improved diplomatic relations with the United States through détente.

Visits to Vietnam were begun during the Sino-Vietnamese War of 1979. Table 19 shows that by the end of 1980, Vietnam ranked as the second most visited country by the Soviet Navy in the Pacific, surpassed only by Singapore. The *Minsk* visited Cam Ranh Bay in September 1980, and a naval presence, including submarines, at Cam Ranh Bay and Haiphong was almost constant throughout the year. The Soviets have also based long-range reconnaissance aircraft in Vietnam. There were also visits to Kompong Som, Kampuchea, in 1980.

Crisis Response — The Sino-Vietnamese War of 1979

The Soviet Union's aid to Vietnam during the Sino-Vietnamese War of 1979 was the first time the Soviet Union defended a Communist state against the People's Republic of China, the USSR's primary competitor in the Communist world. Because of China's assertiveness in the conflict, the USSR proceeded cautiously. Ships returning from duty with the Indian Ocean Squadron or from repairs in Singapore were ordered to take stations off the Vietnamese and Chinese coasts. Other units conducting patrols in the Pacific also proceeded to the South China Sea. Finally, ships were sent from the Pacific Fleet home waters in two major groups. The first was built around a *Kresta II* guided missile cruiser and deployed on February 4. The second, which included the command- and control-equipped *Sverdlov* cruiser *Admiral Senyavin,* was sent in late February. The *Kresta* group operated in the South China Sea off Vietnam, and the *Sverdlov* group was stationed in the East China Sea off the Chinese coast. The ships remained on station until hostilities began to subside, and since President Carter stated that the United States would not become involved in a war between two Asian Communist nations, the ships provided enough power to safeguard ongoing Soviet ventures in Vietnam.

The naval force, which eventually totaled about 30 ships, maintained a naval presence, performed reconnaissance and intelligence collection duties, and protected the Soviet airlift, sealift, and Vietnamese ports.

Naval Presence

As it became evident that the deteriorating Sino-Vietnamese situation might erupt into war, the Soviet Union was faced with the problem of deterring the People's Republic of China. The Soviets attempted to influence the Chinese through propaganda as well as through diplomatic and military means. Soviet troops were moved along the Sino-Soviet border, and naval forces took stations in the East and South China seas.[1] This use of the navy conformed to one of Admiral Gorshkov's precepts: Naval power should be stationed close to a crisis area to influence the conflict through its potential rather than by initiating hostilities.[2] The force was composed of several submarines and 11 surface combatants, including *Kresta II* and *Sverdlov* cruisers, *Kashin* and *Kotlin* guided missile destroyers, a *Krivak* guided missile frigate, 2 *Alligator* tank landing ships, and several auxiliary ships.[3]

Reconnaissance

In order to provide the Soviet leaders with rapid information on the war's developments, a close and accurate monitoring capability was required. This task was fulfilled by three intelligence collectors, naval ships operating along the Chinese and Vietnamese coasts, long-range Tu-95 *Bear D* reconnaissance aircraft, and other surveillance systems.[4]

Protection of the Airlift and Sealift

The Soviets staged an impressive airlift and sealift of supplies to Vietnam immediately before and during the war. Equipment had already been airlifted to Hanoi by February 22 when the fighting started, and Soviet ships subsequently delivered more arms and supplies to Haiphong. Naval units stationed in the East and South China seas patrolled the routes used by those ships.[5]

Protection of Vietnamese Ports

In addition to their offshore activities, the Soviet naval ships also visited the Vietnamese ports of Haiphong, Da Nang, Ho Chi Minh City (formerly

Saigon), and Cam Ranh Bay.[6] The Chinese were capable of launching air and naval attacks on those ports, but the Soviet naval presence increased the possible costs to the Chinese if they did so. If the purpose of the visits was to dissuade the Chinese from attacking those port cities, they had the desired effect.

The Soviet response to the Sino-Vietnamese War was a success, and the Soviet naval presence probably limited the scope of the conflict. In return for their support, the Soviets apparently have been given use of the naval base at Cam Ranh Bay, which could mean a significant shift in the balance of power in the South Pacific, the Indian Ocean, and in South and Southeast Asia. Soviet naval ships no longer would have to travel the hundreds of extra miles to the Soviet port facilities at Vladivostok, passing through restricted straits under Japanese and Korean surveillance. Using Cam Ranh Bay would enable the Soviet Navy to respond much more rapidly to Indian Ocean crises than has been the case in the past. It would also increase the Soviet potential for disrupting Japanese commerce, since Cam Ranh Bay is close to the sea lanes that lead from Japan to the Indian Ocean.

Bolstering the Pacific Fleet

The buildup of the Pacific Fleet during the 1970s made the Soviet Union's Asiatic neighbors, particularly Japan and the People's Republic of China, increasingly uneasy. Late in the decade, the buildup created a rather continuous debate over the adequacy of the Japanese defenses. The Japanese Defense Force (JDF) pointed out repeatedly that the Soviet Pacific Fleet was growing stronger and more threatening to Japan.[7] The JDF reported an increase in the Soviet surveillance of Japanese naval exercises and in sorties by long-range Tu-95 *Bear D* aircraft along the Asian coast,[8] and JDF spokesmen also noted that there had been a Soviet troop buildup in the Far East and that the Soviets had assigned *Backfire* bombers to the Pacific Fleet Naval Air Force.[9]

Arrival of the Minsk, *June 1979*

In the Pacific, an extremely important naval development was the arrival of the aircraft carrier *Minsk* and her escorts in 1979 as that arrival signified a strong increase in Soviet naval power in the Far East.

The composition of the *Minsk* group—a new aircraft carrier, two new *Kara* guided missile cruisers, the prototype *Ivan Rogov* landing platform dock, and a new oiler—was probably politically motivated, and the message was not lost on the Pacific nations. By the time the group arrived at the Socotra Island anchorage in the Indian Ocean, the Chinese were expressing alarm (Map 4.2 shows the route taken by the *Minsk* group to the Pacific).

The transfer of the Soviet Navy's second carrier to the Pacific Fleet graphically illustrates the rising stature of that fleet. The *Minsk* is pictured here, operating off the coast of the Philippines in 1979. (U.S. Navy)

The Chinese linked the *Minsk* group's operations to a larger purpose: "The recent intrusion of the Soviet aircraft carrier "Minsk" and an amphibious vessel for the first time into the approaches of the Red Sea and the Persian Gulf is of strategic significance. As an English magazine pointed out, the Soviet military presence in the Middle East has already threatened the security of the Arabian peninsula."[10] Noting the strategic location and commercial significance of South Asia and the maritime importance of the Indian Ocean, the Chinese alleged Soviet aggression in that area. They concluded that the Soviet endeavor, coupled with Soviet support for Vietnam, was a vivid testament of Soviet expansionist ambitions.[11]

The *Minsk* group entered the Pacific through the Strait of Malacca on June 18 and proceeded northward into the Sea of Japan on June 30. Although the group did not visit a Vietnamese port, it signaled Soviet support for Vietnam and opposition to China by conducting exercises in the East China Sea. Those exercises, which involved air operations by Yak-36 *Forger* aircraft and Ka-25 *Hormone* helicopters and antisubmarine warfare operations by the group, evoked public reaction in both China and Japan.

The most emotional reaction to the *Minsk*'s activities appeared in the Chinese press. This reaction began when the group operated off Socotra Island in May, continued as it entered the Pacific Ocean area, and intensified as it proceeded northward to Vladivostok. The Chinese reports continued to link the group's voyage to an expansionist strategy aimed at developing Soviet power in South Asia and along the coast of East Asia.[12] The method that the Soviets intended to use to develop that power was said to be sea power, specifically a strong navy and modern fleets of commercial ships, fishing vessels, and survey ships. Time and again, China tacitly linked itself to other states in its opposition to the Soviet Union, noting that the *Minsk* threatened the interests of the United States, Japan, and other Asian and Pacific nations.

The importance of the sea lanes to Japan was often mentioned, and the *Minsk*'s exercises in the East China Sea were interpreted as a show of support for Vietnam.[13] Noting that the size of the Pacific Fleet had been increased by 13 "large warships" since 1975, that it was expanding its own naval bases and using Vietnamese ports, and that the Soviet Navy had conducted many large-scale exercises in the Far East in recent years, the Chinese concluded that the arrival of the *Minsk* was yet another manifestation of Soviet expansion.[14] This analysis was considered relevant enough to be repeated in the prestigious *Beijing Review*.[15] The Chinese concluded:

> The arrival of the Minsk in the Far East has worsened the situation in the not-so-pacific Pacific Ocean. It is understandable that all peace-loving people are keeping an eye on the whereabouts of the Minsk.
>
> In sailing to Vladivostok, Minsk has followed precisely that course taken by the tsar's Baltic Fleet when it sailed to the Far East in 1904. A Japanese magazine satirically wrote that the voyage of "Minsk" is just like the Baltic Fleet 75 years ago. Although this magazine did not mention the fate of the tsar's Baltic Fleet, this remark has awakened the memory of past events and provided much food for thought.[16]

By contrast, the Japanese reaction was relatively unemotional, associating the *Minsk*'s arrival with a general increase in Soviet military power in the Far East. The *Minsk*'s presence figured prominently in a White Paper produced by the Japanese Defense Agency.[17] The general consensus was that the strengthened Pacific Fleet did not increase the strategic threat to Japan but that it did increase the military threat. This enhanced military threat was acceptable, provided the United States did not deplete its Seventh Fleet. If such a reduction did occur, Japan would have to take measures to ensure its security. The primary options were either to increase Japan's own military strength or to establish a closer relationship with the USSR.[18]

Summary

It appears that the Soviet Pacific Fleet will become even stronger in the 1980s. Nevertheless, it has some weaknesses; hence, it is important to examine those as well as its strengths, since both will influence the fleet's actions in the 1980s.

Strengths

In 1981, the Pacific Fleet was possibly the strongest of the four Soviet fleets; only the Northern Fleet came close to approximating its power. Each of those two fleets had an aircraft carrier, and together they supported the Soviet Union's nuclear-powered ballistic missile submarine force. The Pacific Fleet, however, had more major surface combatants, large amphibious ships, mine warfare ships and approximately 28 percent of the total naval aircraft inventory. With 121,000 men, the Pacific Fleet was the largest of the four fleets in terms of manpower.

It is also apparent that the fleet was well positioned by 1980, which had not always been the case. It will be shown in Chapter 10 that the northern location of the Pacific Fleet's Soviet ports limited the size of the force that could be stationed in the Indian Ocean and the Soviet naval responses to Indian Ocean crises in the early 1970s must be assessed as failures. However, since the Soviets now have access to Vietnamese ports, they can station naval ships and supplies in Southeast Asia, thus improving the strength and speed of responses to crises in the Indian Ocean.

Weaknesses

The fact that the Pacific Fleet was not more assertive in the 1970s reflects deficiencies in Soviet naval strength, U.S. naval power, and the regional politics of Northeast Asia.

Force Deficiencies. / The Soviet Pacific Fleet's most serious deficiency is its limited ability to project air power. Increasing inventories of navy fighters and bombers—particularly *Backfire* aircraft—the transfer of the aircraft carrier *Minsk* to the Pacific, and access to air bases in Vietnam have improved the position of Soviet naval air power. Nonetheless, the Soviets still lack the air mobility that the United States enjoys through a combination of its Pacific bases and its attack aircraft carriers. This is an important factor, which favors the United States in many potential U.S.-Soviet confrontations, and it probably tempered Soviet actions in the 1970s.

U.S. Naval Power. / The U.S. Seventh Fleet has been a powerful counterforce to the Soviet Pacific Fleet. Ample proof of this assertion can be found in the Vietnam War experience. In other chapters of this book, it is shown that there are trends in the Soviet naval responses to crises. Generally, the Soviets use their navy as a tool of crisis management whenever success seems assured. The strength and complexity of their responses have increased over the years. The most significant exception to that trend was their lack of naval response to the Vietnam War. From the earliest U.S. involvement in Vietnam to the height of U.S. participation and the final U.S. disengagement, the Soviet naval reaction was limited to stationing intelligence collecting ships off Vietnam and Guam to gather information concerning U.S. and South Vietnamese forces. Through all of the operations of the 1960s and 1970s, and in spite of the fact that the Soviet Union developed a strong navy in that period, the USSR never used its naval power in support of North Vietnam. The reason was simple: the vast U.S. naval superiority. The United States had amassed a naval power of such magnitude in Southeast Asia that the Soviet Navy could never hope to seriously challenge it.

Although the Soviet Pacific Fleet was stronger and better positioned in 1980 than during the Vietnam War, and although the Seventh Fleet was reduced after the war ended, the Soviets continued to face a potent force in the U.S. fleet, one with vast wartime experience in Southeast Asia. The U.S. Navy undoubtedly will continue to influence Soviet decisions on the use of its Pacific Fleet into the 1980s.

Regional Politics. / Although the Soviet buildup of its Pacific Fleet intimidated countries in the region, it also created some trends that are not in the Soviet Union's best interests. Japan, which is tied to the United States through a defense pact, signed a peace treaty with China in August 1978. Coupling U.S. and Japanese economic power and a huge Chinese population could be the basis of a new and powerful Pacific alliance system. Such a structure would weaken Soviet security in Northeast Asia and could also impede the expansion of Soviet influence in the region. In 1980, it appeared likely that this nascent Chinese-Japanese-U.S. relationship would act to temper the assertiveness of future Soviet Pacific Fleet operations.

Notes

1. Richard Burt, "Soviet Places Ships Off Vietnam Coast," *New York Times,* 8 February 1979, p. 13; "Soviet Ships Linger Off Vietnam," *Christian Science Monitor,* 8 February 1979, p. 2; and John Cooley, "Soviets Beefing Up Reconnaissance in Far East," *Christian Science Monitor,* 22 February 1979, p. 10.

2. Gorshkov, *Sea Power of the State,* pp. 398, 402–404, 409–410.

3. Burt, "Soviet Places Ships Off Vietnam Coast," p. 13; Henry S. Bradsher, "Soviets Post Ships Off Viet Coast," *Washington Star,* 7 February 1979, p. 1; and Drew Middleton, "Soviet Extends Power of Navy to All Oceans," *New York Times,* 20 March 1979, p. 7.

4. Cooley, "Soviets Beefing Up Reconnaissance in Far East," p. 10, and Barry Kramer, "Regulars of China, Vietnam May Clash, Raising Specter of War Involving Soviets," *Wall Street Journal,* 22 February 1979, p. 3.

5. Don Oberdorfer, "U.S. Sees Little Likelihood of Soviet Attack," *Washington Post,* 22 February 1979, pp. A1, A12; "Soviet Said to Begin Airlift to Vietnam," *Baltimore Sun,* 23 February 1979, p. 2.

6. Don Oberdorfer, "U.S. Concern Grows over Da Nang Visit by Soviet Vessels," *Washington Post,* 10 March 1979, p. A16; L. Edgar Prina, "U.S. Says Hanoi Opens Ports to Soviet Ships," *San Diego Union,* 22 March 1979, p. 2; Charles W. Corddry, "Soviet Sends Warships to Vietnam Base," *Baltimore Sun,* 28 March 1979, p. 1; Richard Burt, "Soviet Ships Arrive at Cam Ranh Bay," *New York Times,* 29 March 1979, p. 7; and "U.S. Warns Soviet over Fleet's Use of Vietnam Base," *Baltimore Sun,* 29 March 1979, p. A4.

7. "Japan Warns of USSR in Far East," *Christian Science Monitor,* 7 August 1980, p. 5.

8. "Soviet Spy Ship Stays Nine Days Off Tsugaru," *Daily Yomiuri,* 30 July 1980, p. 2, and "U.S. Jets Intercept Soviet Aircraft," *Washington Star,* 27 April 1980, p. 16.

9. "Japan Warns of USSR in Far East," p. 5, and "About 30 Soviet Backfire Bombers Stationed in Far East; JDA's View," *Mainichi* (Tokyo), 15 July 1980, p. 2.

10. Ji Yanfeng, "Soviet Expansionist Strategy in the 'Dumbbell' Area," *Renmin Ribao* (Beijing), 22 June 1979, p. 6, translated in *Foreign Broadcast Information Service Daily Report: Vol. 1, People's Republic of China,* no. 127, 29 June 1979, pp. C2–C4.

11. Ibid.

12. Lan Hai, "The Special Task Force of the Soviet Union Is Striving to Dominate the Seas," *Renmin Ribao* (Beijing), 5 July 1979, p. 6, translated in *Foreign Broadcast Information Service Daily Report: Vol. 1, People's Republic of China,* no. 137, 16 July 1979, pp. C1–C2, and "'Myth' Cannot Cover Up Reality," broadcast on Beijing *Xinhua* in English, 19 July 1979, cited in *Foreign Broadcast Information Service Daily Report: Vol. 1, People's Republic of China,* no. 118, 20 June 1979, p. C1.

13. "Soviet Aircraft Carrier Reported in the South China Sea," broadcast on Beijing *Xinhua* in Chinese, 20 June 1979, translated in *Foreign Broadcast Information Service Daily Report: Vol. 1, People's Republic of China,* no. 123, 25 June 1979, p. C1.

14. "Expansion of Soviet Pacific Fleet Enumerated, Discussed," broadcast on Beijing *Xinhua* in English, 7 July 1979, cited in *Foreign Broadcast Information Service Daily Report: Vol. 1, People's Republic of China,* no. 132, 9 July 1979, p. C1.

15. "Moscow Beefs Up Its Pacific Fleet," *Beijing Review* (10 August 1979):26–27.

16. Tan Feng, "Why Does the Minsk Sail the Ocean?" *Renmin Ribao* (Beijing), 26 June 1979, p. 6, translated in *Foreign Broadcast Information Service Daily Report: Vol. 1, People's Republic of China,* no. 130, 5 July 1979, pp. C1–C2.

17. "White Paper on Defense Stresses Soviet Threats," broadcast on Tokyo *Kyodo* in English, 18 June 1979, cited in *Foreign Broadcast Information Service Daily Report: Vol. 4, Asia and Pacific,* no. 119, 19 June 1979, p. C4.

18. "Surprising Buildup of Soviet Warships: Eight Additional Warships of 80,000 Tons Deployed in Far East; Pushing to Three Times 7th Fleet," *Sankei,* 22 December 1979, p. 1; "Not Regarded as Actual Threat, JDA Cautions," *Mainichi* (Tokyo), 2 October 1979, p. 1; "Urges Prudence on 'Soviet Threat' Theory; Unnecessary Subjective Feeling of Fear; Efforts for Friendship Rather Than Emphasis Urged; Peace and Security Institute Executive Director Takuya Kubo," *Asahi,* 15 October 1979, p. 3; "How to View Emergence of Soviet Navy," *Nihon Keizai,* 17 November 1979, p. 2; and "Japan-Soviet Relations," *Daily Yomiuri* (Tokyo), 9 December 1979, p. 2.

10

The Indian Ocean, 1968–1980

The Soviet Navy began continuous operations in the Indian Ocean in 1968. These operations generally have coincided with a major Soviet penetration of Africa and South Asia that is aimed at reducing Western influence along the entire Indian Ocean littoral and limiting Western access to the natural resources—especially the oil—of the Indian Ocean nations. As in other areas, the Soviets have attempted to exploit adversary relationships—the United States versus the Soviet Union and the colonies and former colonies versus their colonial masters.

Aside from controlling the natural resources of the area and the sea routes along which those resources move to the Western industrial nations, the potential benefits of the Indian Ocean Squadron to the Soviets are many. A dominant influence in the area would help in converting regional political systems into socialist systems and would further the encirclement of the People's Republic of China. These goals, if achieved, would enhance the Soviet Union's security and would provide a solid base from which to extend Soviet influence further into South Asia and South Africa. An even more substantial base might be developed by manipulating the Baluchistani independence movement in southeastern Iran and southwestern Pakistan in order to acquire ports along the Indian Ocean coast, or possibly by incorporating Baluchistan into the USSR. Incorporation would extend the Soviet border southward through Afghanistan to the Indian Ocean and vastly improve the strategic position of the Soviet Navy.

As in the Middle East, the relevant Soviet military power in the Indian Ocean has been naval presence. The Indian Ocean Squadron has provided security for Soviet merchant ships, conducted port visits and other diplomatic activities, maintained facilities in Somalia and later Ethiopia, and conducted crisis management operations. Although the squadron had not established Soviet naval hegemony in the area by 1981, its record was impressive. A constant naval presence had been established in an area proximate to both the southern approach to the Suez Canal and to the sea lanes connecting the Persian Gulf with Europe and Japan. Naval ships had made port visits to 39 ports in 23 countries and support facilities had been established in 2 countries. Naval personnel had assisted Indian Ocean countries in several maritime projects, and the navy also had reacted to three regional crises by sending additional forces to the Indian Ocean. Through these operations, the squadron had contributed significantly to the Soviet political offensive.

Soviet Naval Presence in the Indian Ocean, 1968–1980

Prior to 1968, Soviet naval ships occasionally crossed the Indian Ocean, mainly from the western fleets to the Pacific. In 1968, however, the situation changed. Enough surface combatants and auxiliary ships had been built to make possible substantial naval operations in the Indian Ocean. The Soviets may have considered their position in Egypt to be secure enough to warrant the start of a diplomatic, social, and cultural offensive in East Africa and South Asia. At that time, too, the area's traditional outside power—Great Britain—announced it would reduce its presence east of the Suez Canal.

Statistical and Geographic Dimensions of the Presence

The Soviet squadron's presence increased from 1,200 ship days in 1968 (a daily average of approximately 3 ships) to 10,500 ship days in 1974 (a daily average of approximately 29 ships—see Table 2). After 1974, there was a slight decline to approximately 7,000–8,000 ship days per year, but in 1980, the figure rose to 11,800 days—a daily increase of more than 11 ships. This increase was a result of the Iranian crisis (see the next section).[1]

My analysis of the ships deployed indicates a standard Indian Ocean Squadron of 20 to 22 ships composed of the following types:

  1 cruiser
  2 destroyers
0–1 cruise missile submarine
  1 attack submarine
  2 frigates
  1 minesweeper
  2 amphibious ships
0–1 intelligence collector
 10 auxiliary ships
  1 hydrographic research ship

Normally, the squadron is commanded by an admiral, who is often aboard one of the surface combatants. The relatively large number of surface combatants (or relatively small number of submarines) suggests that the squadron's mission is primarily political.

The closure of the Suez Canal in 1967 required that ships for the Indian Ocean operations be staged from the Pacific Fleet rather than from the Black Sea Fleet as the Soviets probably had intended to do. This situation imposed several burdens. It required the transfer of ships from the western fleets to the Pacific, thus effectively removing them from participation in crisis management operations in the Atlantic Ocean or the Mediterranean Sea. In short, the Soviets consciously fragmented their naval power in order to conduct operations in the Indian Ocean. Supply problems also plagued the squadron. The distance from Pacific Fleet ports to the Gulf of Aden was much greater than from the Black Sea, via the Suez Canal. As a result, logistically supporting the Indian Ocean Squadron became vastly more complex and probably limited the size of the force and curtailed the scope of its operations.

In any event, launching operations in the Indian Ocean means that the Soviet Union believes that a gradual geographic expansion of power over the world's oceans, securing one area before further advances are made, is not necessary. Instead, they are willing to leapfrog from one area to another when that is beneficial to their worldwide strategy.

The squadron first concentrated its operations in the Gulf of Aden from Socotra Island to the Bab el Mandeb Strait. From Socotra, naval ships sortied northward into the Persian Gulf, eastward to India, southward into the Indian Ocean for port visits, or southeastward to Diego Garcia for intelligence collection. This geographic focus offered many advantages. Located just west of the sea lanes from the Persian Gulf to the United States, Europe, and Japan, the Soviet force was ideally situated to inderdict supertanker traffic. (That the interruption of oil supplies was a factor in selecting this base of operations was evident when the squadron conducted simulated antishipping maneuvers in these sea lanes during the *Okean* exercise in 1975.)[2] The force was also ideally positioned to interrupt commerce moving to and from the Suez Canal when the waterway was reopened in 1975. It was strategically located close to the Somali and Ethiopian coasts and thus could provide maximum security to Soviet operations in those nations and guarantee the safety of ships delivering arms to Soviet-supported factions in the nations along the Indian Ocean coast. Those deliveries were a significant aspect of Soviet policy. At various times from 1968 through 1980, arms deliveries were made to the Seychelles, Madagascar, Mozambique, Tanzania, Somalia, the People's Democratic Republic of Yemen (South Yemen), Ethiopia, and other Indian Ocean nations. A detailed explanation of those deliveries exceeds the scope of this book, but it is noteworthy that they were an important factor in disputes between the People's Democratic Republic of Yemen and the Yemen Arab Republic (North Yemen) and were of crucial importance to Ethiopia in its war with Somalia in 1978 and 1979.

In contrast to the Mediterranean Fleet, the Indian Ocean Squadron has conducted only a few exercises each year. This probably is due to logistic considerations. Extensive exercise operations would further burden the existing supply capability and are probably not feasible.

The squadron has spent its time primarily at anchor off Socotra Island and Cape Guardafui or conducting surveillance activities. Regular intelligence patrols in the Bab el Mandeb Strait and in the vicinity of Perim Island have enabled the squadron to monitor all traffic passing into and out of the Red Sea and to collect intelligence relevant to the nations along the southern coast of the sea. A patrol in the Strait of Hormuz provides the Soviets with similar information on Persian Gulf traffic. The fact that they often have used a surface combatant to conduct the patrol indicates its importance to the Soviets. A third patrol is near the U.S. base on Diego Garcia. Also, U.S., British, and French naval ships have been monitored closely whenever they have operated in the Gulf of Aden and the northern Arabian Sea. This Soviet interest in the approaches to the Suez Canal may presage intentions to more actively influence the use of the waterway.

Bilateral U.S.-Soviet Crisis Responses, 1968–1980

From 1968 to 1980, a rather unique balance of naval power between the two superpowers existed in the Indian Ocean. The Soviet squadron managed to maintain a sizable constant naval presence, and thus from the early 1970s onward, the Soviet Navy routinely had a more impressive standing capability in the Indian Ocean than did the U.S. Navy's Middle East Force, which normally consisted of a minor combatant flagship and two destroyers. Although the naval balance of power favored the Soviet Union during most of the period, this situation was often reversed during times of crisis and periods of exercise activity. By moving Seventh Fleet attack carrier task groups from the vicinity of Japan and the Philippines into the Indian Ocean, the United States could establish strategic and naval superiority in the area. The U.S. Navy had greater sea power projection and logistic support capabilities than the Soviet Navy, which had to stage from its Pacific Fleet ports. The Soviets' relatively weak crisis management capability in the Indian Ocean was most evident during the Indo-Pakistani War of 1971, the Arab-Israeli War of 1973, and the Iranian crisis of 1979.

On the eve of the Indo-Pakistani War, both the United States and the Soviet Union had relatively small forces in the Indian Ocean. The U.S. force consisted of three ships, and the Soviet force included a destroyer, a *Foxtrot* submarine, an *Alligator* tank landing ship, and a minesweeper. The Soviet force was augmented on December 5, two days after the war began, when a guided missile destroyer and another minesweeper entered the Indian

Ocean to relieve ships of the squadron that were nearing the end of their deployment.

Both the United States and the Soviet Union immediately bolstered their forces in the Indian Ocean. The Soviets sent two groups. The first, consisting of a *Kynda* guided missile cruiser and a *Juliett* cruise missile submarine, left the Sea of Japan on December 9. The second group, which comprised a *Kresta* guided missile cruiser, a *Kashin* guided missile destroyer, and two submarines, departed from the same area on December 15. The United States responded by assembling Task Group 74 on December 10 and positioning it in a holding area off Singapore. That task group, composed of the nuclear-powered attack aircraft carrier *Enterprise,* the helicopter carrier *Tripoli,* three missile-equipped and several conventionally armed destroyers, and a nuclear-powered attack submarine, entered the Andaman Sea south of Burma on December 14. This U.S. augmentation force, which arrived on station three days earlier than the first Soviet group, gave the United States naval superiority, which it maintained throughout the war. In terms of response time and potency of the responding force, the Soviets showed poorly in comparison to the United States.[3]

The crisis management capabilities of the United States and the Soviet Union appeared unchanged in the Indian Ocean two years later. During the Arab-Israeli War of October 1973, the United States ordered the *Hancock* task group into the Arabian Sea, which guaranteed U.S. naval superiority along the southern littoral of the Arabian peninsula. In contrast to the tremendous naval power the Soviets assembled in the eastern Mediterranean, they were unable to develop a comparable counterforce to the U.S. task group in the Indian Ocean. Once again, the inadequacy of Soviet logistic facilities in the Indian Ocean and the handicap of distance from home ports were demonstrated.

The crisis management capability of the Soviet Indian Ocean Squadron improved considerably from 1974 to 1980. Nonetheless, in the 1970s, the squadron never matched the U.S. Navy's ability to respond in the Indian Ocean. This was evident in 1979 when the U.S. Embassy in Teheran was seized. The initial U.S. action was to dispatch sea power to the northern Arabian Sea while attempting a diplomatic settlement. This naval power was of such magnitude that the Soviet Union had no hope of challenging the United States. The Soviet reaction, therefore, was in consonance with established Soviet naval crisis response patterns. The prerequisites for any Soviet naval response are that it have a reasonable probability of success and that it reflect a Soviet commitment to a contending faction. Neither prerequisite existed in 1979. Since the United States had already established control of the Arabian Sea, the Soviets considerably bolstered their squadron but scrapped a naval riposte in favor of other foreign policy options.

The Squadron's Use of Port Facilities

Somalia

The squadron's distance from Soviet home ports in the Pacific and the closure of the Suez Canal, which effectively isolated the Indian Ocean Squadron from the Black Sea Fleet, made port facilities in the Indian Ocean essential if the Soviets were to increase their naval operations in that area. Admiral Zumwalt has observed that politically, it mattered little to the Soviets which nation they gained a foothold in; the most relevant factor was geographic location.[4] In the late 1960s, the Soviets gained influence in two African nations, Somalia and Guinea, and Somalia became the focus of Indian Ocean Squadron activity for several years.

The assassination of Somali President Abd-i-rashid Ali Shermarke on October 15, 1969, started a chain of events that led to both a radical reorientation of the Somali political system and a significant influx of Soviet influence. Following the assassination, a military faction quickly captured key telecommunications and transportation facilities; dissolved the national assembly; suspended the constitution; arrested the prime minister, the cabinet, and other political leaders; dissolved the political parties; and proclaimed a state of emergency. A new government was formed under President Siyad Barre, and Somalia was later declared to be a socialist state. The extent of Soviet involvement in the coup d'etat remains undetermined. However, the replacement of the pro-Western government with a pro-Soviet regime, the dramatic increase in Soviet involvement in Somalia after the coup, the Marxist structure of the new government, and the extent and nature of the economic and social reforms indicate that Soviet influence in the coup was significant.

At first, Soviet naval involvement with the new Somali government was limited to a few port calls. This low-profile approach may have been an attempt to minimize accusations that the Soviets had participated in the takeover. Tables 20–22 demonstrate that Soviet port visits to Somalia began to exceed the established four-to-six-day pattern in 1970. The tables also show that the Soviets probably began significant use of Berbera for logistic purposes as early as 1972. This naval presence would eventually be the high point in Soviet port visit activity in the Indian Ocean, and Somalia was the seventh most visited nation in the world by the Soviet Navy through 1980 (see Table 25).

From 1969 through 1977, Soviet involvement in Somalia grew significantly. In return for general assistance, they were given permission to establish facilities in Somalia and to stage ships and aircraft from that country. Soviet assistance to Somalia rose during the early 1970s and was codified in 1974 with a Treaty of Friendship and Cooperation, which provided for

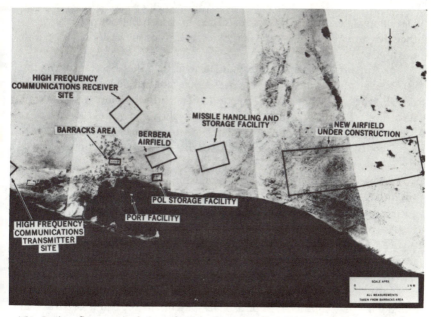

The Soviets first acquired shore facilities in the Indian Ocean at Berbera, Somalia. The proximity of the various facilities supports the theory that they were part of a larger planned complex that would have supported extensive Soviet naval operations in the Indian Ocean. (U.S. Navy)

significant economic, scientific, and cultural aid as well as military assistance and training. From 1969 until 1974, Somalia received naval aircraft, ground equipment, and dozens of other aircraft. In return, the Soviets were allowed to build a port facility, an airfield, a missile depot, and a communications complex in the country.[5]

The Port Facility. / The Soviets made extensive improvements to the Berbera port facilities. Tables 20–22 show that the number of Soviet naval ships to visit Berbera rose rather consistently from 1969 through 1976, and the average duration of those visits exceeded the normal pattern as early as 1970. It appears that the Soviet squadron was using Berbera as a supply base in the early 1970s and that dependence on the port for logistic support increased continually until 1977. The Soviets added a barracks, a repair barge, a floating pier, and a floating drydock to the port. These additions, especially the floating drydock, enabled them to repair and overhaul naval ships as large as guided missile cruisers. The port's petroleum storage facilities were also expanded extensively.[6]

The Soviet squadron did not make full use of these facilities, however. There is no evidence that any major Soviet combatants underwent overhaul in the floating drydock or that Soviet naval ships refueled at the port.

Developing a capability that far exceeded immediate Soviet needs suggests that they intended to deploy a larger force of ships to the Indian Ocean in the 1980s.

The Airfield. / The Soviets expanded an airfield near Berbera during the 1970s. One runway measured well over 4,000 yards in length and could handle all types of Soviet planes, including Tu-95 *Bear D* long-range reconnaissance aircraft.[7] Like the Berbera port facility, the airfield capacity exceeded Soviet and Somali needs. In fact, existing Somali airfields were adequate for the Il-38 *May* aircraft operations that were conducted frequently in the 1970s.

The Missile Support Facility. / The missile handling and storage facility could have been used to replenish Soviet combatants in wartime. Without such a facility, warships would have had to return to Vladivostok or Black Sea ports or rearm at sea.[8]

The Communications Station. / Finally, the Soviets constructed a communications station in the vicinity of Berbera for command and control of the Indian Ocean Squadron.[9]

The Soviets invested heavily in Somalia, and they gained considerable influence in that country. Political developments in the Horn of Africa in 1977, however, drastically altered apparent Soviet intentions to use Somalia as a base for greatly expanded operations.

Ethiopia

The Soviets' success in extending their influence within Somalia was achieved at least in part by exploiting the traditional Somali-Ethiopian animosity over a disputed area known as the Ogaden. However, the radical reorientation of Ethiopian politics between 1974 and 1977, which saw Mengistu Haile Mariam emerge as the leader of a Marxist Ethiopia in early 1977, presented the Soviet Union with an opportunity to make inroads into another African country. For a time, the USSR was supporting both contending pro-Marxist nations. The Soviet leadership may have assessed this dual support as a major tactical blunder, and President Nikolai Podgorny's retirement in June 1977 may have been linked to the role he played in formulating that policy.

Soviet support to the Ethiopians caused a rupture in Soviet-Somali relations. Beset not only by the Ogaden problem, but also by the more immediate issue of uprisings in Ethiopia's Red Sea province of Eritrea, Ethiopia appealed to the Soviet Union for arms and assistance. The USSR supplied both. Cubans were first observed in Ethiopia in May 1977; in July, fierce fighting occurred in the Ogaden area; and in August, the Soviet Union attempted to mediate as Ethiopia was suffering losses on both the Ogaden and Eritrean fronts. When that effort failed, extensive aid—including forces and equipment—was sent to Ethiopia, thus destroying the Soviet-Somali relationship. The initial Cuban contingent was expanded, and in February 1978, Soviet General Vasiliy Petrov became the senior military adviser in Ethiopia, commanding approximately 10,000–11,000 Cuban and Soviet military personnel.[10]

After the Soviets were ordered out of Somalia in November 1977, they mounted a massive airlift of supplies to Ethiopia, overflying some countries without permission. Equipment was flown either to Addis Ababa or to Aden, then transshipped to Ethiopia by sea. A sealift directly to the Ethiopian port of Assab had an even greater effect. On November 17, the *New York Times* reported that the Soviets had pledged $800 million in military aid—including tanks, missiles, and 48 MiG-21 aircraft.[11]

Those measures not only enabled Ethiopia to stem the Somali offensive, but also to counterattack in early February 1978. The Ethiopians' subsequent successes aroused U.S. alarm concerning their intentions. Those fears were somewhat assuaged when the Soviet Union assured the United States that Ethiopia would not invade Somalia, but merely intended to occupy the Ogaden. The occupation was complete by late March 1978, although fighting continued into the following months. Cuban forces were then transferred to the Eritrean front, where Ethiopia launched an offensive in May.[12]

Soviet Naval Involvement. / The Soviet naval reaction was an ambitious attempt to perform a variety of tasks. Following the expulsion of the Indian Ocean Squadron from Berbera in November 1977, Soviet ships were staged from Aden, South Yemen (People's Democratic Republic of Yemen), for their Ethiopian operations. The force level of the squadron was increased from a normal complement of 22 ships to an unprecedented 32 on March 26, 1978. The force, which was concentrated in the Red Sea and the western Gulf of Aden, was composed of 2 destroyers, 2 submarines, 4 frigates, 4 amphibious ships, 1 minesweeper, and 19 auxiliary ships. Several of these ships came from the Soviet western fleets through the Suez Canal. Soviet naval ships had rarely used the canal since its reopening in 1975, but the situation in Ethiopia was apparently thought sufficiently urgent to warrant an exception to that policy. The squadron's missions were to safeguard and assist Soviet operations in Ethiopia. These missions included the following tasks.

1. Sea control in the southern Red Sea and the western Gulf of Aden. A single U.S. attack carrier task group could have denied the Soviets control of the seas off Ethiopia. However, since the United States did not deploy such a group in response to either the Ogaden War or the Eritrean crisis, the Soviet force was adequate to control the seas and perform the other tasks assigned to it.

2. Protect shipping to Ethiopia. The primary mission was to assure that the flow of supplies into Assab was not disrupted. Since there was no opposition, the mission was successful, thereby enabling the Ethiopian forces to continue operations on both the Ogaden and the Eritrean fronts.

3. Assist in transporting Cuban military personnel to Ethiopia. In early 1978, the Soviet Union transported thousands of Cubans to Ethiopia, many of whom had fought in Angola. The Soviet Navy also assured the safe passage of Soviet passenger ships carrying Cubans. The Cuban troops, which numbered 16,000–17,000 in April 1978, were a decisive factor in the Ethiopian victory.

4. Protect Soviet personnel. During the autumn and winter of 1977, when the numbers of Soviet and Cuban personnel in Ethiopia were small and Ethiopia still was losing on both fronts, the navy stood ready to evacuate Soviets and Cubans in the event the Ethiopian effort collapsed.

5. Conduct reconnaissance. An additional task was to patrol the southern Red Sea and the western Gulf of Aden in order to detect enemy movements.

6. Conduct shore bombardment operations. The information concerning these operations is both spotty and unconfirmed. In January 1978, Michael Wells reported in the *Manchester Guardian* that Soviet naval ships, including an *Alligator* tank landing ship, fired shells and rockets at Eritrean forces assaulting Massawa. Wells also quoted the captain of a Greek freighter who said he had seen landing craft unloading *Katyusha* rocket launchers from the *Alligator* and that the ship's crew was firing rocket salvos at the Eritreans.[13] David Fairhall, a respected commentator on Soviet naval matters, also has discussed the shelling, but in more guarded terms. He cited Eritrean sources who claimed that "'Soviet destroyers' were shelling their soldiers in an effort to raise the siege of the Ethiopian port." Fairhall concluded that those reports were inconclusive and that the shellings remain unsubstantiated.[14]

The Soviet policy toward Ethiopia was successful. The only setback, the loss of naval access to Somali ports, has been temporary. In July 1978, intelligence analysts were quoted as saying that Soviet access to Ethiopian facilities should eventually more than compensate for the loss of those in Somalia.[15] On the positive side, the Ethiopians' success in both the Ogaden War and against the Eritreans demonstrated the Soviets' ability to successfully support a client. In addition, in operating from Ethiopia, the Soviet Navy is excellently positioned to influence affairs in the southern Red Sea and maritime traffic through the Bab el Mandeb Strait should it choose to do so. Admiral Zumwalt feels that access to Ethiopian facilities also has put the USSR in a better position to exert its influence through the Sudan into southern Egypt. In concert with the threat from Libya's Colonel Qaddafi, that possibility has amounted to considerable pressure on Sadat. Furthermore, from Ethiopia and South Yemen, the Soviets could interdict traffic in the southern approaches to the Suez Canal and exert increased pressure on Israel's southern flank.[16] Admiral Moorer has expressed similar observations.

> An accomplishment of Dr. Kissinger after the October 1973 War was to prevail upon President Sadat to expel the Soviets. The Soviets require a presence along the Red Sea coast, and they were willing to sacrifice their position in Somalia for one in Ethiopia. Ethiopia provides the Soviets access to ports along the Red Sea coast which they need, enables them to keep pressure on Egypt, and provides them with an alternative to Egypt as a base for Soviet operations in the Middle East.[17]

Perhaps the most dramatic demonstration of the enhanced position the Soviets gained through their activities in Ethiopia was Saudi Arabia's vacillating policy in the late 1970s. Faced with a strong Soviet presence and 17,000 Cuban troops in Ethiopia; an emerging, introspective Iran following the shah's departure and death; hostilities between North and South Yemen; and, as the Saudis perceived it, a cautious, uncertain U.S. administration reluctant to become involved in the problems of the Horn of Africa, the Saudis almost certainly decided to reexamine their foreign policy options.

Finally, as in other crisis reactions, the Soviet naval presence has remained at a higher level following the Ethiopian conflicts. As the new decade began, the Soviet Navy, along with 16,000–17,000 Cubans still in Africa, stood ready to exploit future opportunities that might arise in East Africa or South Asia.

The Squadron's Other Political Activities

Soviet involvement in Somalia and Ethiopia and the strategic value of those endeavors have tended to overshadow the Indian Ocean Squadron's other political activities. These have been varied, and many are impressive examples of superior coordination and control. The majority of these activities have been aimed at curtailing Western, particularly U.S., influence in the Indian Ocean.

From 1969 through 1980, the Soviet Navy participated in several endeavors that can be classified as assistance to the Third World. These operations include helping Iraq expand the port of Umm Qasr and training the North Yemen Navy. However, two of the Soviet Navy's activities stand out because of their scope and ambition: clearing the port of Chittagong, Bangladesh, and removing mines from the southern approaches to the Suez Canal.

The Chittagong Port-Clearing Operation

The Soviets, enjoying favorable relations with India, saw an opportunity to further their influence in South Asia by assisting the newly independent Bangladesh (formerly East Pakistan). India wanted to see its new neighbor get back on its feet economically in order to lighten the burden of Indian assistance to that country. In 1972, Bangladesh's only seaports, Chalna and Chittagong, were inoperable. Their approaches were heavily mined and littered with sunken wrecks, and their facilities had been severely damaged in the war with Pakistan. A Soviet offer to clear those harbors was accepted. Twenty-two ships—including an *Amur* repair ship, three salvage tugs, a *Sura* buoy tender, a diving tender, floating cranes, from four to nine minesweepers, and a tanker—were sent to Bangladesh and conducted operations in 1972 and 1973. This force encountered many difficulties. It finished the Chittagong operation months behind schedule and did not even begin clearing the Chalna port. (That task was done by a Western group in a few months.)[18]

The success of the project was mixed. On the one hand, the slow, laborious effort reflects a relatively primitive salvage capability and resulted in embarrassment as the Soviets failed to meet deadlines. The slow progress, in turn, created impatience on the part of Bengalis, which resulted in a loss of Soviet prestige. On the other hand, in the immediate aftermath of the war, only the Soviets stepped forward to offer assistance, and that fact was probably beneficial to their image, regardless of the problems subsequently encountered.

Mine-Clearing Operations in the Gulf of Suez

The mine-clearing operations in the Gulf of Suez were similar to the operations at Chittagong. In both cases, the Soviets agreed to undertake an ambitious program, mine clearing was involved, and the Soviets clearly overextended themselves and encountered unexpected difficulties. In both cases, also, the Soviets failed to meet the proposed timetables, and, finally, both operations were completed without any clear-cut benefits to the Soviets.

When Egypt announced in January 1974 that it intended to reopen the canal, the Soviet Union failed to make a firm commitment to help clear the waterway. That failure was probably due to a Soviet misreading of the situation; they believed that the Western nations would not assist Sadat and that Egypt would have to seek help from the Soviet Union. However, the United States and other Western nations unexpectedly agreed to sweep the canal, and the Egyptians accepted a U.S. proposal on March 18. The Soviets thus found themselves in danger of being excluded from a high-visibility Third

The Soviet Navy participated in the Suez Canal mine-clearing operation by sweeping the Gulf of Suez. The antisubmarine helicopter cruiser *Leningrad* is pictured proceeding to the Gulf of Suez with two Mi-8 *Hip* helicopters on deck. Since these helicopters are not normally used by the Soviet Navy, it is believed that the helicopters were variants equipped for mine-countermeasure operations. (U.S. Navy)

World assistance operation. On May 31, they agreed to clear the Strait of Gubal and the Gulf of Suez by August 15.[19]

Once committed, the Soviet Navy responded rapidly. By June 3, a task force of five minesweepers departed Vladivostok for the Gulf of Suez, and an *Amur* repair ship joined that force when it reached the Indian Ocean. Meanwhile, a task group composed of the guided missile helicopter cruiser *Leningrad,* a *Kashin* guided missile destroyer, and a replenishment oiler made a high-speed run from the Black Sea to the gulf. The minesweeper task force arrived on July 14 with some experienced personnel from the Chittagong port-clearing operation aboard.

As in the Chittagong episode, the Soviets met many problems. By August 15, they had cleared only the Strait of Gubal and still had to clear the Gulf of Suez. That latter operation was completed on November 29, three and a half months after the agreed-on deadline.[20]

The Gulf of Suez operation failed to retard or reverse the deterioration of Soviet-Egyptian relations. The Egyptians openly criticized and insulted the Soviets, and Sadat praised the U.S. and British minesweeping efforts while ignoring those of the Soviets. The Egyptians even failed to invite the Soviet Navy to participate in the Suez Canal reopening ceremonies on June 5. The

U.S. Navy was invited and the USS *Little Rock* participated in a ceremonial transit of the canal.

Soviet Naval Port Visit Activity

Port calls have been an important political activity of the squadron. The visits appear to have been associated with foreign policy objectives in the area and can be subdivided by regions: East Africa and the Middle East, the Persian Gulf, and South Asia.

Soviet Port Visits to East Africa and the Middle East. / The first three calls to this area were to Hodeida, North Yemen, in 1963. No additional calls were made at Hodeida until 1969, denoting more than anything else the sparse Soviet naval presence in the Indian Ocean in the intervening years.

In 1965, the Soviets began making yearly calls to Ethiopia, a pattern that continued through 1974. Rather than signifying Soviet influence in Ethiopia, the visits merely reflected the Soviet Navy's participation in the Ethiopian Navy Day, an annual event of considerable regional significance. These celebrations usually also included U.S., British, and French naval participation, in addition to participation by most of the region's navies. The Soviets attached considerable importance to the event, often sending ships from the Pacific Fleet. An admiral knowledgeable in international relations was often the senior officer aboard, and the ships' crews were composed of men selected for their conduct and professionalism.

When the Soviets established a constant Indian Ocean presence in 1968, port visit activity in East Africa and the Middle East picked up. By that time, the Soviet Navy had enough ships to make such visits, and given the logistic problems associated with the Indian Ocean operations, frequent port visits were required to replenish provisions and water. During 1968, the first visits to Kenya, the Malagasy Republic, Tanzania, South Yemen, Somalia, and Egyptian Red Sea ports were made. As the Soviet diplomatic offensive into Africa and South Asia increased, so did the number of port visits. Somalia very quickly claimed the lion's share of the visits in the area, which reflected the meteoric rise of Soviet influence in that country. Use of the Egyptian ports from 1968 through 1974 betokened the tremendous increase in Soviet influence in Egypt after the June 1967 war.

The beginning of Soviet naval visits to Aden in 1968 and the return to Hodeida in 1969 coincided with the start of active naval operations in the Indian Ocean and also indicate the increased Soviet prestige in the Arab world that resulted from the Soviet Union's support of Egypt and Syria during the June 1967 war. Aden soon was second only to Berbera in importance as a logistic base for the squadron. Aden also could be of vital strategic importance in controlling or influencing maritime commerce to and from the Red

Port visits are an important part of the Soviet Navy's political operations in the Indian Ocean. Until the fall of Haile Selassie, which spelled an end to the annual Ethiopian Navy Day, Soviet naval ships, like the one pictured in Massawa in 1974, participated in that international event. (C. Sills)

Sea and the Suez Canal. Similarly, Hodeida, located just north of the Bab el Mandeb Strait, has great strategic significance, but that port was only used intermittently by the Soviets from 1969 until 1976, when they began assisting the North Yemeni Navy. There have been unconfirmed reports that the Soviets have been seen repairing Yemeni naval ships on several occasions. Whether those reports are true or not, the dramatic increase in the Soviet use of the port reflects substantial progress in extending Soviet influence in North Yemen.

The visits to Port Sudan from 1969 to 1971 all conformed to the four-to-six-day pattern, signifying that relations with Sudan remained formal. Since there were no visits during the next five years, the Soviets may have assessed the initial visits as unproductive. Finally, the dramatic increase in visits to Ethiopian ports, particularly Dahlak Island in 1978–1980, indicates that Ethiopia has replaced Somalia as the squadron's supply base.

In the remaining countries of Africa, the prevalent visit pattern demonstrates that the Soviets have taken advantage of opportunities to show their support for people's movements but were only beginning a serious penetration of southern Africa in 1976–1980. Visits to the Malagasy

A Yak-36 *Forger* approaches the deck of the *Kiev*. Her sister ship, the *Minsk*, conducted carrier operations off Aden on May 29, 1979, during one of the Soviet Navy's most elaborate port visits. (U.S. Navy)

Republic and Tanzania in 1968–1970 conformed roughly to the standard Soviet pattern and reflected the formality of diplomatic relations. The Soviets have seemed to enjoy greater access to Kenya, where their visits have been much more frequent. Further south, frequent visits to Port-aux-Français in the Kerguelen Islands and Port Louis, Mauritius, may have been for operational support. Calls to Mozambique, which began in 1977, denote cordial relations with that nation.

In 1979, an interesting series of calls was conducted by the *Minsk* task group as it proceeded through the Indian Ocean to its new home port in the Pacific. In Chapter 4, it was noted that the Soviets exploited to the fullest the *Minsk*'s political effect during her voyage along the West Coast of Africa. This tactic was continued in the Indian Ocean and involved a lengthy detour northward to the Gulf of Aden (Map 4.2 shows the route of the *Minsk*'s voyage). During her stay in the Indian Ocean, the *Minsk* visited Maputo, Mozambique; Port Louis, Mauritius; and Aden, South Yemen. The *Minsk* and two of her escorts spent five days at Maputo while two other

MAP 10.1   Indian Ocean ports visited by Soviet naval ships from 1962 through 1980.

escorts visited Nacala, Mozambique. The Maputo visit, from April 16 to April 20, conformed to the five-day format. Considerable planning was evident as the ships were open to the public, and Soviet crews toured the city and visited the Museum of the Revolution.[21] The visit demonstrated Soviet support for Mozambique vis-à-vis Rhodesia and South Africa. The *Minsk*'s visit to Port Louis, from April 26 to April 28, was low key and lasted only three days.

The *Minsk*'s final Indian Ocean port visit, to Aden, was one of the most impressive Soviet calls in recent history. Leaving Mauritius, the *Minsk* group proceeded northward to the Socotra Island anchorage. There, the group conducted exercises, including air operations in the vicinity of the sea lanes leading from the Persian Gulf to Europe. The group then moved westward for an eight-day visit to Aden, from May 26 to June 2, which was highlighted by an impressive naval demonstration on May 29. The *Minsk* group, with many South Yemeni officials aboard, conducted flight operations with Yak-36 *Forger* aircraft and Ka-25 *Hormone* helicopters and amphibious operations. The landing platform dock *Ivan Rogov* flooded her well deck and launched both air-cushioned vehicles and landing craft.[22] The activities were a vivid demonstration of the navy's ability to conduct power projection operations after traveling for weeks on the high seas.

Soviet Port Visits to the Persian Gulf. / For several reasons, there have been relatively few Soviet calls to Persian Gulf ports. The most important of the reasons are lingering pro-British sentiment; the conservative orientation of many of the monarchical Persian Gulf states; the emergence of a pro-West Iran as a regional power, which could have viewed a large Soviet presence as a threat to its security; and Western sensitivity concerning the free flow of oil from the gulf to Japan, Europe, and the United States. As a result, the squadron has visited only four gulf nations—Iraq, Iran, Kuwait, and the United Arab Emirates—and those, infrequently.

The initial visits to Iraq from 1968 to 1970 were a prelude to longer visits at Basra and Umm Qasr, which began in 1971. Assistance in expanding the port facilities at Umm Qasr in the early 1970s led to speculation that the Soviets might be establishing a naval facility in the Persian Gulf. However, the ease with which the gulf can be blockaded at the Strait of Hormuz, Iranian and Western sensitiveness, and possibly even an Iraqi refusal to allow the Soviets access to that country precluded the development of such a base.

Tables 20–22 show that a total of 18 ships visited Iran from 1968 through 1976. The visits conformed fairly well to the four-to-six-day pattern and could have been intended to assure the Iranians that the Indian Ocean Squadron meant to conduct its operations in a traditional manner and did not intend to participate in subversive operations.

Elsewhere in the Persian Gulf, Kuwait was visited by three Soviet ships in 1969–1970, accounting for 21 ship days, but no visits to Kuwait have been made since 1970. Kuwait has long-standing disputes with Iraq, and it is likely that the Soviets see no advantage in jeopardizing their relationship with the Iraqis. Visits to Dubai began in 1976.

Soviet Port Visits to South Asia. / Naval port visit activity in South Asia from 1968 through 1980 was a near-perfect reflection of the status of Soviet diplomatic relations. Visits to Indian ports began in 1966, and from 1968 onward Soviet ships have visited India every year. In the early 1970s, sizable transfers of Soviet naval equipment to the Indian Navy and rumors of assistance in improving the port of Vishakhapatnam led to the speculation that that port was to become a support facility for the Indian Ocean Squadron. However, Soviet ships have made only moderate use of the Indian ports, and the average length of their visits has generally conformed to the standard pattern. Although the Soviets may have relied on Indian ports for limited logistic support, the Indian Ocean Squadron has never been dependent on them.

Following an isolated port call at Ceylon (later Sri Lanka) in 1962, Soviet naval ships visited Colombo, the country's major port, every year from 1967 through 1980. These visits generally lasted from four to six days. In 1968–1970, eight naval ships visited Karachi, Pakistan. Those visits ended with the Indo-Pakistani War of 1971 as the Soviet Union supported India in that war. Soviet port visits to Karachi began again in 1975, and more visits occurred in 1976 and 1979, but none lasted any longer than six days. Almost all the visits to Bangladesh in 1972–1974 were associated with the port-clearing operation at Chittagong. The lack of calls after 1974 probably reflects a Soviet loss of interest in Bangladesh.

Summary

The record of Soviet naval operations in the Indian Ocean from 1968 through 1980 is a mixture of success and failure. The Soviets stationed a squadron in the Indian Ocean and thus enjoyed naval superiority for most of the period. However, the United States could have wrested this superiority from them at will, simply by dispatching a carrier task group to the area. Soviet success in Somalia led to establishing a naval support facility and other installations there that proved invaluable both as a logistic base and as a staging area for Soviet aircraft. However, those assets were lost when the Soviets were expelled from Somalia in 1977, and by 1980, the loss had been only partially offset by the use of Ethiopian facilities. The most significant political operations, the port clearing of Chittagong and the mine clearing of the Gulf of Suez, also showed mixed results. Although both operations had propaganda value, both were completed considerably behind schedule, earned scant praise for the USSR, and resulted in no significant inroads into either Bangladesh or Egypt. Finally, the Soviet port visit program in the Indian Ocean has been an incomplete success. Greatly enhanced Soviet influence in South Yemen and Ethiopia could be claimed as significant achievements, and it seems that Mozambique might soon fall into the Soviet success column. Alternatively, Soviet naval power has had little impact on affairs in the Persian Gulf or South Asia.

In the early 1980s, serious problems confronted the Soviet Navy as it pursued its goals in the Indian Ocean. Of these, the following seem most important.

1. Control of the Suez Canal. In Part 2 of this book, it is assumed that a major goal of the Soviet Mediterranean Fleet has been control of the Suez Canal. In spite of a great deal of effort going back to 1956, the Soviet Union still had not reached that goal in 1980. That failure has created a serious problem for the Indian Ocean Squadron, which has to draw on the Pacific Fleet for ships and support. Although Soviet naval ships were brought from the Mediterranean through the canal during the Ethiopian-Somali War, operating patterns in the Indian Ocean show continued reliance on the Pacific Fleet. Until the Suez Canal is judged secure by the USSR, Soviet naval power will continue to be fragmented. If the Pacific Fleet's regional responsibilities increase in the 1980s, the Indian Ocean Squadron will become an increasing burden. As a result, control over the canal will remain an objective of Soviet policy.

2. Inadequate crisis response. During the Indo-Pakistani War of 1971, the Arab Israeli War of 1973, and the Iranian crisis of 1979, the United States chose to respond with naval power. On all those occasions, the Soviet squadron was overwhelmed, and the United States enjoyed regional superiority, based on its strength and rapid response. If the Soviet Navy is to counter U.S. naval power in the Indian Ocean, it must develop a capability to augment its squadron more generously and more rapidly. Great fluctuations in the squadron's presence (see Table 2) reflect the difficulties in consistently maintaining a large force in the Indian Ocean. The extensive facilities built at Berbera indicate an intention to do just that, but the loss of those facilities in 1977 has been offset only partially by later access to the less extensive facilities in Ethiopia. Also, the facilities at Dahlak Island are north of the narrow Bab el Mandeb Strait at the southern entrance to the Red Sea; hence, elements of the squadron could easily be bottled up in that sea.

Developing a truly effective Indian Ocean presence thus depends on continued naval construction to enlarge the overall size of the Soviet Navy, use of the Suez Canal by Soviet warships, expanded use of port facilities in Vietnam, and acquisition of additional facilities along the Indian Ocean littoral.

3. U.S. naval power. Throughout the 1970s, the United States demonstrated that it could establish regional control in the Indian Ocean when it chose to do so. A hint of future U.S. intentions to play a more significant role in the area was evident in August 1980, when the United States announced that it was considering agreements with Somalia, Kenya, and Oman for use of facilities in those countries, including the Soviet-built air and naval facilities at Berbera.[23] The availability of those bases would widen the disparity between Soviet and U.S. naval power in the region.

At least through the early 1980s, the Soviet Navy will have to operate with the liabilities those problems impose. The squadron will not reach maturity and long-range goals for the region will not be realized until solutions to the problems are found. In the interim, the problems will dominate Soviet Indian Ocean Squadron operations.

Notes

1. U.S., Department of the Navy, Office of the Chief of Naval Operations, *Understanding Soviet Naval Developments,* pp. 15–16.

2. Watson and Walton, "Okean-75," p. 94.

3. James M. McConnell and Anne M. Kelly, *Naval Diplomacy in the Indo-Pakistani Crisis* (Arlington, Va.: Center for Naval Analyses, 1973), pp. 1–3, 5–6.

4. Interview with Admiral Zumwalt, 22 October 1977.

5. Stockholm International Peace Research Institute, *The Arms Trade Registers,* pp. 85–86.

6. Interview with Admiral Zumwalt, 22 October 1977.

7. Ibid.

8. Ibid., and Richard L. Homan, "New Soviet Base Perturbs Hill Unit," *Washington Post,* 9 July 1975, p. A31.

9. Interview with Admiral Zumwalt, 22 October 1977.

10. Graham Hovey, "Brzezinski Asserts That Soviet General Leads Ethiopia Units," *New York Times,* 25 February 1978, p. 1.

11. Hedrick Smith, "U.S. Says Castro Has Transferred 60's Policy of Intervention to Africa," *New York Times,* 17 November 1977, pp. A1, A11, and Graham Hovey, "U.S. Officials Say Soviet Mounts a Major Arms Airlift to Ethiopia," *New York Times,* 14 December 1977, p. 1.

12. "Sadat Says Soviet Pilots are Flying for Ethiopia in Fighting with Somalia," *New York Times,* 7 February 1978, p. 4; "More Cubans Reported on Way," *New York Times,* 8 February 1978, p. A5; Graham Hovey, "Soviet Assures U.S. Ethiopians Will Stop at Somalia's Border," *New York Times,* 11 February 1978, pp. 1, 3; Michael Kaufman, "Somalis Abandoning Northern Ogaden," *New York Times,* 9 March 1978, p. A4; "Cubans Said to Fight in Eritrea," *New York Times,* 17 March 1978, p. A7; "Ethiopia Says It Now Holds Entire Ogaden Region," *New York Times,* 25 March 1978, p. 4; and "Somalis Say They Killed 1000 in Ogaden Battles," *New York Times,* 16 April 1978, p. 8.

13. Michael Wells, "Russians Shelling Massawa?" *Manchester Guardian Weekly,* 29 January 1978, p. 7.

14. David Fairhall, "Transformed Role for the Soviet Navy," *Manchester Guardian Weekly,* 29 January 1978, p. 7.

15. Drew Middleton, "Soviet Position in Aden and Kabul Seen Improving," *New York Times,* 31 July 1978, p. A2.

16. Interview with Admiral Zumwalt, 22 October 1977.

17. Interview with Admiral Moorer, 9 January 1978.

18. Charles C. Petersen, *The Soviet Port Clearing Operation in Bangladesh, March 1972–December 1973* (Arlington, Va.: Center for Naval Analyses, 1974), pp. 1, 7, 10, 15–21, 29.

19. Charles C. Petersen, *The Soviet Union and the Reopening of the Suez Canal: Mineclearing Operations in the Gulf of Suez* (Arlington, Va.: Center for Naval Analyses, 1975), pp. 1, 3–6.

20. Ibid., pp. 9–10.

21. G. Savichev, "Soviet Ships' Mozambique Call," *Red Star,* 22 April 1979, p. 3.

22. "Soviet Carrier at Aden," *New York Times,* 31 May 1979, cited by *U.S. Naval Institute Proceedings* 105 (August 1979):124.

23. Don Oberdorfer, "Somalia Agrees to Let U.S. Use Ports, Airfields," *Washington Post,* 22 August 1980, pp. A1, A20.

11
Summary and Forecast

Summary of Soviet Naval Operations Through 1980

From 1956 through 1980, the Soviet Navy's strength grew from a coastal defense force to a major sea power; its presence was extended outward from the nation's coasts into most of the world's major ocean areas; its firepower was increased impressively and now includes many classes of missile-equipped surface combatants and submarines; its propulsion systems became much more reliable in both nuclear-powered and conventionally powered ships; and its operations reached a degree of sophistication that makes it a powerful offensive and defensive weapon. This navy has evolved into an important element of Soviet foreign policy, which traditionally has relied on exploiting long- and short-range adversary relationships to achieve the four long-range strategic goals outlined in Chapter 1. With these goals and the power of the Soviet Navy in mind, some conclusions can be drawn that can help explain past actions and forecast future trends.

First, the Soviets have understood that the ability to successfully defend their nation is basic to political operations anywhere in the world. In the 1950s, any Soviet foreign maneuver could be countered by the tacit threat of a U.S. strategic assault directly on the Soviet homeland. As a result, the Soviets built a fleet of submarines, a naval air force, and thousands of major and minor surface combatants in order to defend the nation's sea approaches and coasts in depth. The ability to successfully defend the nation has remained a dominant requirement; hence, submarine construction and deployment to the Atlantic and Pacific oceans continued to be a major element in the composition of and the out-of-area operations of the navy through 1980.

Second, Soviet naval strategy has been based on a combination of traditional naval thought and Soviet perceptions. Admiral Zumwalt believes that Soviet external political objectives have been pursued behind advanced naval screens, which accounts for a naval presence in the Indian Ocean, the Mediterranean Sea, and along the coast of West Africa.[1] This strategy is, on the one hand, similar to that of the traditional British use of sea power.

Although Great Britain often did not have complete control over the internal affairs of its colonies in the eighteenth and nineteenth centuries, its sea power generally was adequate to prevent foreign interference into its colonial affairs. On the other hand, the USSR differs from Great Britain, since the Soviet naval power can be used in conjunction with a Soviet-sponsored insurgent or national liberation movement to form an extranational force, one that is rooted in the Communist doctrine and the Russian revolutionary tradition.

At least the first stage of the Soviet naval strategy was formulated completely in the mid-1950s. The repetitiveness of Soviet naval actions and reactions supports this conclusion. For example, there was little difference in their use of naval facilities in Valona in 1958, Alexandria in 1968, and Berbera in the early 1970s, and their response to expulsion from all those ports was similar. Likewise, the conduct of their port visit program has remained rather static. The fundamental four-to-six-day pattern and port visit schedules became apparent in the 1950s; subsequent visits have been merely expansions and variations on those basic themes. Although the first stage of Soviet naval strategy—defending the nation and establishing a naval presence on the world's oceans—was formulated and initiated in the mid-1950s, it still remained operable in 1980.

Third, crisis response and access to foreign port facilities are important aspects of naval strategy. Through its response to crises, the Soviet Navy has been able to expand dramatically its presence on the world's oceans. Crisis responses have their own prerequisites, character, and intended results. They are not defense oriented; rather, they are a part of Soviet foreign policy. The Soviets have responded only to those crises in which they seemed to have a significant foreign policy commitment, and the amount of available power used often has reflected the degree of that commitment.

Each reaction has to stand a good chance of influencing a crisis for the benefit of the Soviet Union. If that probability does not exist, a different foreign policy option is used. If the probability of success is high and the Soviets believe they have enough naval power for a successful response, a naval reaction often occurs. The mission of the response force has never exceeded its capabilities. The prerequisites have been binding. The Soviet failure to respond to crises in the Suez in 1956, Lebanon in 1958, Cuba in 1962, and the Vietnam War in the 1960s and early 1970s was a result of their navy's inability to influence those events.

On eight occasions, the Soviet naval force level has remained larger in the crisis region after the crisis has ended—Lebanon (1958), the Arab-Israeli War (1967), Jordan (1970), Guinea (1970), the Indo-Pakistani War (1971), the Angolan Civil War (1976), Ethiopia (1978), and Vietnam (1979)—which amounts to a postcrisis increase in 73 percent of the Soviet responses to the major crises since 1956 in which I feel Soviet naval power should have been employed. The figure is even larger if one considers that in three additional Mediterranean crises—1973, 1974, and 1976—the Soviet Mediterranean Fleet had already reached its full size and needed no further expansion. With this adjustment, the Soviet naval force level after a crisis has been higher in *all* incidents. Apparently the Soviets believe that naval response to a crisis is an important foreign policy option, and they intend to use such responses to justify bolstering a naval force already stationed in an area, or stationing a force in areas where Soviet naval power has not previously existed. These force level escalations have occurred so often in the past that future Soviet naval reactions should not be viewed as temporary. Responses often are part of the initial stage of a complex program aimed at expanding Soviet influence in an area.

On four occasions, a Soviet naval reaction has led to the use of foreign naval facilities: after the June 1967 Arab-Israeli War, when the Soviets were granted permission to use Egyptian and Syrian ports; after the Angolan Civil War, when Soviet ships used Luanda; after the Ethiopian crisis, when they used Ethiopian ports and increased their use of neighboring South Yemeni ports; and after the Sino-Vietnamese War, when they began using Vietnamese facilities, including Cam Ranh Bay. This record supports the conclusion that the Soviets actively seek access to ports during postcrisis periods.

Extrapolations from Tables 2 and 3 demonstrate significant increases in area naval activity during postcrisis periods. In the Mediterranean, for example, activity increased more than 112 percent between 1967 and 1971, and similar increases have occurred in the Indian Ocean. The increases have been made possible by using indigenous port facilities to ease the logistic burden of supporting a distant naval force. A larger force permits more sophisticated operating patterns, command and control procedures, and, of course, more naval power to be employed in future crises. Using the Mediterranean as an example, it appears that the USSR has built its naval strength progressively from crisis to crisis until it has what it considers to be a fully adequate force in the area. Varying circumstances could rule out a comparable progression in other areas, but the Mediterranean experience does support some conclusions and guarded predictions concerning future Soviet operations.

Soviet naval responses fit into the scheme of Soviet naval operations in the following manner:

- precrisis operations
- crisis responses
- increased postcrisis operations
- increased postcrisis port visit activity
- postcrisis use of port facilities

That scheme in turn supports several further conclusions. First, Soviet precrisis operations have almost always been less intense than Soviet operations in postcrisis periods. In some cases, such as Angola and Vietnam, there was no precrisis activity at all. Next, the Soviet naval force in a crisis area has always been increased during a response, and in the majority of cases, the naval force has remained stronger than it was before the crisis. Also, the tempo of the Soviet port visit program in a crisis region has often increased after a settlement, which may have enhanced Soviet influence. Finally, the Soviet Navy has gained access to port facilities so many times in postcrisis periods that it is reasonable to believe that such access is often the price a nation must pay for Soviet support.

In summary, Soviet naval crisis responses are integral elements in the foreign policy–oriented operations of the Soviet Navy, through which considerable influence has been wrested from the West. The responses often have improved the Soviet Navy's ability to operate in distant areas. Rather than dreading crises, the Soviet leadership probably welcomes and may even stimulate them since they have so often advanced Soviet foreign policy objectives.

A strong U.S. Navy has precluded more assertive Soviet naval operations. However, Soviet naval construction, which began in 1956 and continues today, has narrowed the gap between Soviet and U.S. naval power, and the USSR could have naval superiority over the United States in future decades.

An Assessment of Soviet Naval Operations in Relation to Long-Range Goals

Soviet naval operations from 1956 to 1980 have contributed, with varying degrees of success, to achieving the long-range goals stated in Chapter 1. To recapitulate, these goals are (1) to provide for the defense of the Soviet Union, (2) to improve the country's international stature, (3) to develop an ability to project power in the international arena, and (4) to bring about changes in the international political structure. In this assessment, an examination of the operations relative to the second and third goals is included in one section, since those goals are closely related.

Defense of the Soviet Union

Soviet naval operations after 1956 increased the USSR's security by contributing to countering the U.S. nuclear strike advantage of the 1950s and fragmenting the NATO alliance. At the end of World War II and throughout the 1950s, the United States had absolute strategic and naval superiority, projected by the U.S. Navy's attack aircraft carrier and nuclear-powered ballistic missile–equipped submarine forces. Soviet naval construction has been focused on countering those two forces. Antishipping missiles deployed on submarines and surface combatants have created a potent anti-carrier capability, which has helped secure the Soviet Union's approaches from seaborne air strikes.

The Soviets have attempted to neutralize the U.S. ballistic missile submarine force through an ambitious antisubmarine warfare program and by building a fleet of ballistic missile–equipped submarines. In the first instance, inadequate antisubmarine warfare capabilities remained a primary Soviet liability in 1980. However, the Soviets have been more successful in developing a missile-equipped submarine force that has erased much of the United States' early advantage. Indeed, many U.S. authorities feel, incorrectly, that the only relevant Soviet naval threat is its submarine force and that the surface combatant operations in the Mediterranean, along West Africa, and in the Indian Ocean are of little importance. In fact, by achieving a shift in the U.S.-Soviet strategic balance, the Soviet Navy has enabled the USSR to launch political offensives in the Middle East, Africa, and Asia without the threat of overwhelming U.S. strategic power. These initiatives have enhanced Soviet influence in strategically vital areas at the expense of the United States.

The Soviet Navy also has helped to reduce NATO's warfighting capability. For example, Admiral Moorer has stated that although all contingency plans for the defense of NATO countries are predicated on an allied control of the North Atlantic sea lanes, the Soviets could deny the use of those lanes in wartime, thus reducing or preventing the reinforcement of Europe.[2] Admiral Zumwalt believes that regardless of the reallocation of U.S. naval power, the allies would probably lose a war in Europe in six weeks.[3] A similarly adverse shift has occurred in the Mediterranean. In wartime, the Sixth Fleet, the primary defender of NATO's southern flank, could not immediately begin operations against a Soviet overland invasion of southern Europe as it would first have to defeat the Soviet naval forces in the Mediterranean.[4] In wartime, NATO would find it difficult, if not impossible, to defend either the coastline of the Scandinavian Peninsula north and east of the North Sea or the coastline of NATO's southeastern front east of the Strait of Sicily.

In addition, Soviet naval forces have been stationed in the Gulf of Aden and along the west coast of Africa where they might control the sea lanes from the Persian Gulf to Europe if the United States had to commit all of its available naval power to the Atlantic and the Mediterranean. The potential effects of such a tactic were evident in 1973 when the Arab oil boycott swiftly and dramatically neutralized European and Japanese support for the U.S. pro-Israeli policy.

The Soviet Navy has seriously weakened NATO's military position while increasing both Soviet security and the navy's ability to operate with impunity in other areas of the world. The dramatic shift in the balance of strategic and theater power, to which the Soviet Navy has been a major contributor, probably more than justifies the huge cost of the USSR's postwar naval construction program.

Improving the Soviet Union's International Stature
Through a Capability to Project Power
in the International Arena

The Soviet appreciation of the value of the seas has been stated most cogently by Admiral Gorshkov. Combining a traditional understanding of sea power with Marxist-Leninist dialectics, Gorshkov has envisioned an imperialist-socialist struggle on both land and at sea. He has advocated developing a naval presence in the maritime approaches to those countries or areas selected for Soviet penetration, since naval forces make possible the application of military power without initiating hostilities; hence, with less danger of Western intervention. Gorshkov's strategy has been apparent in several aspects of Soviet naval operations, including the navy's eastern Mediterranean presence during ventures in Egypt and Syria; the naval presence in the Indian Ocean when policy initiatives began in Somalia, South Yemen, Iraq, and Ethiopia; and the navy's presence along the coast of West Africa during the major Soviet-sponsored offensive in Angola.

The degree to which this strategy has affected events is difficult to assess. However, it is clear that since 1964, the Soviets have steadily expanded their operations on the high seas. Operations in specific areas have not been independent operations, but have occurred in concert with and as a part of the comprehensive Soviet foreign policy thrusts into the Third World.

Critics of the standing-naval-force concept often ask what the Soviets hope to achieve by maintaining a far-flung naval presence, thus implying their belief that the Soviet naval forces have been deployed in accordance with a detailed plan and have been expected to achieve specific benefits for the Soviet Union. It is true that the naval deployments generally have been concurrent with the initiation of major policy objectives in a given area, but those deployments have not been expected to conform to preconceived schemes with clear-cut objectives. Rather, naval power has been considered an important part of Soviet foreign policy implementation. Initially, their forces have established a military presence in support of political ventures, and the future utility of those forces has depended on the progression of events. For example, the Soviet presence along West Africa was static for several years, then played a major role in the Angolan Civil War. Soviet naval power has been detailed widely to ensure that sufficient military power is available if needed.

Once established, the standing naval force in an area often participates in political activities, including port visits and acquiring port facilities. The port visit program accustoms nations in an area to the presence of Soviet naval power, and the development of port facilities often has provided the host country with a degree of security, while easing the Soviets' logistic problem of supporting a distant naval force.

Exercising Power to Encourage Changes in the International Arena

From 1956 through 1980, the Soviets used their navy whenever possible to encourage changes in the international political system. That none of these applications of naval power resulted in more dramatic successes reflects the existing balance of power. However, toward the end of the period, the Soviets became more assertive in their operations. This was particularly true in Angola in 1975–1976 and in Ethiopia in 1977–1978, when the United States chose not to react to those crises with naval power.

Although Soviet naval power has been employed effectively on many occasions, none has led to socialist systems conforming to the Soviet model. That fact does not spell failure for the Soviets. Indeed, they have experienced some success in Angola, Ethiopia, Mozambique, and South Yemen. Rather, it reflects the influence of U.S. naval power in international affairs. A continued relative shift in the naval balance of power away from the United States is a prerequisite for Soviet operations that are sufficiently aggressive to cause more dramatic changes.

Future Soviet Naval Construction and Operations

Naval Construction

Submarine construction will continue to play a dominant role in Soviet shipbuilding, first to maintain a strategic balance with the United States and second to disrupt the maritime traffic through the North Atlantic between the United States and Europe in time of war. Submarine construction will continue to have the highest priority for the resources allotted to naval shipbuilding.

In surface combatant construction, the Soviets will continue to build cruisers, destroyers, and frigates, since those ships have a high-visibility political value as well as a combat capability. More effective antisubmarine warfare equipment and missile systems should be anticipated on those ships. In naval propulsion, the Soviets began building nuclear-powered surface combatant ships in the late 1970s, although the first unit did not become operational until 1980. Such ships will be a distinct asset as naval operations are staged farther and farther away from home ports and as logistic support is improved. The Soviets are reportedly building new aircraft carriers as

The Soviet Navy is now building nuclear-powered surface ships, which will significantly enhance its sea projection capability. The first such ship, the guided missile cruiser *Kirov*, is pictured on sea trials in the Baltic Sea in 1980. (U.S. Navy)

Soviet naval infantry is expected to expand along with the naval amphibious force. These forces may be extremely valuable in some Soviet operations in Africa and South Asia. (U.S. Navy)

follow-ups to the *Kiev* carriers, and those ships will provide the Soviets with better air cover, which is crucial to many naval operations, and will contribute to the Soviet antisubmarine warfare capability. Finally, because of the politically and geographically expanding Soviet naval operations, new classes of amphibious ships will be built. The *Alligator* and *Ropucha* tank landing ships clearly have not provided a great amphibious capability, and larger amphibious ships, like the *Ivan Rogov* landing platform dock, will be required to enable the USSR to exploit opportunities that may arise in the closing decades of this century.

Naval Operations

Soviet naval operations since 1956 suggest how and for what purposes Soviet naval operations will be conducted in the 1980s and 1990s. The Soviet policy of pursuing political initiatives behind naval screens will continue and the Soviet naval presence on the high seas will expand as the Soviets extend their influence in Africa, Asia, and Latin America.

In the Mediterranean, the Soviet Navy is expected to maintain a considerable force for the next several decades in order to continue to defend the Soviet Union, exert pressure on NATO's southern flank, support Soviet policy in the Middle East, and influence maritime affairs in the approaches to the Suez Canal. Since the Soviet fleet has declined somewhat in size since 1973, the leaders may have decided to reduce the size of the Mediterranean Fleet. It is probable, however, that the navy will keep enough combatants in the Black Sea to dramatically augment the Mediterranean Fleet during times of crisis.

As the size of the Indian Ocean Squadron increases, the Soviet Union probably will decide to deploy ships to that force in peacetime through the Suez Canal. That maneuver would greatly simplify the squadron's logistic problem and provide more versatility in the composition of both the Mediterranean Fleet and the Indian Ocean Squadron.

The Soviets can be expected to expand their influence in Ethiopia and South Yemen. From those outposts, they could exert pressure northward from Ethiopia and eastward from Libya in order to try to regain influence in Egypt. Increased influence in Egypt, in turn, might lead to greater influence over the Suez Canal. The Soviets also could exert pressure on oil rich Saudi Arabia. If that were successful, pressure could then be applied on other Persian Gulf countries to isolate Iran. Soviet gains in the Arabian Peninsula and the Persian Gulf would weaken the West by affecting its access to Middle East oil.

In respect to Africa, the events of the 1970s in Somalia, Ethiopia, Mozambique, Guinea, and Angola have amounted to a major Soviet assault on that continent. Unless countered, the assault is likely to continue, supported by ships from both the Indian Ocean Squadron and the naval force positioned off the coast of West Africa. The chief target will be South Africa; the ultimate aims will be the expansion of communism and the concomitant weakening of the United States and the Western world through their loss of strategic position and the natural resources of the continent.

Finally, in Latin America, the Soviet Navy is capable of establishing a naval force in the Caribbean in the 1980s. Whether such an offensive will be launched concurrently with the ongoing African operations or will be delayed until the penetration of Africa has been completed is conjectural. However, it appears certain that a Soviet naval force operating out of Cuba will play a major role in any future Latin American offensive.

The Soviet decision to use sea power as a major force in achieving its long-range goals has been backed up by a naval construction program that began in 1956 and has produced one of the two most powerful navies in the world. Today, Soviet and U.S. naval forces compete for supremacy on the high seas. Lacking a preponderance of sea power, the Soviet naval forces have conformed to international maritime law. If they gain naval preponderance, Soviet actions are likely to become more aggressive, lawless, and destructive. Angola may be a harbinger of future trends: a recognized, legitimate Soviet naval force actively supporting an unrecognized, illegitimate Soviet-sponsored movement — a mixture of legitimacy and lawlessness.

Notes

1. Interview with Admiral Zumwalt, 22 October 1977.
2. Interview with Admiral Moorer, 9 January 1978.
3. Interview with Admiral Zumwalt, 22 October 1977.
4. Ibid.

Appendix

Tables

Table 1

Soviet Naval Order of Battle, October 1, 1981[a]

Part I - Ships

Type	Class	Northern Fleet	Baltic Fleet	Black Sea[b] Fleet	Pacific Fleet	Total
Submarines						
Ballistic Missile	Delta SSBN	---	---	---	---	35
Equipped	Yankee SSBN	---	---	---	---	27
Submarines	Typhoon SSBN	---	---	---	---	1
	Hotel SSBN	---	---	---	---	7
	Golf/Zulu SSB	---	---	---	---	15
Cruise Missile	Charlie/Echo/Oscar/					
Equipped	Papa SSGN	---	---	---	---	50
Submarines	Juliet/Whiskey SSG	---	---	---	---	20
Attack Submarines	Alfa/Echo/November/					
	Victor/Yankee SSN	---	---	---	---	60
	Bravo/Foxtrot/Golf/					
	Quebec/Romeo/Tango/					
	Whiskey/Zulu SS	---	---	---	---	160
Total Submarines		188	34	26	127	375
<u>Aircraft Carriers</u>	Kiev CVHG	1	0	0	1	2
<u>Principal Surface Combatants</u>						
Cruisers	Kirov CGN	1	0	0	0	1
	Moskva CHG	0	0	2	0	2
	Kara CG	0	0	5	2	7
	Kresta I CG	1	1	0	2	4
	Kresta II CG	6	1	0	3	10
	Kynda CG	0	0	2	2	4
	Sverdlov CG	0	0	1	0	1
	Sverdlov CL	2	1	3	3	9
Destroyers	Kanin DDG	5	0	0	3	8
	Kashin/Mod Kashin DDG	2	3	10	4	19
	Kildin DDG	0	0	0	1	1
	Kotlin DDG	2	1	3	2	8
	Sovremennyy DDG	0	1	0	0	1
	Udaloy DDG	0	2	0	0	2
	Kotlin/Mod Kildin/					
	Skoryy DD	5	5	10	10	30
Frigates	Krivak FFG	8	7	5	9	29
	Koni/Riga FF, Grisha/					
	Mirka/Petya FFL	40	25	35	40	140
Total		72	47	76	81	276
<u>Amphibious Warfare Ships</u>	Ivan Rogov LPD	0	0	0	1	1
	Ropucha LST	4	2	0	5	11
	Alligator LST	2	2	5	5	14
	MP-4/Polnocny LSM	5	20	20	15	60
Total		11	24	25	26	86

[a]This table presents the latest figures issued by the Department of Defense. However, recent issues of professional naval journals contain much speculation of new classes of ships and submarines. If this speculation is true, then the information on this table is already dated. Thus, these figures should be used cautiously, and are most valuable in conveying an idea of the relative strengths of the four Soviet Fleets.

[b]Includes units assigned to the Caspian Sea Flotilla.

Table 1 (Continued)

Soviet Naval Order of Battle, October 1, 1981

Type	Class	Northern Fleet	Baltic Fleet	Black Sea Fleet	Pacific Fleet	Total
Patrol Combatants	Sarancha PGGH Nanuchka/					
	Tarantul PGG	---	---	---	---	25
	Pauk/Poti PG	---	---	---	---	70
	Ivan Susanin/Purga Okhtenskiy/Sorum/					
	T-58 PGF	---	---	---	---	35
Total		30	35	25	40	130
Coastal Patrol-River/ Roadstead Craft	Matka PTGH, Osa PTG,	---	---	---	---	130
	Babochka PCSH, S.O.1					
	PCS, Stenka WPCS	---	---	---	---	120
	Turya PTH, Shershen PT	---	---	---	---	60
	PCF, WPBH, PM	---	---	---	---	120
Total		35	125	120	150	430
Mine Warfare Ships	Natya/T-43/T-58/ Yurka MSF	35	35	40	50	160
Mine Warfare Craft	MSC, MHC, MSI, MSB, MSD	40	90	55	45	230
Underway Replenishment Ships	AO	---	---	---	---	35
	AOR	---	---	---	---	20
	AF, AW	---	---	---	---	25
Total		25	10	20	25	80
Material Support Ships	AEM, AGP, AR, AS	30	10	10	20	70
Fleet Support Ships	ATA, ASR, ARS	35	25	35	35	130
Other Auxiliaries[c]		110	110	110	150	480
Total Ships		612	545	542	750	2,449

Part II - Naval Aircraft

	Northern Fleet	Baltic Fleet	Black Sea Fleet	Pacific Fleet	Total
Tactical					
Strike/Bombers (Backfire, Badger, Blinder)	---	---	---	---	390
Fighter/Fighter-Bombers (Forger, Fitter)	---	---	---	---	70
Total	95	130	100	135	460
Tactical Support					
Tankers (Badger)	---	---	---	---	80
Reconnaissance/Electronic Warfare (Bear D, Badger, Blinder)	---	---	---	---	185
Total	85	45	45	90	265
Antisubmarine Warfare (ASW)					
Bear F, May, Mail, Hormone A, Haze A	120	50	110	130	410
Utility					
Transport/Training (Various)	85	45	130[d]	65	325
Total Naval Aircraft	385	270	385	420	1,460

Part III - Personnel Strength

	Northern Fleet	Baltic Fleet	Black Sea Fleet	Pacific Fleet	Total
Afloat	---	---	---	---	185,000
Naval Aviation	---	---	---	---	59,000
Coastal Defense	---	---	---	---	8,000
Naval Infantry	---	---	---	---	12,000
Training	---	---	---	---	54,000
Shore Support	---	---	---	---	125,000
Total Personnel Strength	118,000	105,000	99,000[e]	121,000	443,000

[c]Includes intelligence collection ships, hydrographic survey ships, cargo ships, and other miscellaneous auxiliaries.

[d]Includes training aircraft at the Soviet Naval Aviation School.

[e]Includes personnel assigned to the Caspian Sea Flotilla.

Table 2

Out-of-Area Ship Days – Distribution by Geographical Area, 1956–1980[a]

Year	Atlantic Ocean	Mediterranean Sea	Pacific Ocean	Indian Ocean	Caribbean Sea	Total
1956	500	100	200	0	0	800
1957	1,500	600	200	0	0	2,300
1958	1,300	1,000	900	0	0	3,200
1959	2,100	4,100	900	0	0	7,100
1960	1,600	5,600	400	200	0	7,800
1961	2,200	2,300	700	0	0	5,200
1962	4,300	800	1,400	100	0	6,600
1963	3,600	600	1,800	100	0	6,100
1964	5,300	1,800	2,000	0	0	9,100
1965	5,400	3,700	2,500	0	0	11,600
1966	5,500	5,400	2,800	0	0	13,700
1967	5,800	8,800	3,600	200	0	18,400
1968	5,900	11,700	4,200	1,200	0	23,000
1969	9,600	15,400	5,900	4,100	300	35,300
1970	13,600	17,400	7,100	4,900	700	43,700
1971	14,800	18,700	6,200	4,000	700	44,400
1972	14,500	17,700	5,900	8,900	1,900	48,900
1973	13,000	20,600	6,300	8,900	1,400	50,200
1974	13,900	20,200	7,400	10,500	1,200	53,200
1975	13,200	20,000	6,800	7,100	1,100	48,200
1976	14,000	18,600	6,500	7,300	1,000	47,400
1977	15,800	16,300	7,500	6,700	1,200	47,500
1978	16,100	16,600	6,900	8,500	1,300	49,400
1979	16,900	16,600	10,400	7,600	1,100	52,600
1980	16,900	16,600	11,800	11,800	700	57,800

[a]Data for the years prior to 1969 have been extrapolated from approximative information and are not considered as valid as those for the years 1969–1980. Ship days in the Indian Ocean prior to 1967 reflect ship transits through the ocean and are not ships deployed specifically for Indian Ocean operations.

Table 3

Out-of-Area Ship Days – Percentage Distribution by Geographical Area, 1956–1980[a]

Year	Atlantic Ocean	Mediterranean Sea	Pacific Ocean	Indian Ocean	Caribbean Sea
1956	62%	13%	25%	0%	0%
1957	65	26	9	0	0
1958	41	31	28	0	0
1959	29	58	13	0	0
1960	20	72	5	3	0
1961	42	44	14	0	0
1962	65	12	21	2	0
1963	59	10	29	2	0
1964	58	20	22	0	0
1965	47	32	21	0	0
1966	40	39	21	0	0
1967	31	48	20	1	0
1968	26	51	18	5	0
1969	27	44	17	11	1
1970	31	40	16	11	2
1971	33	42	14	9	2
1972	30	36	12	18	4
1973	26	41	12	18	3
1974	26	38	14	20	2
1975	27	42	14	15	2
1976	30	39	14	15	2
1977	33	34	16	14	3
1978	32	34	14	17	3
1979	32	32	19	15	2
1980	29	29	20.5	20.5	1

[a]Data for the years prior to 1969 have been extrapolated from approximative information and are not considered as valid as those for the years 1969–1980. Ship days in the Indian Ocean prior to 1967 reflect ship transits through the Indian Ocean and are not ships deployed specifically for Indian Ocean operations.

Table 4

Number of Soviet Naval Ships Visiting Atlantic Area Ports, 1953-1980[a]

COUNTRY/PORT	53	54	55	56	57	58	59	60	61	62	63	64	65	66	67	68	69	70	71	72	73	74	75	76	77	78	79	80
Angola																												
Luanda	0	0	0	0	0	0	0	0	0	0	0	0	0	0	0	0	0	0	0	0	0	0	0	5	31	31	33	21
Argentina																												
Buenos Aires	0	0	0	0	0	0	0	0	0	0	0	0	0	0	0	0	0	0	0	0	0	0	0	0	0	0	1	0
Ushuaia	0	0	0	0	0	0	0	0	0	0	0	0	0	0	0	0	0	0	0	0	0	0	0	0	0	0	0	1
Aruba																												
Oranjestad	0	0	0	0	0	0	0	0	0	0	0	0	0	0	0	0	0	0	0	0	0	0	0	0	0	1	0	0
Azores																												
Ponta Delgada	0	0	0	0	0	0	0	0	0	0	0	0	0	0	0	0	0	0	0	0	0	0	0	0	0	1	0	0
São Miguel	0	0	0	0	0	0	0	0	0	0	0	0	0	0	0	0	0	0	0	0	0	0	0	0	0	1	0	0
Barbados																												
Bridgetown	0	0	0	0	0	0	0	0	0	0	0	0	0	0	0	0	3	0	0	0	0	0	0	0	0	0	1	0
Benin (Dahomey)																												
Cotonou	0	0	0	0	0	0	0	0	0	0	0	0	0	0	0	0	0	0	1	0	0	0	0	0	15	11	7	7
Bermuda																												
Hamilton	0	0	0	0	0	0	0	2	3	2	3	0	0	0	0	0	0	0	0	0	0	1	2	0	0	1	1	0
St. George	0	0	0	0	0	0	0	0	0	0	0	0	0	0	0	0	0	0	0	0	0	0	2	0	0	0	0	0
Brazil																												
Fernando de Noronha	0	0	0	0	0	0	0	0	0	0	0	0	0	0	0	0	0	3	0	0	0	0	0	0	0	0	0	0
Natal	0	0	0	0	0	0	0	0	0	0	0	0	0	0	0	0	0	1	0	0	0	0	0	0	0	0	0	0
Recife	0	0	0	0	0	0	0	0	0	0	0	0	0	0	0	0	0	1	0	0	0	1	0	0	0	0	0	0
Rio de Janeiro	0	0	0	0	0	0	0	0	0	0	0	0	0	1	0	2	0	0	4	0	0	0	0	0	0	0	0	0
Cameroon																												
Douala	0	0	0	0	0	0	0	0	0	0	0	0	0	0	0	0	0	0	0	0	0	1	0	0	0	0	0	0
Canada																												
Halifax	0	0	0	0	0	0	0	2	0	0	0	2	1	0	0	0	1	1	4	6	2	9	6	4	5	2	0	0
St. John's	0	0	0	0	0	0	0	1	0	0	0	0	2	0	0	0	0	1	0	0	0	5	0	6	0	1	7	0
Canary Islands																												
Las Palmas	0	0	0	0	0	0	0	0	0	0	0	0	0	0	0	0	1	8	12	6	7	8	23	26	35	45	58	30
Santa Cruz de Tenerife	0	0	0	0	0	0	0	0	0	0	0	0	0	0	0	0	0	0	0	0	5	9	4	5	4	6	2	0
Cape Verde Islands																												
Praia	0	0	0	0	0	0	0	0	0	0	0	0	0	0	0	0	0	0	0	0	0	0	0	0	0	0	4	0
São Vicente	0	0	0	0	0	0	0	0	0	0	0	0	0	0	0	0	0	0	0	0	0	0	0	0	0	0	1	0
Colombia																												
Cartagena	0	0	0	0	0	0	0	0	0	0	0	0	0	0	0	0	0	0	0	0	1	1	0	3	0	3	0	0
Congo																												
Pointe-Noire	0	0	0	0	0	0	0	0	0	0	0	0	0	0	0	0	0	0	0	4	2	0	2	1	0	0	0	0
Cuba																												
Antilla	0	0	0	0	0	0	0	0	0	0	0	0	0	0	0	0	0	4	8	0	1	0	0	0	3	0	0	0
Bahia de Cadiz	0	0	0	0	0	0	0	0	0	0	0	0	0	0	0	0	0	0	0	0	0	0	0	0	0	0	0	1
Bahia de Nipe	0	0	0	0	0	0	0	0	0	0	0	0	0	0	0	0	0	0	1	5	2	1	1	0	0	0	0	0
Caibarién	0	0	0	0	0	0	0	0	0	0	0	0	0	0	0	0	0	0	0	0	0	0	0	0	0	0	0	2
Casilda	0	0	0	0	0	0	0	0	0	0	0	0	0	0	0	0	0	2	0	2	0	0	0	0	0	0	0	0
Cienfuegos	0	0	0	0	0	0	0	0	0	0	0	0	0	0	0	0	0	29	19	27	18	21	20	15	20	35	28	16
Havana	0	0	0	0	0	0	0	0	0	0	0	0	0	2	0	0	9	13	18	32	26	39	33	23	36	25	12	14
Manzanillo	0	0	0	0	0	0	0	0	0	0	0	0	0	0	0	0	0	0	0	2	0	0	0	0	0	0	0	0
Mariel	0	0	0	0	0	0	0	0	0	0	0	0	0	0	0	0	0	3	4	6	9	6	0	2	0	0	0	0
Moa	0	0	0	0	0	0	0	0	0	0	0	0	0	0	0	0	0	0	0	0	0	0	0	0	0	0	1	0

[a]Includes visits to non-Soviet-Bloc Baltic nations and nations in the Gulf of Guinea, Caribbean Sea, and Gulf of Mexico.

Table 4 (Continued)

Number of Soviet Naval Ships Visiting Atlantic Area Ports, 1953–1980

COUNTRY/PORT	53	54	55	56	57	58	59	60	61	62	63	64	65	66	67	68	69	70	71	72	73	74	75	76	77	78	79	80
Cuba																												
Nuevitas	0	0	0	0	0	0	0	0	0	0	0	0	0	0	0	0	0	0	0	3	0	0	0	2	0	0	0	0
Puerto Cabañas	0	0	0	0	0	0	0	0	0	0	0	0	0	0	0	0	0	0	1	0	0	0	0	0	0	0	0	0
Puerto Manati	0	0	0	0	0	0	0	0	0	0	0	0	0	0	0	0	0	0	0	2	0	0	0	0	0	0	0	0
Puerto Padre	0	0	0	0	0	0	0	0	0	0	0	0	0	0	0	0	0	0	0	3	0	0	0	0	0	0	0	0
Santa Cruz del Norte	0	0	0	0	0	0	0	0	0	0	0	0	0	0	0	0	0	0	0	0	0	0	0	0	1	0	0	0
Santiago de Cuba	0	0	0	0	0	0	0	0	0	0	0	0	0	0	0	0	0	3	0	3	0	1	1	4	0	0	0	1
Curaçao																												
Willemstad	0	0	0	0	0	0	0	0	0	0	0	0	0	0	0	0	0	0	0	1	1	1	0	3	3	3	3	2
Denmark																												
Copenhagen	0	0	0	3	0	0	0	0	0	0	0	3	0	0	0	0	0	0	2	0	2	0	1	1	0	3	0	0
Equatorial Guinea																												
Bata	0	0	0	0	0	0	0	0	0	0	0	0	0	0	0	0	0	0	0	0	0	1	0	0	0	0	0	0
Luba	0	0	0	0	0	0	0	0	0	0	0	0	0	0	0	0	0	0	0	0	3	0	0	0	0	0	0	0
Santa Isabel	0	0	0	0	0	0	0	0	0	0	0	0	0	0	0	0	0	3	0	3	0	2	0	0	0	0	0	0
Faeroe Islands																												
Thorshavn	0	0	0	0	0	0	0	0	0	0	0	0	0	0	0	0	0	0	0	0	2	7	6	6	3	1	2	1
Falkland Islands																												
Port Stanley	0	0	0	0	0	0	0	0	0	0	0	0	0	0	0	0	0	0	0	3	0	0	0	0	0	0	0	0
Finland																												
Helsinki	0	2	0	0	0	3	0	2	0	0	0	0	0	1	1	2	0	0	2	0	0	0	0	0	0	2	0	0
Kotka	0	0	0	0	0	0	0	0	0	0	2	0	0	0	0	0	0	0	0	0	0	0	0	0	0	0	0	0
Oulu	0	0	0	0	0	0	0	0	0	0	0	0	0	0	0	0	0	0	0	0	0	0	2	0	0	0	0	0
Rauma	0	0	0	0	0	0	0	0	0	0	0	0	0	0	0	0	0	0	0	0	0	0	0	0	0	0	2	0
Turku	0	0	0	0	0	0	0	0	2	0	0	0	0	0	0	0	0	0	0	0	0	3	0	0	0	0	0	0
France																												
Barfleur	0	0	0	0	0	0	0	0	0	0	0	0	0	0	0	0	0	3	0	0	0	0	0	0	0	0	0	0
Bordeaux	0	0	0	0	0	0	0	0	0	0	0	0	0	0	0	0	0	0	0	0	0	0	0	2	0	2	0	0
Cherbourg	0	0	0	0	0	0	0	0	0	0	0	0	0	0	0	0	0	2	0	0	3	0	0	2	0	0	0	0
Le Havre	0	0	0	0	0	0	0	0	0	0	0	0	0	0	3	1	3	1	1	0	0	0	0	0	0	0	0	0
Nantes	0	0	0	0	0	0	0	0	0	0	0	0	0	0	0	0	0	0	0	1	0	0	0	0	0	0	0	0
Gambia																												
Bathurst (Banjul)	0	0	0	0	0	0	0	0	0	0	0	0	0	0	0	0	0	0	1	0	0	0	0	0	0	0	0	0
Guinea																												
Conakry	0	0	0	0	0	0	0	0	0	0	0	0	0	0	0	0	9	7	26	52	38	33	27	50	77	83	51	36
Guinea-Bissau																												
Bissau	0	0	0	0	0	0	0	0	0	0	0	0	0	0	0	0	0	0	0	0	0	0	0	1	0	0	2	0
Iceland																												
Reykjavik	0	0	0	0	0	0	0	0	0	0	0	1	0	3	0	0	4	1	0	0	0	0	3	7	9	2	1	3
Ireland																												
Cork	0	0	0	0	0	0	0	0	0	0	0	0	0	0	0	3	0	0	0	0	0	0	0	0	0	0	0	0
Dublin	0	0	0	0	0	0	0	0	0	0	0	0	0	0	0	0	0	0	0	0	0	0	3	0	0	0	0	0
Ivory Coast																												
Abidjan	0	0	0	0	0	0	0	0	0	0	0	0	0	0	0	0	0	2	2	1	1	4	4	1	3	2	0	1
Jamaica																												
Kingston	0	0	0	0	0	0	0	0	2	0	0	0	0	0	0	0	0	2	0	0	0	0	0	0	0	0	0	0
Liberia																												
Monrovia	0	0	0	0	0	0	0	0	0	0	0	0	0	0	0	0	0	0	0	0	0	1	0	1	0	0	1	0

Table 4 (Continued)

Number of Soviet Naval Ships Visiting Atlantic Area Ports, 1953–1980

COUNTRY/PORT	53	54	55	56	57	58	59	60	61	62	63	64	65	66	67	68	69	70	71	72	73	74	75	76	77	78	79	80
Martinique																												
Fort-de-France	0	0	0	0	0	0	0	0	0	0	0	0	0	0	0	0	0	2	0	0	0	0	0	0	0	0	0	0
Mauritania																												
Nouadhibou	0	0	0	0	0	0	0	0	0	0	0	0	0	0	0	0	0	0	0	1	0	0	0	0	0	0	0	0
Mexico																												
Veracruz	0	0	0	0	0	0	0	0	0	0	0	0	0	0	1	0	0	0	0	4	0	2	1	2	4	3	2	1
Morocco																												
Casablanca	0	0	0	0	0	0	0	0	0	0	2	0	3	0	5	0	0	8	1	6	9	12	15	6	4	4	3	4
Rabat	0	0	0	0	0	0	0	0	0	0	0	0	0	0	0	0	0	0	0	0	0	0	0	1	0	0	0	0
Safi	0	0	0	0	0	0	0	0	0	0	0	0	0	0	0	0	0	0	0	0	3	1	0	0	0	0	0	0
Tangier	0	0	0	0	0	0	0	0	0	0	0	0	0	0	0	0	7	6	12	6	14	6	1	1	1	0	3	1
Netherlands																												
Amsterdam	0	0	0	0	0	0	0	0	0	0	0	0	0	0	0	0	1	0	0	0	0	0	0	0	0	2	0	0
Rotterdam	0	0	0	5	0	0	0	0	0	0	0	0	0	0	0	0	0	0	2	0	0	0	0	0	0	0	0	0
Nigeria																												
Lagos	0	0	0	0	0	0	0	0	0	0	0	0	0	0	0	0	8	3	0	0	0	0	0	3	2	0	0	0
Norway																												
Bergen	0	0	0	0	2	2	0	0	2	1	0	4	0	0	0	0	0	0	1	0	0	0	0	0	0	0	0	0
Haugesund	0	0	0	0	0	0	0	0	0	0	0	0	0	0	0	0	2	1	0	0	0	0	0	0	0	0	0	0
Oslo	0	0	0	3	0	0	0	0	0	0	0	0	0	0	0	0	0	2	0	0	2	0	0	2	0	0	0	0
Tromsö	0	0	0	0	0	0	0	0	0	0	0	0	0	0	0	0	1	0	0	0	0	0	0	0	0	0	0	0
Trondheim	0	0	0	0	0	0	0	0	0	0	2	0	0	0	0	0	0	0	0	0	0	0	0	0	0	0	0	0
St. Helena																												
Jamestown	0	0	0	0	0	0	0	0	0	0	0	0	0	0	0	0	1	5	4	1	0	3	0	0	1	0	0	0
São Thomé																												
São Thomé	0	0	0	0	0	0	0	0	0	0	0	0	0	0	0	0	0	0	0	0	0	0	0	0	0	5	7	0
Senegal																												
Dakar	0	0	0	0	0	1	0	0	0	0	0	2	0	0	0	0	3	8	5	15	7	15	3	8	3	7	8	8
Sierra Leone																												
Freetown	0	0	0	0	0	0	1	0	0	0	0	0	0	0	0	1	1	0	4	6	4	7	1	3	0	0	0	0
Southwest Africa																												
Walvis Bay	0	0	0	0	0	0	0	0	0	0	0	0	0	0	0	0	0	0	0	2	0	0	0	0	0	0	0	0
Spain																												
La Coruña	0	0	0	0	0	0	0	0	0	0	0	0	0	0	0	0	0	0	0	0	0	0	0	0	0	4	4	0
Vigo	0	0	0	0	0	0	0	0	0	0	0	0	0	0	0	0	0	0	0	0	0	0	0	0	0	0	2	0
Surinam																												
Paramaribo	0	0	0	0	0	0	0	0	0	0	0	0	0	0	0	0	0	0	0	0	0	0	0	0	1	0	0	0
Sweden																												
Gothenburg	0	0	0	3	0	2	0	0	0	0	0	0	0	0	0	0	0	0	0	0	0	4	1	1	2	3	4	2
Stockholm	0	5	0	0	0	2	0	0	0	4	0	0	3	0	0	0	0	0	0	0	3	0	0	0	0	0	0	0
Trinidad																												
Port of Spain	0	0	0	0	0	0	0	0	0	0	0	0	0	0	0	0	0	0	0	0	0	1	0	1	0	0	0	0
United Kingdom																												
Belfast	0	0	0	0	0	0	0	0	0	0	0	0	0	0	0	2	0	0	0	0	0	0	0	0	0	0	0	0
Bristol	0	0	0	0	0	0	0	0	0	0	0	0	0	4	0	2	0	0	0	0	0	0	0	0	0	0	0	0
Glasgow	0	0	0	0	0	0	0	0	0	0	0	0	3	0	0	0	0	0	0	0	0	0	0	0	0	0	0	0
Leith	0	0	0	0	0	0	0	0	0	0	0	0	0	0	0	1	0	2	0	0	0	0	0	0	0	0	0	0
London	0	0	0	0	0	0	0	0	0	0	0	0	1	0	0	0	0	0	0	0	0	0	0	0	1	0	0	0
Portsmouth	1	0	6	3	0	0	0	0	0	0	0	0	0	0	0	0	0	0	0	0	0	0	0	0	0	0	0	0
Southampton	0	0	0	0	0	0	0	0	0	0	0	3	0	0	2	0	0	0	0	0	0	0	0	0	0	0	0	0
Spithead	1	0	0	0	0	0	0	0	0	0	0	0	0	0	0	0	0	0	0	0	0	0	0	0	0	0	0	0
United States																												
Baltimore	0	0	0	0	0	0	0	0	0	0	0	0	0	0	0	0	0	0	0	0	0	2	0	1	0	0	0	0
Boston	0	0	0	0	0	0	0	0	0	0	0	0	0	0	0	0	0	0	0	0	0	0	2	0	0	0	0	0
Philadelphia	0	0	0	0	0	0	0	0	0	0	0	0	0	0	0	0	0	0	0	0	0	1	0	1	0	0	0	0
Savannah	0	0	0	0	0	0	0	0	0	0	0	0	0	0	0	0	0	0	0	0	0	2	2	0	0	0	0	0
Uruguay																												
Montevideo	0	0	0	0	0	0	0	0	0	0	0	0	0	0	1	3	1	5	5	9	6	5	9	4	5	7	3	8
Venezuela																												
La Guaira	0	0	0	0	0	0	0	0	0	0	0	0	0	0	0	0	0	0	0	0	0	0	0	0	0	0	2	0
Puerto Cabello	0	0	0	0	0	0	0	0	0	0	0	0	0	0	0	0	0	0	0	0	0	0	1	0	0	1	0	0

Table 5

Soviet Naval Ship Days Spent in Atlantic Area Ports, 1953–1980[a]

COUNTRY/PORT	53	54	55	56	57	58	59	60	61	62	63	64	65	66	67	68	69	70	71	72	73	74	75	76	77	78	79	80
Angola																												
Luanda	0	0	0	0	0	0	0	0	0	0	0	0	0	0	0	0	0	0	0	0	0	0	0	42	856	941	749	806
Argentina																												
Buenos Aires	0	0	0	0	0	0	0	0	0	0	0	0	0	0	0	0	0	0	0	0	0	0	0	0	0	0	6	0
Ushuaia	0	0	0	0	0	0	0	0	0	0	0	0	0	0	0	0	0	0	0	0	0	0	0	0	0	0	0	6
Aruba																												
Oranjestad	0	0	0	0	0	0	0	0	0	0	0	0	0	0	0	0	0	0	0	0	0	0	0	0	0	2	0	0
Azores																												
Ponta Delgada	0	0	0	0	0	0	0	0	0	0	0	0	0	0	0	0	0	0	0	0	0	0	0	0	0	0	5	0
São Miguel	0	0	0	0	0	0	0	0	0	0	0	0	0	0	0	0	0	0	0	0	0	0	0	0	0	4	0	0
Barbados																												
Bridgetown	0	0	0	0	0	0	0	0	0	0	0	0	0	0	0	8	0	0	0	0	0	0	0	0	0	0	2	0
Benin (Dahomey)																												
Cotonou	0	0	0	0	0	0	0	0	0	0	0	0	0	0	0	0	0	1	0	0	0	0	0	0	170	191	48	52
Bermuda																												
Hamilton	0	0	0	0	0	0	0	8	6	8	15	0	0	0	0	0	0	0	0	0	0	1	12	0	0	7	1	0
St. George	0	0	0	0	0	0	0	0	0	0	0	0	0	0	0	0	0	0	0	0	0	0	12	0	0	0	0	0
Brazil																												
Fernando de Noronha	0	0	0	0	0	0	0	0	0	0	0	0	0	0	0	0	0	21	0	0	0	0	0	0	0	0	0	0
Natal	0	0	0	0	0	0	0	0	0	0	0	0	0	0	0	0	0	4	0	0	0	0	0	0	0	0	0	0
Recife	0	0	0	0	0	0	0	0	0	0	0	0	0	0	0	0	0	4	0	0	0	1	0	0	0	0	0	0
Rio de Janeiro	0	0	0	0	0	0	0	0	0	0	0	0	0	4	0	10	0	0	0	17	0	0	0	0	0	0	0	0
Cameroon																												
Douala	0	0	0	0	0	0	0	0	0	0	0	0	0	0	0	0	0	0	0	0	0	0	5	0	0	0	0	0
Canada																												
Halifax	0	0	0	0	0	0	0	4	0	0	12	3	0	0	0	5	0	2	22	31	9	45	30	12	16	8	0	0
St. John's	0	0	0	0	0	0	0	7	0	0	0	0	10	0	0	0	0	3	0	0	0	29	0	29	0	4	36	0
Canary Islands																												
Las Palmas	0	0	0	0	0	0	0	0	0	0	0	0	0	0	0	0	5	15	41	22	31	30	75	78	100	156	239	102
Santa Cruz de Tenerife	0	0	0	0	0	0	0	0	0	0	0	0	0	0	0	0	0	0	0	0	16	29	14	15	16	21	6	0
Cape Verde Islands																												
Praia	0	0	0	0	0	0	0	0	0	0	0	0	0	0	0	0	0	0	0	0	0	0	0	0	0	0	23	0
São Vicente	0	0	0	0	0	0	0	0	0	0	0	0	0	0	0	0	0	0	0	0	0	0	0	0	0	0	2	0
Colombia																												
Cartagena	0	0	0	0	0	0	0	0	0	0	0	0	0	0	0	0	0	0	0	0	4	6	0	15	0	18	0	0
Congo																												
Pointe-Noire	0	0	0	0	0	0	0	0	0	0	0	0	0	0	0	0	0	0	0	21	14	0	9	3	0	0	0	0
Cuba																												
Antilla	0	0	0	0	0	0	0	0	0	0	0	0	0	0	0	0	0	23	62	0	7	0	0	0	18	0	0	0
Bahia de Cadiz	0	0	0	0	0	0	0	0	0	0	0	0	0	0	0	0	0	0	0	0	0	0	0	0	0	0	0	3
Bahia de Nipe	0	0	0	0	0	0	0	0	0	0	0	0	0	0	0	0	0	0	2	41	13	25	15	35	0	0	0	9
Caibarién	0	0	0	0	0	0	0	0	0	0	0	0	0	0	0	0	0	0	0	0	0	0	0	0	0	0	0	10
Casilda	0	0	0	0	0	0	0	0	0	0	0	0	0	0	0	0	0	11	0	4	0	0	0	0	0	0	0	0
Cienfuegos	0	0	0	0	0	0	0	0	0	0	0	0	0	0	0	0	0	365	243	457	241	342	263	137	117	578	311	99
Havana	0	0	0	0	0	0	0	0	0	0	0	0	0	0	7	0	80	91	126	301	210	398	451	355	575	377	325	338
Manzanillo	0	0	0	0	0	0	0	0	0	0	0	0	0	0	0	0	0	0	10	0	0	0	0	0	0	0	0	0
Mariel	0	0	0	0	0	0	0	0	0	0	0	0	0	0	0	0	0	19	184	100	247	45	0	11	0	0	0	0
Moa	0	0	0	0	0	0	0	0	0	0	0	0	0	0	0	0	0	0	0	0	0	0	0	0	0	0	2	0
Nuevitas	0	0	0	0	0	0	0	0	0	0	0	0	0	0	0	0	0	0	13	0	0	0	0	4	0	0	0	0
Puerto Cabañas	0	0	0	0	0	0	0	0	0	0	0	0	0	0	0	0	0	0	5	0	0	0	0	0	0	0	0	0
Puerto Manati	0	0	0	0	0	0	0	0	0	0	0	0	0	0	0	0	0	0	0	2	0	0	0	0	0	0	0	0
Puerto Padre	0	0	0	0	0	0	0	0	0	0	0	0	0	0	0	0	0	0	0	14	0	0	0	0	0	0	0	0
Santa Cruz del Norte	0	0	0	0	0	0	0	0	0	0	0	0	0	0	0	0	0	0	0	0	0	0	0	0	4	0	0	0
Santiago de Cuba	0	0	0	0	0	0	0	0	0	0	0	0	0	0	0	0	0	14	0	20	0	2	2	13	0	0	0	5
Curaçao																												
Willemstad	0	0	0	0	0	0	0	0	0	0	0	0	0	0	0	0	0	0	0	6	4	3	0	12	16	12	11	10
Denmark																												
Copenhagen	0	0	0	15	0	0	0	0	0	0	0	15	0	0	0	0	0	0	10	0	10	0	5	6	0	18	0	0

[a]Includes visits to non-Soviet-Bloc Baltic nations and nations in the Gulf of Guinea, Caribbean Sea, and Gulf of Mexico.

Table 5 (Continued)

Soviet Naval Ship Days Spent in Atlantic Area Ports, 1953–1980

COUNTRY/PORT	53	54	55	56	57	58	59	60	61	62	63	64	65	66	67	68	69	70	71	72	73	74	75	76	77	78	79	80
Equatorial Guinea																												
Bata	0	0	0	0	0	0	0	0	0	0	0	0	0	0	0	0	0	0	0	0	0	2	0	0	0	0	0	0
Luba	0	0	0	0	0	0	0	0	0	0	0	0	0	0	0	0	0	0	0	0	0	21	0	0	0	0	0	0
Santa Isabel	0	0	0	0	0	0	0	0	0	0	0	0	0	0	0	0	0	18	0	18	0	7	0	0	0	0	0	0
Faeroe Islands																												
Thorshavn	0	0	0	0	0	0	0	0	0	0	0	0	0	0	0	0	0	0	0	0	9	35	27	28	14	4	11	2
Falkland Islands																												
Port Stanley	0	0	0	0	0	0	0	0	0	0	0	0	0	0	0	0	0	0	0	12	0	0	0	0	0	0	0	0
Finland																												
Helsinki	0	10	0	0	0	15	0	10	0	0	0	0	0	0	6	3	10	0	0	12	0	0	0	0	0	0	12	0
Kotka	0	0	0	0	0	0	0	0	0	0	0	10	0	0	0	0	0	0	0	0	0	0	0	0	0	0	0	0
Oulu	0	0	0	0	0	0	0	0	0	0	0	0	0	0	0	0	0	0	0	0	0	0	0	12	0	0	0	0
Rauma	0	0	0	0	0	0	0	0	0	0	0	0	0	0	0	0	0	0	0	0	0	0	0	0	0	0	130	0
Turku	0	0	0	0	0	0	0	0	10	0	0	0	0	0	0	0	0	0	0	0	0	18	0	0	0	0	0	0
France																												
Barfleur	0	0	0	0	0	0	0	0	0	0	0	0	0	0	0	0	0	12	0	0	0	0	0	0	0	0	0	0
Bordeaux	0	0	0	0	0	0	0	0	0	0	0	0	0	0	0	0	0	0	0	0	0	0	0	12	0	10	0	0
Cherbourg	0	0	0	0	0	0	0	0	0	0	0	0	0	0	0	0	0	12	0	0	0	13	0	0	12	0	0	0
Le Havre	0	0	0	0	0	0	0	0	0	0	0	0	0	0	21	2	13	3	5	0	0	0	0	0	0	0	0	0
Nantes	0	0	0	0	0	0	0	0	0	0	0	0	0	0	0	0	0	0	0	5	0	0	0	0	0	0	0	0
Gambia																												
Bathurst (Banjul)	0	0	0	0	0	0	0	0	0	0	0	0	0	0	0	0	0	0	3	0	0	0	0	0	0	0	0	0
Guinea																												
Conakry	0	0	0	0	0	0	0	0	0	0	0	0	0	0	44	0	0	60	334	546	401	902	633	998	1410	1432	1042	686
Guinea-Bissau																												
Bissau	0	0	0	0	0	0	0	0	0	0	0	0	0	0	0	0	0	0	0	0	0	0	0	5	0	0	11	0
Iceland																												
Reykjavik	0	0	0	0	0	0	0	0	0	0	0	0	5	0	18	0	19	4	0	0	0	0	15	30	37	9	6	16
Ireland																												
Cork	0	0	0	0	0	0	0	0	0	0	0	0	0	0	0	18	0	0	0	0	0	0	0	0	0	0	0	0
Dublin	0	0	0	0	0	0	0	0	0	0	0	0	0	0	0	0	0	0	0	0	0	8	0	0	0	0	0	0
Ivory Coast																												
Abidjan	0	0	0	0	0	0	0	0	0	0	0	0	0	0	0	0	0	14	4	3	2	24	15	5	10	8	0	4
Jamaica																												
Kingston	0	0	0	0	0	0	0	0	8	0	0	0	0	0	0	0	0	5	0	0	0	0	0	0	0	0	0	0
Liberia																												
Monrovia	0	0	0	0	0	0	0	0	0	0	0	0	0	0	0	0	0	0	0	0	0	0	6	0	3	0	0	4
Martinique																												
Fort-de-France	0	0	0	0	0	0	0	0	0	0	0	0	0	0	0	6	0	0	0	0	0	0	0	0	0	0	0	0
Mauritania																												
Nouadhibou	0	0	0	0	0	0	0	0	0	0	0	0	0	0	0	0	0	0	0	5	0	0	0	0	0	0	0	0
Mexico																												
Veracruz	0	0	0	0	0	0	0	0	0	0	0	0	0	0	6	0	0	0	0	7	0	12	4	8	17	12	7	6
Morocco																												
Casablanca	0	0	0	0	0	0	0	0	0	0	0	12	0	15	0	30	0	31	5	34	39	51	77	27	23	16	7	22
Rabat	0	0	0	0	0	0	0	0	0	0	0	0	0	0	0	0	0	0	0	0	0	0	0	1	0	0	0	0
Safi	0	0	0	0	0	0	0	0	0	0	0	0	0	0	0	0	0	0	0	0	19	1	0	0	0	0	0	0
Tangier	0	0	0	0	0	0	0	0	0	0	0	0	0	0	0	0	29	22	59	31	61	22	5	5	5	0	13	4

Table 5 (Continued)

Soviet Naval Ship Days Spent in Atlantic Area Ports, 1953–1980

COUNTRY/PORT	53	54	55	56	57	58	59	60	61	62	63	64	65	66	67	68	69	70	71	72	73	74	75	76	77	78	79	80
Netherlands																												
Amsterdam	0	0	0	0	0	0	0	0	0	0	0	0	0	0	0	0	0	6	0	0	0	0	0	0	0	10	0	0
Rotterdam	0	0	0	25	0	0	0	0	0	0	0	0	0	0	0	0	0	0	15	0	0	0	0	0	0	0	0	0
Nigeria																												
Lagos	0	0	0	0	0	0	0	0	0	0	0	0	0	0	0	0	44	15	0	0	0	0	18	12	0	0	0	0
Norway																												
Bergen	0	0	0	0	0	8	10	0	0	0	10	6	0	20	0	0	0	0	3	0	0	0	0	0	0	0	0	0
Haugesund	0	0	0	0	0	0	0	0	0	0	0	0	0	0	0	0	12	4	0	0	0	0	0	0	0	0	0	0
Oslo	0	0	0	15	0	0	0	0	0	0	0	0	0	0	0	0	0	0	12	0	0	10	0	0	12	0	0	0
Tromsö	0	0	0	0	0	0	0	0	0	0	0	0	0	0	0	0	0	0	4	0	0	0	0	0	0	0	0	0
Trondheim	0	0	0	0	0	0	0	0	0	0	10	0	0	0	0	0	0	0	0	0	0	0	0	0	0	0	0	0
St. Helena																												
Jamestown	0	0	0	0	0	0	0	0	0	0	0	0	0	0	0	0	1	12	15	5	0	14	0	0	2	0	0	0
São Thomé																												
São Thomé	0	0	0	0	0	0	0	0	0	0	0	0	0	0	0	0	0	0	0	0	0	0	0	0	0	59	44	0
Senegal																												
Dakar	0	0	0	0	0	6	0	0	0	0	0	12	0	0	0	0	18	41	18	122	32	68	13	26	13	23	30	24
Sierra Leone																												
Freetown	0	0	0	0	0	0	2	0	0	0	0	0	0	0	0	6	4	0	24	28	14	31	3	7	0	0	0	0
Southwest Africa																												
Walvis Bay	0	0	0	0	0	0	0	0	0	0	0	0	0	0	0	0	0	0	0	0	8	0	0	0	0	0	0	0
Spain																												
La Coruña	0	0	0	0	0	0	0	0	0	0	0	0	0	0	0	0	0	0	0	0	0	0	0	0	0	17	19	0
Vigo	0	0	0	0	0	0	0	0	0	0	0	0	0	0	0	0	0	0	0	0	0	0	0	0	0	0	6	0
Surinam																												
Paramaribo	0	0	0	0	0	0	0	0	0	0	0	0	0	0	0	0	0	0	0	0	0	0	3	0	0	0	0	0
Sweden																												
Gothenburg	0	0	0	15	0	6	0	0	0	0	0	0	0	0	0	0	0	0	0	0	0	22	1	71	94	74	75	91
Stockholm	0	33	0	0	0	12	0	0	0	16	0	0	12	0	0	0	0	0	0	18	0	0	0	0	0	0	0	0
Trinidad																												
Port of Spain	0	0	0	0	0	0	0	0	0	0	0	0	0	0	0	0	0	0	0	0	0	5	0	3	0	0	0	0
United Kingdom																												
Belfast	0	0	0	0	0	0	0	0	0	0	0	0	0	0	0	4	0	0	0	0	0	0	0	0	0	0	0	0
Bristol	0	0	0	0	0	0	0	0	0	0	0	0	0	0	20	0	16	0	0	0	0	0	0	0	0	0	0	0
Glasgow	0	0	0	0	0	0	0	0	0	0	0	6	0	0	0	0	0	0	0	0	0	0	0	0	0	0	0	0
Leith	0	0	0	0	0	0	0	0	0	0	0	0	0	0	2	0	12	0	0	0	0	0	0	0	0	0	0	0
London	0	0	0	0	0	0	0	0	0	0	0	0	5	0	0	0	0	0	0	0	0	0	0	0	0	0	0	0
Portsmouth	13	0	36	33	0	0	0	0	0	0	0	0	0	0	0	0	0	0	0	0	0	0	0	5	0	0	0	0
Southampton	0	0	0	0	0	0	0	0	0	0	6	0	0	10	0	0	0	0	0	0	0	0	0	0	0	0	0	0
Spithead	2	0	0	0	0	0	0	0	0	0	0	0	0	0	0	0	0	0	0	0	0	0	0	0	0	0	0	0
United States																												
Baltimore	0	0	0	0	0	0	0	0	0	0	0	0	0	0	0	0	0	0	0	0	10	0	0	6	0	0	0	0
Boston	0	0	0	0	0	0	0	0	0	0	0	0	0	0	0	0	0	0	0	0	0	0	0	0	12	0	0	0
Philadelphia	0	0	0	0	0	0	0	0	0	0	0	0	0	0	0	0	0	0	0	0	0	0	5	0	5	0	0	0
Savannah	0	0	0	0	0	0	0	0	0	0	0	0	0	0	0	0	0	0	0	0	0	10	12	0	0	0	0	0
Uruguay																												
Montevideo	0	0	0	0	0	0	0	0	0	0	0	0	0	0	2	9	11	19	35	37	25	16	36	14	22	25	11	38
Venezuela																												
La Guaira	0	0	0	0	0	0	0	0	0	0	0	0	0	0	0	0	0	0	0	0	0	0	0	0	0	0	12	0
Puerto Cabello	0	0	0	0	0	0	0	0	0	0	0	0	0	0	0	0	0	0	0	0	0	0	0	6	0	0	2	0

Table 6

Average Length of Soviet Naval Ship Visits in Atlantic Area Ports, 1953-1980[a]

COUNTRY/PORT	53	54	55	56	57	58	59	60	61	62	63	64	65	66	67	68	69	70	71	72	73	74	75	76	77	78	79	80
Angola																												
Luanda	0	0	0	0	0	0	0	0	0	0	0	0	0	0	0	0	0	0	0	0	0	0	0	8	28	30	23	38
Argentina																												
Buenos Aires	0	0	0	0	0	0	0	0	0	0	0	0	0	0	0	0	0	0	0	0	0	0	0	0	0	0	6	0
Ushuaia	0	0	0	0	0	0	0	0	0	0	0	0	0	0	0	0	0	0	0	0	0	0	0	0	0	0	0	6
Aruba																												
Oranjestad	0	0	0	0	0	0	0	0	0	0	0	0	0	0	0	0	0	0	0	0	0	0	0	0	0	2	0	0
Azores																												
Ponta Delgada	0	0	0	0	0	0	0	0	0	0	0	0	0	0	0	0	0	0	0	0	0	0	0	0	0	5	0	0
São Miguel	0	0	0	0	0	0	0	0	0	0	0	0	0	0	0	0	0	0	0	0	0	0	0	0	0	4	0	0
Barbados																												
Bridgetown	0	0	0	0	0	0	0	0	0	0	0	0	0	0	0	0	3	0	0	0	0	0	0	0	0	0	2	0
Benin (Dahomey)																												
Cotonou	0	0	0	0	0	0	0	0	0	0	0	0	0	0	0	0	0	0	1	0	0	0	0	0	11	17	7	7
Bermuda																												
Hamilton	0	0	0	0	0	0	4	2	4	5	0	0	0	0	0	0	0	0	0	0	0	1	6	0	0	7	1	0
St. George	0	0	0	0	0	0	0	0	0	0	0	0	0	0	0	0	0	0	0	0	0	0	6	0	0	0	0	0
Brazil																												
Fernando de Noronha	0	0	0	0	0	0	0	0	0	0	0	0	0	0	0	0	0	7	0	0	0	0	0	0	0	0	0	0
Natal	0	0	0	0	0	0	0	0	0	0	0	0	0	0	0	0	0	4	0	0	0	0	0	0	0	0	0	0
Recife	0	0	0	0	0	0	0	0	0	0	0	0	0	0	0	0	0	4	0	0	0	1	0	0	0	0	0	0
Rio de Janeiro	0	0	0	0	0	0	0	0	0	0	0	0	0	4	0	5	0	0	0	4	0	0	0	0	0	0	0	0
Cameroon																												
Douala	0	0	0	0	0	0	0	0	0	0	0	0	0	0	0	0	0	0	0	0	0	0	5	0	0	0	0	0
Canada																												
Halifax	0	0	0	0	0	0	0	2	0	0	0	6	3	0	0	0	5	2	6	5	5	5	5	3	3	4	0	0
St. John's	0	0	0	0	0	0	0	7	0	0	0	0	5	0	0	0	0	3	0	0	0	6	0	5	0	4	5	0
Canary Islands																												
Las Palmas	0	0	0	0	0	0	0	0	0	0	0	0	0	0	0	0	5	2	3	4	4	4	3	3	3	3	4	3
Santa Cruz de Tenerife	0	0	0	0	0	0	0	0	0	0	0	0	0	0	0	0	0	0	0	0	3	3	4	3	4	4	3	0
Cape Verde Islands																												
Praia	0	0	0	0	0	0	0	0	0	0	0	0	0	0	0	0	0	0	0	0	0	0	0	0	0	0	6	0
São Vicente	0	0	0	0	0	0	0	0	0	0	0	0	0	0	0	0	0	0	0	0	0	0	0	0	0	0	2	0
Colombia																												
Cartagena	0	0	0	0	0	0	0	0	0	0	0	0	0	0	0	0	0	0	0	0	4	6	0	5	0	6	0	0
Congo																												
Pointe-Noire	0	0	0	0	0	0	0	0	0	0	0	0	0	0	0	0	0	0	0	5	7	0	5	3	0	0	0	0
Cuba																												
Antilla	0	0	0	0	0	0	0	0	0	0	0	0	0	0	0	0	0	6	8	0	7	0	0	0	6	0	0	0
Bahia de Cadiz	0	0	0	0	0	0	0	0	0	0	0	0	0	0	0	0	0	0	0	0	0	0	0	0	0	0	0	3
Bahia de Nipe	0	0	0	0	0	0	0	0	0	0	0	0	0	0	0	0	0	0	2	8	7	25	15	35	0	0	0	9
Caibarién	0	0	0	0	0	0	0	0	0	0	0	0	0	0	0	0	0	0	0	0	0	0	0	0	0	0	0	5
Casilda	0	0	0	0	0	0	0	0	0	0	0	0	0	0	0	0	0	6	0	2	0	0	0	0	0	0	0	0
Cienfuegos	0	0	0	0	0	0	0	0	0	0	0	0	0	4	0	9	0	7	7	9	8	10	14	15	16	15	27	24
Havana	0	0	0	0	0	0	0	0	0	0	0	0	0	0	0	0	0	13	13	17	13	16	13	9	6	17	11	6
Manzanillo	0	0	0	0	0	0	0	0	0	0	0	0	0	0	0	0	0	0	0	5	0	0	0	0	0	0	0	0
Mariel	0	0	0	0	0	0	0	0	0	0	0	0	0	0	0	0	6	46	17	27	8	0	6	0	0	0	0	0
Moa	0	0	0	0	0	0	0	0	0	0	0	0	0	0	0	0	0	0	0	0	0	0	0	0	0	0	2	0

[a] Includes visits to non-Soviet-Bloc Baltic nations and nations in the Gulf of Guinea, Caribbean Sea, and Gulf of Mexico.

Table 6 (Continued)

Average Length of Soviet Naval Ship Visits in Atlantic Area Ports, 1953–1980

COUNTRY/PORT	53	54	55	56	57	58	59	60	61	62	63	64	65	66	67	68	69	70	71	72	73	74	75	76	77	78	79	80
Cuba																												
Nuevitas	0	0	0	0	0	0	0	0	0	0	0	0	0	0	0	0	0	0	0	4	0	0	0	2	0	0	0	0
Puerto Cabañas	0	0	0	0	0	0	0	0	0	0	0	0	0	0	0	0	0	0	5	0	0	0	0	0	0	0	0	0
Puerto Manati	0	0	0	0	0	0	0	0	0	0	0	0	0	0	0	0	0	0	0	1	0	0	0	0	0	0	0	0
Puerto Padre	0	0	0	0	0	0	0	0	0	0	0	0	0	0	0	0	0	0	0	5	0	0	0	0	0	0	0	0
Santa Cruz del Norte	0	0	0	0	0	0	0	0	0	0	0	0	0	0	0	0	0	0	0	0	0	0	0	0	4	0	0	0
Santiago de Cuba	0	0	0	0	0	0	0	0	0	0	0	0	0	0	0	0	0	5	0	7	0	2	2	3	0	0	0	5
Curaçao																												
Willemstad	0	0	0	0	0	0	0	0	0	0	0	0	0	0	0	0	0	0	0	6	4	3	0	4	5	4	4	5
Denmark																												
Copenhagen	0	0	0	5	0	0	0	0	0	0	0	5	0	0	0	0	0	5	0	5	0	5	6	0	6	0	0	
Equatorial Guinea																												
Bata	0	0	0	0	0	0	0	0	0	0	0	0	0	0	0	0	0	0	0	0	0	2	0	0	0	0	0	0
Luba	0	0	0	0	0	0	0	0	0	0	0	0	0	0	0	0	0	0	0	0	0	7	0	0	0	0	0	0
Santa Isabel	0	0	0	0	0	0	0	0	0	0	0	0	0	0	0	0	0	6	0	6	0	4	0	0	0	0	0	0
Faeroe Islands																												
Thorshavn	0	0	0	0	0	0	0	0	0	0	0	0	0	0	0	0	0	0	0	0	5	5	5	5	5	4	6	2
Falkland Islands																												
Port Stanley	0	0	0	0	0	0	0	0	0	0	0	0	0	0	0	0	0	0	0	4	0	0	0	0	0	0	0	0
Finland																												
Helsinki	0	5	0	0	0	5	0	5	0	0	0	0	0	6	3	5	0	0	6	0	0	0	0	0	0	0	6	0
Kotka	0	0	0	0	0	0	0	0	0	0	5	0	0	0	0	0	0	0	0	0	0	0	0	0	0	0	0	0
Oulu	0	0	0	0	0	0	0	0	0	0	0	0	0	0	0	0	0	0	0	0	0	0	0	6	0	0	0	0
Rauma	0	0	0	0	0	0	0	0	0	0	0	0	0	0	0	0	0	0	0	0	0	0	0	0	0	0	65	0
Turku	0	0	0	0	0	0	0	5	0	0	0	0	0	0	0	0	0	0	0	0	0	6	0	0	0	0	0	0
France																												
Barfleur	0	0	0	0	0	0	0	0	0	0	0	0	0	0	0	0	0	4	0	0	0	0	0	0	0	0	0	0
Bordeaux	0	0	0	0	0	0	0	0	0	0	0	0	0	0	0	0	0	0	0	0	0	0	0	6	0	5	0	0
Cherbourg	0	0	0	0	0	0	0	0	0	0	0	0	0	0	0	0	0	6	0	0	0	4	0	0	6	0	0	0
Le Havre	0	0	0	0	0	0	0	0	0	0	0	0	0	0	7	2	4	3	5	0	0	0	0	0	0	0	0	0
Nantes	0	0	0	0	0	0	0	0	0	0	0	0	0	0	0	0	0	0	0	5	0	0	0	0	0	0	0	0
Gambia																												
Bathurst (Banjul)	0	0	0	0	0	0	0	0	0	0	0	0	0	0	0	0	0	0	3	0	0	0	0	0	0	0	0	0
Guinea																												
Conakry	0	0	0	0	0	0	0	0	0	0	0	0	0	0	0	0	5	9	13	11	11	27	23	20	18	17	20	19
Guinea-Bissau																												
Bissau	0	0	0	0	0	0	0	0	0	0	0	0	0	0	0	0	0	0	0	0	0	0	0	5	0	0	6	0
Iceland																												
Reykjavik	0	0	0	0	0	0	0	0	0	0	0	5	0	6	0	0	5	4	0	0	0	0	5	4	4	5	6	5
Ireland																												
Cork	0	0	0	0	0	0	0	0	0	0	0	0	0	0	6	0	0	0	0	0	0	0	0	0	0	0	0	0
Dublin	0	0	0	0	0	0	0	0	0	0	0	0	0	0	0	0	0	0	0	0	0	3	0	0	0	0	0	0
Ivory Coast																												
Abidjan	0	0	0	0	0	0	0	0	0	0	0	0	0	0	0	0	0	7	2	3	2	6	4	5	3	4	0	4
Jamaica																												
Kingston	0	0	0	0	0	0	0	0	0	4	0	0	0	0	0	0	0	3	0	0	0	0	0	0	0	0	0	0
Liberia																												
Monrovia	0	0	0	0	0	0	0	0	0	0	0	0	0	0	0	0	0	0	0	0	0	0	6	0	3	0	0	4

Table 6 (Continued)

Average Length of Soviet Naval Ship Visits in Atlantic Area Ports, 1953–1980

COUNTRY/PORT	53	54	55	56	57	58	59	60	61	62	63	64	65	66	67	68	69	70	71	72	73	74	75	76	77	78	79	80
Martinique																												
Fort-de-France	0	0	0	0	0	0	0	0	0	0	0	0	0	0	0	0	3	0	0	0	0	0	0	0	0	0	0	0
Mauritania																												
Nouadhibou	0	0	0	0	0	0	0	0	0	0	0	0	0	0	0	0	0	0	5	0	0	0	0	0	0	0	0	0
Mexico																												
Veracruz	0	0	0	0	0	0	0	0	0	0	0	0	0	0	0	6	0	0	0	2	0	6	4	4	4	4	4	6
Morocco																												
Casablanca	0	0	0	0	0	0	0	0	0	0	0	6	0	5	0	6	0	4	5	6	4	4	5	5	6	4	2	6
Rabat	0	0	0	0	0	0	0	0	0	0	0	0	0	0	0	0	0	0	0	0	0	0	1	0	0	0	0	0
Safi	0	0	0	0	0	0	0	0	0	0	0	0	0	0	0	0	0	0	0	0	0	6	1	0	0	0	0	0
Tangier	0	0	0	0	0	0	0	0	0	0	0	0	0	0	0	0	4	4	5	5	4	4	5	5	5	0	4	4
Netherlands																												
Amsterdam	0	0	0	0	0	0	0	0	0	0	0	0	0	0	0	0	0	6	0	0	0	0	0	0	0	5	0	0
Rotterdam	0	0	0	5	0	0	0	0	0	0	0	0	0	0	0	0	0	0	8	0	0	0	0	0	0	0	0	0
Nigeria																												
Lagos	0	0	0	0	0	0	0	0	0	0	0	0	0	0	0	0	6	5	0	0	0	0	6	6	0	0	0	0
Norway																												
Bergen	0	0	0	0	0	4	5	0	0	0	5	6	0	5	0	0	0	0	3	0	0	0	0	0	0	0	0	0
Haugesund	0	0	0	0	0	0	0	0	0	0	0	0	0	0	0	0	6	4	0	0	0	0	0	0	0	0	0	0
Oslo	0	0	0	5	0	0	0	0	0	0	0	0	0	0	0	0	0	6	0	0	5	0	0	6	0	0	0	0
Tromsö	0	0	0	0	0	0	0	0	0	0	0	0	0	0	0	0	0	4	0	0	0	0	0	0	0	0	0	0
Trondheim	0	0	0	0	0	0	0	0	0	0	0	5	0	0	0	0	0	0	0	0	0	0	0	0	0	0	0	0
St. Helena																												
Jamestown	0	0	0	0	0	0	0	0	0	0	0	0	0	0	0	0	0	1	2	4	5	0	5	0	0	2	0	0
São Thomé	0	0	0	0	0	0	0	0	0	0	0	0	0	0	0	0	0	0	0	0	0	0	0	0	0	12	6	0
Senegal																												
Dakar	0	0	0	0	0	6	0	0	0	0	0	6	0	0	0	0	6	5	4	8	5	5	4	3	4	3	4	3
Sierra Leone																												
Freetown	0	0	0	0	0	0	2	0	0	0	0	0	0	0	0	0	6	4	0	6	5	4	4	3	2	0	0	0
Southwest Africa																												
Walvis Bay	0	0	0	0	0	0	0	0	0	0	0	0	0	0	0	0	0	0	0	4	0	0	0	0	0	0	0	0
Spain																												
La Coruña	0	0	0	0	0	0	0	0	0	0	0	0	0	0	0	0	0	0	0	0	0	0	0	0	0	4	5	0
Vigo	0	0	0	0	0	0	0	0	0	0	0	0	0	0	0	0	0	0	0	0	0	0	0	0	0	0	3	0
Surinam																												
Paramaribo	0	0	0	0	0	0	0	0	0	0	0	0	0	0	0	0	0	0	0	0	0	0	0	3	0	0	0	0
Sweden																												
Gothenburg	0	0	0	5	0	3	0	0	0	0	0	0	0	0	0	0	0	0	0	0	0	6	1	71	47	25	19	46
Stockholm	0	7	0	0	0	6	0	0	0	4	0	0	4	0	0	0	0	0	0	6	0	0	0	0	0	0	0	0
Trinidad																												
Port of Spain	0	0	0	0	0	0	0	0	0	0	0	0	0	0	0	0	0	0	0	0	0	5	0	3	0	0	0	0
United Kingdom																												
Belfast	0	0	0	0	0	0	0	0	0	0	0	0	0	0	0	2	0	0	0	0	0	0	0	0	0	0	0	0
Bristol	0	0	0	0	0	0	0	0	0	0	0	0	0	0	0	5	0	8	0	0	0	0	0	0	0	0	0	0
Glasgow	0	0	0	0	0	0	0	0	0	0	2	0	0	0	0	0	0	0	0	0	0	0	0	0	0	0	0	0
Leith	0	0	0	0	0	0	0	0	0	0	0	0	0	0	0	2	0	6	0	0	0	0	0	0	0	0	0	0
London	0	0	0	0	0	0	0	0	0	0	0	0	0	5	0	0	0	0	0	0	0	0	0	0	0	0	0	0
Portsmouth	13	0	6	11	0	0	0	0	0	0	0	0	0	0	0	0	0	0	0	0	0	0	0	0	5	0	0	0
Southampton	0	0	0	0	0	0	0	0	0	0	0	2	0	0	5	0	0	0	0	0	0	0	0	0	0	0	0	0
Spithead	2	0	0	0	0	0	0	0	0	0	0	0	0	0	0	0	0	0	0	0	0	0	0	0	0	0	0	0
United States																												
Baltimore	0	0	0	0	0	0	0	0	0	0	0	0	0	0	0	0	0	0	0	0	0	5	0	6	0	0	0	0
Boston	0	0	0	0	0	0	0	0	0	0	0	0	0	0	0	0	0	0	0	0	0	0	6	0	0	0	0	0
Philadelphia	0	0	0	0	0	0	0	0	0	0	0	0	0	0	0	0	0	0	0	0	0	5	0	5	0	0	0	0
Savannah	0	0	0	0	0	0	0	0	0	0	0	0	0	0	0	0	0	0	0	0	0	5	6	0	0	0	0	0
Uruguay																												
Montevideo	0	0	0	0	0	0	0	0	0	0	0	0	0	0	0	2	3	11	4	7	4	4	3	4	4	4	4	5
Venezuela																												
La Guaira	0	0	0	0	0	0	0	0	0	0	0	0	0	0	0	0	0	0	0	0	0	0	0	0	0	0	6	0
Puerto Cabello	0	0	0	0	0	0	0	0	0	0	0	0	0	0	0	0	0	0	0	0	0	0	6	0	0	2	0	0

Table 7

Cumulative Totals of Soviet Naval Port Visits
in the Atlantic Area by Port, 1953–1980

	Port	Total Ship Days	Comments
1.	Conakry, Guinea	8,488	Visits began in 1969. The naval presence began in 1970, when the navy established a patrol in response to Guinean requests for assistance. In 1975 and 1976 Conakry was used as a staging area for Soviet naval forces during the Angolan Civil War. A heightened naval presence was maintained at Conakry from 1976 through 1979.
2.	Havana, Cuba	3,634	The first naval combatant deployment to Cuba occurred in 1969. There had been twenty-one such deployments by May 1981 and the Soviets had also established a modest but constant non-combatant presence in the area. Many Cuban ports have been visited, but Soviet activity has centered around Havana, Cienfuegos, and Mariel. Activity in Cienfuegos has prompted speculation that the Soviets are establishing a permanent facility there. However, such a base was not operational in 1980.
3.	Luanda, Angola	3,394	Since the conclusion of the Angolan Civil War, the Soviet naval presence in Angola has been fairly constant. The Soviets apparently have unrestricted access to the port and intend to use it as a base of operations in the Gulf of Guinea to augment their use of Conakry. The base is particularly suited to operations that might be launched against South Africa.
4.	Cienfuegos, Cuba	3,153	See entry 2.
5.	Las Palmas, Canary, Islands	894	Since the Soviets began using this port in 1969, it has been used by auxiliary ships to support naval operations in Guinea and elsewhere in the Atlantic.
6.	Mariel, Cuba	606	See entry 2.
7.	Cotonou, Benin	462	Many of these have been good will/operational visits by Soviet naval combatants. The port has also been used by naval auxiliaries for support of operations in the Atlantic Ocean and along West Africa.
8.	Gothenburg, Sweden	449	Overhaul/yard work on Soviet auxiliary ships.
9.	Dakar, Senegal	446	Good will/operational visits, primarily for support of hydrographic ships and space support ships operating in the Atlantic Ocean.
10.	Casablanca, Morocco	389	Many of these good will/operational visits, which were begun in 1964, were by hydrographic ships and were in support of operations in the Atlantic. Some good will/operational visits were made by naval combatants to the port.
11.	Montevideo, Uruguay	300	Good will/operational visits by space support ships.
12.	Tangier, Morocco	256	Most of these were good will/operational visits by naval auxiliaries, which were begun in 1969 and were in support of naval operations in the Atlantic Ocean and along West Africa.
13.	Halifax, Canada	199	See entry 9.
14.	Reykjavik, Iceland	159	Good will/operational visits by hydrographic ships.
15.	Bahia de Nipe, Cuba	140	See entry 2.
16.	Rauma, Finland	130	Overhaul/yard work of an auxiliary ship in 1979.
17.	Thorshavn, Faeroe Islands	130	See entry 14.
18.	Freetown, Sierra Leone	119	Official visits by naval combatants and good will/operational visits by space support ships, which began in 1959.

Table 7 (Continued)

Cumulative Totals of Soviet Naval Port Visits
in the Atlantic Area by Port, 1953–1980

Port	Total Ship Days	Comments
19. St. John's, Canada	118	See entry 9.
20. Santa Cruz de Tenerife, Canary Islands	117	See entry 9.
21. Antilla, Cuba	110	See entry 2.
22. São Thomé	103	Good will/operational visits by naval combatants which began in 1978.
23. Stockholm, Sweden	91	Official visits by naval combatants from 1954 to 1972.
24. Lagos, Nigeria	89	Good will/operational visits by naval combatants from 1969 to 1976.
25. Abidjan, Ivory Coast	89	See entry 11.
26. Portsmouth, United Kingdom	87	Official visits by naval combatants, probably as part of the port visit program to NATO nations discussed in Chapter 2.
27. Vera Cruz, Mexico	79	See entry 11.
28. Copenhagen, Denmark	79	See entry 26.
29. Helsinki, Finland	78	Official naval visits which began in 1954.
30. Willemstad, Curaçao	74	See entry 9.
31. Hamilton, Bermuda	58	See entry 9.
32. Bergen, Norway	57	An official visit in 1958 and several good will/operational visits by hydrographic ships.
33. Santiago, Cuba	56	See entry 2.
34. Jamestown, St. Helena	49	Good will/operational visits, mostly by space support ships, which began in 1969.
35. Oslo, Norway	49	See entry 26.
36. Pointe-Noire, Congo	47	Good will/operational visits by naval combatants from 1972 to 1976.
37. Le Havre, France	44	See entry 14.
38. Santa Isabel, Equatorial Guinea	43	Good will/operational and official visits by naval combatants from 1970 to 1974.
39. Cartagena, Colombia	43	Two official visits in 1974 and 1978, and several good will/operational visits from 1973 to 1978, all by hydrographic ships.
40. Rotterdam, Netherlands	40	See entry 26.
41. Cherbourg, France	37	See entry 26.
42. La Coruña, Spain	36	See entry 14.
43. Bristol, United Kingdom	36	See entry 14.
44. Rio de Janeiro, Brazil	31	Good will/operational visits, mostly by hydrographic ships.
45. Turku, Finland	28	Good will/operational by naval combatants in 1961 and 1974.
46. Praia, Cape Verde Islands	23	Good will/operational visits by naval combatants in 1979.

Table 7 (Continued)

Cumulative Totals of Soviet Naval Port Visits
in the Atlantic Area by Port, 1953–1980

	Port	Total Ship Days	Comments
47.	Savannah, United States	22	See entry 14.
48.	Bordeaux, France	22	See entry 26.
49.	Fernando de Noronha, Brazil	21	Visit in 1970 associated with repairs on naval ships.
50.	Luba, Equatorial Guinea	21	Official visits by naval combatant groups in 1974.
51.	Safi, Morocco	20	Good will/operational visits.
52.	Cork, Ireland	18	See entry 14.
53.	Nuevitas, Cuba	17	See entry 2.
54.	Haugesund, Norway	16	See entry 14.
55.	Bissau, Guinea–Bissau	16	Official and good will/operational visits by naval combatants from 1976 to 1979.
56.	Southampton, United Kingdom	16	See entry 14.
57.	Baltimore, United States	16	See entry 14.
58.	Amsterdam, Netherlands	16	See entry 26.
59.	Casilda, Cuba	15	See entry 2.
60.	Leith, United Kingdom	14	See entry 14.
61.	Puerto Padre, Cuba	14	See entry 2.
62.	Kingston, Jamaica	13	Good will/operational visits, which began in 1962.
63.	Monrovia, Liberia	13	See entry 9.
64.	St. George, Bermuda	12	See entry 14.
65.	Port Stanley, Falkland Islands	12	Good will/operational visit in 1972.
66.	Barfleur, France	12	Good will/operational visit in 1970.
67.	Boston, United States	12	Official naval combatant visit in 1975.
68.	La Guaira, Venezuela	12	See entry 14.
69.	Oulu, Finland	12	Good will visit in 1976.
70.	Manzanillo, Cuba	10	See entry 2.
71.	Trondheim, Norway	10	Good will/operational visit in 1964.
72.	Philadelphia, United States	10	See entry 14.
73.	Kotka, Finland	10	Good will/operational visit in 1964.
74.	Bridgetown, Barbados	10	Good will/operational visits, which began in 1969.
75.	Caibarién, Cuba	10	See entry 2.
76.	Walvis Bay, Southwest Africa	8	Good will/operational visit in 1972.
77.	Dublin, Ireland	8	Good will/operational visits in 1975.
78.	Port of Spain, Trinidad	8	See entry 9.

Table 7 (Continued)

Cumulative Totals of Soviet Naval Port Visits
in the Atlantic Area by Port, 1953-1980

	Port	Total Ship Days	Comments
79.	Puerto Cabello, Venezuela	8	See entry 14.
80.	Vigo, Spain	6	See entry 14.
81.	Fort-de-France, Martinique	6	Good will/operational visit by a naval combatant in 1969.
82.	Glasgow, United Kingdom	6	See entry 14.
83.	Buenos Aires, Argentina	6	See entry 14.
84.	Ushuaia, Argentina	6	See entry 14.
85.	Recife, Brazil	5	See entry 11.
86.	Douala, Cameroon	5	Good will/operational visit by a naval combatant in 1975.
87.	Puerto Cabañas, Cuba	5	See entry 2.
88.	Nantes, France	5	See entry 14.
89.	London, United Kingdom	5	See entry 14.
90.	Ponta Delgada, Azores	5	See entry 14.
91.	Nouadhibou, Mauritania	5	Good will/operational visit in 1972.
92.	Natal, Brazil	4	Good will/operational visit in 1970.
93.	Tromsö, Norway	4	See entry 14.
94.	Belfast, United Kingdom	4	See entry 14.
95.	Santa Cruz del Norte, Cuba	4	See entry 2.
96.	São Miguel, Azores	4	See entry 14.
97.	Bathurst (Banjul), Gambia	3	Good will/operational visit in 1971.
98.	Paramaribo, Surinam	3	See entry 11.
99.	Bahia de Cadiz, Cuba	3	See entry 2.
100.	Puerto Manati, Cuba	2	See entry 2.
101.	Bata, Equatorial Guinea	2	Good will/operational visit by a naval combatant in 1974.
102.	Moa, Cuba	2	See entry 2.
103.	Spithead, United Kingdom	2	See entry 26.
104.	Oranjestad, Aruba	2	Good will/operational visit in 1978.
105.	São Vicente, Cape Verde Islands	2	Good will/operational visit in 1979.
106.	Rabat, Morocco	1	See entry 14.

Table 8

Cumulative Totals of Soviet Naval Port Visits

in the Atlantic Area By Country, 1953–1980

	Country	Total Ship Days
1.	Guinea	8,488
2.	Cuba	7,781
3.	Angola	3,394
4.	Canary Islands	1,011
5.	Morocco	666
6.	Sweden	540
7.	Benin	462
8.	Senegal	446
9.	Canada (Atlantic coast only)	317
10.	Uruguay	300
11.	Finland	258
12.	United Kingdom	170
13.	Iceland	159
14.	Norway	136
15.	Faeroe Islands	130
16.	France (Atlantic coast only)	120
17.	Sierra Leone	119
18.	São Thomé	103
19.	Nigeria	89
20.	Ivory Coast	89
21.	Mexico (Gulf coast only)	79
22.	Denmark	79
23.	Curaçao	74
24.	Bermuda	70

Table 8 (Continued)

Cumulative Totals of Soviet Naval Port Visits

in the Atlantic Area By Country, 1953–1980

	Country	Total Ship Days
25.	Equatorial Guinea	66
26.	Brazil	61
27.	United States (Atlantic coast only)	60
28.	Netherlands	56
29.	St. Helena	49
30.	Congo	47
31.	Colombia (Gulf coast only)	43
32.	Spain (Atlantic coast only)	42
33.	Ireland	26
34.	Cape Verde Islands	25
35.	Venezuela	20
36.	Guinea-Bissau	16
37.	Jamaica	13
38.	Liberia	13
39.	Falkland Islands	12
40.	Argentina	12
41.	Barbados	10
42.	Azores	9
43.	Southwest Africa	8
44.	Trinidad	8
45.	Martinique	6
46.	Cameroon	5
47.	Mauritania	5
48.	Gambia	3
49.	Surinam	3
50.	Aruba	2

Table 9

Soviet Naval Combatant Deployments to the Caribbean, 1969-1981

Deployment Number	Dates	Participants
1	July 10-August 13, 1969	1 Kynda guided missile cruiser, 1 Kashin guided missile destroyer, 1 Kildin guided missile destroyer, 1 November nuclear-powered attack submarine, 2 Foxtrot attack submarines, 1 Ugra submarine tender, 1 Uda oiler, and 1 merchant tanker.
2	May 6-June 10, 1970	1 Kresta guided missile cruiser, 1 Kanin guided missile destroyer, 1 Echo-II nuclear-powered cruise missile submarine, 2 Foxtrot attack submarines, 1 Ugra submarine tender, and 1 merchant tanker.
3	September 4, 1970-January 8, 1971	1 Kresta-I guided missile cruiser, 1 Kanin guided missile destroyer, 1 Alligator tank landing ship, 1 Ugra submarine tender, 1 hydrographic survey ship, 2 oiler/tankers, 1 tug, and 1 buoy tender.
4	November 30-December 29, 1970	1 Kashin guided missile destroyer, 1 Foxtrot attack submarine, 1 Ugra submarine tender, and 1 naval oiler.
5	February 9-February 28, 1971	1 Kresta-I guided missile cruiser, 1 November nuclear-powered attack submarine, 1 Ugra submarine tender, and 1 merchant tanker.
6	May 22-June 11, 1971	1 Echo-II nuclear-powered cruise missile submarine, and 1 Ugra submarine tender.
7	October 30-November 20, 1971	1 Kresta-I guided missile cruiser, 1 Kashin guided missile destroyer, 2 Foxtrot attack submarines, and 1 naval oiler.
8	February 26-May 8, 1972	1 Kotlin destroyer, 1 Golf-II ballistic missile submarine, 1 Foxtrot attack submarine, 1 Ugra submarine tender, and 2 oiler/tankers.
9	November 24, 1972-February 16, 1973	1 Kresta-I guided missile cruiser, 1 Kanin guided missile destroyer, 1 Echo-II nuclear-powered cruise missile submarine, 1 Foxtrot attack submarine, 1 Ugra submarine tender, and 1 merchant tanker.
10	August 2-October 16, 1973	1 Kresta-II guided missile cruiser, 1 Kanin guided missile destroyer, 1 Echo-II nuclear-powered cruise missile submarine, 1 Foxtrot attack submarine, and 1 merchant tanker.
11	April 28-June 2, 1974	2 Krivak guided missile frigates, 1 Golf-II ballistic missile submarine, and 1 merchant tanker.
12	September 24-November 11, 1974	2 Kresta-II guided missile cruisers and 1 naval oiler.
13	February 26-April 5, 1975	2 Krivak guided missile frigates and 1 merchant tanker.
14	May 21-June 7, 1975	2 Kanin guided missile destroyers and 1 naval oiler.
15	August 16-September 21, 1976	2 Krivak guided missile frigates and 1 naval oiler.
16	June 26-July 22, 1977	1 Kresta-II guided missile cruiser, 2 Krivak guided missile frigates, and 1 naval oiler.
17	December 16, 1977-January 16, 1978	2 Krivak guided missile frigates, 1 Foxtrot submarine, and 1 naval oiler.
18	March 14-May 7, 1978	1 Mod-Kashin guided missile destroyer, 1 Natya fleet minesweeper, and 1 oiler.
19	September 12-December 11, 1978	1 Mod-Kashin guided missile destroyer, 2 Krivak guided missile frigates, 1 Foxtrot attack submarine, and 1 oiler.
20	August 12-August 19, 1979	1 Kresta-II guided missile cruiser, 1 Krivak-II guided missile frigate, possibly 1 or 2 submarines, and 1 merchant tanker.
21	April 10-May 11, 1981	1 Kara guided missile cruiser, 2 Krivak-I guided missile frigates, and 1 oiler.

Table 10

Number of Soviet Naval Ships Visiting Mediterranean Area Ports, 1954-1980[a]

COUNTRY/PORT	54	55	56	57	58	59	60	61	62	63	64	65	66	67	68	69	70	71	72	73	74	75	76	77	78	79	80
Albania																											
Durres (Durazzo)	5	2	3	8	7	0	0	0	0	0	0	0	0	0	0	0	0	0	0	0	0	0	0	0	0	0	0
Valona	0	0	0	0	26	42	52	24	0	0	0	0	0	0	0	0	0	0	0	0	0	0	0	0	0	0	0
Algeria																											
Algiers	0	0	0	0	0	0	0	0	0	0	0	0	9	25	22	6	7	5	1	0	3	0	0	0	7	0	2
Annaba	0	0	0	0	0	0	0	0	0	0	0	0	0	0	0	5	14	21	26	23	14	16	20	22	18	17	15
Mers-el-Kebir	0	0	0	0	0	0	0	0	0	0	0	0	0	1	0	0	0	0	0	0	0	0	0	0	0	0	0
Oran	0	0	0	0	0	0	0	0	0	0	0	0	8	0	0	0	2	1	0	6	1	1	2	2	2	0	0
Cyprus																											
Larnaca	0	0	0	0	0	0	0	0	0	0	0	0	0	0	0	0	0	0	0	0	0	0	1	0	0	1	0
Egypt																											
Alexandria	0	0	0	1	3	2	0	2	2	0	0	3	5	40	55	71	89	101	135	190	194	198	63	0	0	0	0
Matrûh	0	0	0	0	0	0	0	0	0	0	0	0	0	0	0	0	1	67	14	25	101	45	0	0	0	0	0
Port Said	0	0	0	1	0	1	0	0	0	0	0	5	6	14	0	20	5	35	18	11	2	2	4	0	0	0	0
Ras al Kanis	0	0	0	0	0	0	0	0	0	0	0	0	0	0	0	0	0	1	7	1	2	1	0	0	0	0	0
France																											
Marseille	0	0	0	0	0	0	0	0	0	0	0	0	1	0	0	2	0	0	1	3	0	0	0	0	0	0	0
Toulon	0	0	0	0	0	0	0	0	0	0	0	0	2	0	0	0	0	0	0	0	2	0	0	0	2	0	0
Gibraltar	0	0	0	0	0	1	0	0	0	5	1	9	0	3	0	6	13	16	6	16	15	18	6	7	1	1	0
Greece																											
Ermoúpolis	0	0	0	0	0	0	0	0	0	0	0	0	0	0	0	0	0	0	0	0	0	0	0	0	0	9	6
Iráklion	0	0	0	0	0	0	0	0	0	0	0	0	0	0	0	0	0	0	1	0	0	0	5	17	11	13	5
Patrai	0	0	0	0	0	0	0	0	0	0	0	0	0	0	0	0	0	0	0	0	0	1	0	0	0	0	0
Piraeus	0	0	0	0	0	0	0	0	0	0	0	0	0	0	0	0	0	0	0	0	0	0	2	3	5	2	2
Pylos	0	0	0	0	0	0	0	0	0	0	0	0	0	0	0	0	0	0	0	0	0	0	0	0	1	1	1
Thessaloniki	0	0	0	0	0	0	0	0	0	0	0	0	0	0	0	0	0	0	0	0	0	0	0	0	0	0	1
Zakros	0	0	0	0	0	0	0	0	0	0	0	0	0	0	0	0	0	0	1	0	0	0	0	0	0	0	0
Italy																											
Augusta	0	0	0	0	0	0	0	0	0	0	0	0	0	0	0	0	0	0	0	0	0	0	1	0	0	0	0
Bari	0	0	0	0	0	0	0	0	0	0	0	0	0	0	0	0	0	0	0	0	1	2	0	0	0	0	0
Cagliari	0	0	0	0	0	0	0	0	0	0	0	0	0	0	0	0	0	0	0	0	1	1	0	2	0	1	0
Catania	0	0	0	0	0	0	0	0	0	0	0	0	0	0	0	0	0	0	0	0	0	1	0	0	0	0	0
Civitavecchia	0	0	0	0	0	0	0	0	0	0	0	0	1	1	0	0	3	0	1	2	2	1	0	0	0	0	0
Genoa	0	0	0	0	0	0	0	0	0	0	0	3	1	0	0	0	0	0	0	0	0	1	0	0	0	0	0
Livorno	0	0	0	0	0	0	0	0	0	0	0	0	0	0	0	0	0	0	0	0	0	0	0	0	1	0	0
Messina	0	0	0	0	0	0	0	0	0	0	0	0	0	0	1	0	0	0	0	2	0	0	2	1	1	0	0
Naples	0	0	0	0	0	0	0	0	0	2	1	1	0	0	1	0	0	0	0	0	0	0	0	0	0	0	0

[a]The above is believed to be the most accurate and comprehensive list of Soviet naval port visits to Mediterranean ports tabulated by number of ships ever compiled. However, some of the figures, particularly for numbers of ships in Albanian, Egyptian, and Syrian ports, are estimates based on incomplete data. This listing includes visits to ports in the Alboran, Balearic, Tyrrhenian, Adriatic, Ionian, and Aegean Seas.

Table 10 (Continued)

Number of Soviet Naval Ships Visiting Mediterranean Area Ports, 1954–1980

COUNTRY/PORT	54	55	56	57	58	59	60	61	62	63	64	65	66	67	68	69	70	71	72	73	74	75	76	77	78	79	80
Palermo	0	0	0	0	0	0	0	0	0	0	0	0	2	0	2	2	2	1	1	2	1	5	21	24	27	35	17
Pantelleria	0	0	0	0	0	0	0	0	0	0	0	0	0	0	0	4	0	0	0	0	0	0	0	0	0	0	0
Reggio di Calabria	0	0	0	0	0	0	0	0	0	0	0	0	0	0	0	0	3	0	0	0	1	0	0	0	0	0	0
Salerno	0	0	0	0	0	0	0	0	0	0	0	0	0	0	0	1	2	0	0	1	2	1	0	0	0	0	0
Taranto	0	0	0	0	0	0	0	0	0	0	0	0	0	0	0	0	0	1	0	2	1	0	1	0	0	1	0
Trapani	0	0	0	0	0	0	0	0	0	0	0	0	0	0	0	0	0	0	0	0	1	0	0	0	0	0	0
Venice	0	0	0	0	0	0	0	0	0	0	0	0	0	0	0	1	0	0	0	0	1	0	0	0	0	0	0
Libya																											
Tobruk	0	0	0	0	0	0	0	0	0	0	0	0	0	0	0	1	0	0	0	0	0	0	0	0	0	0	0
Tripoli	0	0	0	0	0	0	0	0	0	0	0	0	0	0	0	1	1	0	0	0	0	0	0	0	0	0	0
Malta																											
Valetta	0	0	0	0	0	0	0	0	0	0	0	0	0	0	0	0	0	0	0	0	0	0	0	0	2	0	1
Spain																											
Algeciras	0	0	0	0	0	0	0	0	0	0	0	0	0	0	0	0	0	0	2	0	12	6	5	1	0	0	0
Alicante	0	0	0	0	0	0	0	0	0	0	0	0	0	0	0	0	0	0	0	0	0	1	0	0	0	0	0
Cartagena	0	0	0	0	0	0	0	0	0	0	0	0	0	0	0	0	0	0	0	0	0	0	0	1	0	0	0
Ceuta	0	0	0	0	0	0	0	0	0	0	0	0	0	0	0	0	0	0	0	0	0	7	11	13	14	9	8
Málaga	0	0	0	0	0	0	0	0	0	0	0	0	0	0	0	0	0	0	0	0	0	1	0	0	0	0	0
Syria																											
Latakia	0	0	0	7	2	0	0	0	0	0	0	0	0	18	40	9	19	18	25	14	25	0	1	0	3	0	5
Tartus	0	0	0	0	0	0	0	0	0	0	0	0	0	0	0	8	0	0	16	18	20	67	81	86	95	84	79
Tunisia																											
Bizerte	0	0	0	0	0	0	0	0	0	0	0	0	0	0	0	0	0	0	0	0	2	2	10	5	4	8	12
La Goulette	0	0	0	0	0	0	0	0	0	0	0	0	0	0	0	0	0	0	0	0	1	4	2	0	0	0	3
Menzel-Bourguiba	0	0	0	0	0	0	0	0	0	0	0	0	0	0	0	0	0	0	0	0	0	0	0	8	14	13	9
Sfax	0	0	0	0	0	0	0	0	0	0	0	0	0	0	0	0	3	0	0	0	3	0	0	0	0	0	0
Sousse	0	0	0	0	0	0	0	0	0	0	0	0	0	0	0	0	0	0	0	0	0	2	0	0	0	0	0
Tunis	0	0	0	0	0	0	0	0	0	0	0	0	0	0	1	5	0	4	1	0	5	3	4	3	0	0	3
Turkey																											
Antalya	0	0	0	0	0	0	0	0	0	0	0	0	0	0	0	0	0	0	0	0	0	2	0	0	0	0	0
Istanbul	0	0	0	0	0	0	0	0	0	0	0	0	0	0	0	0	0	0	0	0	0	0	0	0	2	0	0
Yugoslavia																											
Bijela	0	0	0	0	0	0	0	0	0	0	0	0	0	0	0	0	0	0	0	0	0	0	2	0	1	0	0
Dubrovnik	0	0	0	0	0	0	0	0	0	0	0	0	0	0	0	0	0	3	3	3	2	3	0	6	3	4	4
Gruz	0	0	0	0	0	0	0	0	0	0	0	0	0	0	0	0	0	0	0	0	0	0	1	0	0	0	0
Hercegnovi	0	0	0	0	0	0	0	0	0	0	0	0	0	0	0	0	0	0	1	1	0	0	0	0	0	0	0
Kotor	0	0	0	2	0	0	0	0	0	0	0	0	3	6	3	0	1	0	0	0	1	0	0	0	1	0	0
Kraljevica	0	0	0	0	0	0	0	0	0	0	0	0	0	0	0	0	0	0	0	0	0	0	0	0	0	1	0
Novi Sad	0	0	0	0	0	0	0	0	0	0	0	0	0	0	0	0	0	0	0	0	0	0	0	0	0	0	4
Rijeka	0	0	0	0	0	0	0	0	0	0	0	0	0	0	0	0	3	0	3	3	0	0	3	4	3	0	0
Split	0	0	3	7	3	0	0	0	0	3	0	5	11	1	6	6	0	3	2	4	5	7	0	4	5	0	9
Tivat	0	0	0	0	0	0	0	0	0	0	0	0	0	5	0	0	0	0	0	0	2	8	11	9	12	7	10
Trogir	0	0	0	0	0	0	0	0	0	0	0	0	0	0	0	0	0	0	0	0	1	1	2	3	2	4	3
Zadar	0	0	0	0	0	0	0	0	0	0	0	0	0	0	0	0	0	0	0	1	1	0	0	0	2	0	0

Table 11

Soviet Naval Ship Days Spent in Mediterranean Area Ports, 1954-1980[a]

COUNTRY/PORT	54	55	56	57	58	59	60	61	62	63	64	65	66	67	68	69	70	71	72	73	74	75	76	77	78	79
Albania																										
Durazzo	10	0	0	25	8	0	0	0	0	0	0	0	0	0	0	0	0	0	0	0	0	0	0	0	0	
Durres	15	2	18	13	31	0	0	0	0	0	0	0	0	0	0	0	0	0	0	0	0	0	0	0	0	
Valona	0	0	0	0	2035	2994	4380	1752	0	0	0	0	0	0	0	0	0	0	0	0	0	0	0	0	0	
Algeria																										
Algiers	0	0	0	0	0	0	0	0	0	0	0	0	54	171	269	31	40	35	2	0	18	0	0	0	37	
Annaba	0	0	0	0	0	0	0	0	0	0	0	0	0	0	0	24	87	110	156	117	88	80	116	176	164	199
Mers-el-Kebir	0	0	0	0	0	0	0	0	0	0	0	0	0	0	0	2	0	0	0	0	0	0	0	0	0	
Oran	0	0	0	0	0	0	0	0	0	0	0	0	30	0	0	0	11	1	0	18	2	1	8	10	8	
Cyprus																										
Larnaca	0	0	0	0	0	0	0	0	0	0	0	0	0	0	0	0	0	0	0	0	0	0	1	0	0	1
Egypt																										
Alexandria	0	0	0	8	24	22	0	21	10	0	0	13	30	1224	2190	2920	3285	3650	3758	4043	4197	4554	1321	0	0	
Matruh	0	0	0	0	0	0	0	0	0	0	0	0	0	0	0	0	235	1227	779	923	987	280	0	0	0	
Port Said	0	0	0	34	0	3	0	0	0	0	0	25	30	306	0	197	46	740	924	838	2	4	12	0	0	
Ras al Kanis	0	0	0	0	0	0	0	0	0	0	0	0	0	0	0	0	0	5	32	48	11	8	0	0	0	
France																										
Marseille	0	0	0	0	0	0	0	0	0	0	0	0	6	0	0	12	0	0	2	18	0	0	0	0	0	
Toulon	0	0	0	0	0	0	0	0	0	0	0	0	12	0	0	0	0	0	0	0	10	0	0	0	12	
Gibraltar	0	0	0	0	0	1	0	0	0	13	6	49	0	18	0	20	56	49	11	29	45	57	17	37	3	14
Greece																										
Ermoupolis	0	0	0	0	0	0	0	0	0	0	0	0	0	0	0	0	0	0	0	0	0	0	0	0	0	134
Iraklion	0	0	0	0	0	0	0	0	0	0	0	0	0	0	0	0	0	1	0	0	0	6	23	14	32	
Patrai	0	0	0	0	0	0	0	0	0	0	0	0	0	0	0	0	0	0	0	0	5	0	0	0		
Piraeus	0	0	0	0	0	0	0	0	0	0	0	0	0	0	0	0	0	0	0	0	0	0	12	8	29	
Pylos	0	0	0	0	0	0	0	0	0	0	0	0	0	0	0	0	0	0	0	0	0	0	0	0	4	5
Thessaloniki	0	0	0	0	0	0	0	0	0	0	0	0	0	0	0	0	0	0	0	0	0	0	0	0	0	
Zakros	0	0	0	0	0	0	0	0	0	0	0	0	0	0	0	0	0	5	0	0	0	0	0	0	0	
Italy																										
Augusta	0	0	0	0	0	0	0	0	0	0	0	0	0	0	0	0	0	0	0	0	0	1	0	0		
Bari	0	0	0	0	0	0	0	0	0	0	0	0	0	0	0	0	0	0	0	4	10	0	0	0		
Cagliari	0	0	0	0	0	0	0	0	0	0	0	0	0	0	0	0	0	0	0	2	1	0	9	0		
Catania	0	0	0	0	0	0	0	0	0	0	0	0	0	0	0	0	0	0	0	2	0	0	0	0		
Civitavecchia	0	0	0	0	0	0	0	0	0	0	0	0	6	6	0	16	0	5	10	12	5	0	0	0		
Genoa	0	0	0	0	0	0	0	0	0	0	0	16	6	0	0	0	0	0	0	0	5	0	0	0		
Livorno	0	0	0	0	0	0	0	0	0	0	0	0	0	0	0	0	0	0	0	0	0	0	6	0		
Messina	0	0	0	0	0	0	0	0	0	0	0	0	0	0	7	0	0	0	8	0	0	12	6	4		
Naples	0	0	0	0	0	0	0	0	0	0	12	6	6	0	0	1	0	0	0	0	0	0	0	0		
Palermo	0	0	0	0	0	0	0	0	0	0	0	0	12	0	6	8	7	1	5	11	2	37	44	48	50	62
Pantelleria	0	0	0	0	0	0	0	0	0	0	0	0	0	0	0	6	0	0	0	0	0	0	0	0		
Reggio di Calabria	0	0	0	0	0	0	0	0	0	0	0	0	0	0	0	6	0	0	0	3	0	0	0			
Salerno	0	0	0	0	0	0	0	0	0	0	0	0	0	0	0	5	10	0	5	12	5	0	0	0		
Taranto	0	0	0	0	0	0	0	0	0	0	0	0	0	0	0	0	0	3	0	8	6	0	1	0	0	1
Trapani	0	0	0	0	0	0	0	0	0	0	0	0	0	0	0	0	0	0	0	6	0	0	0	0		
Venice	0	0	0	0	0	0	0	0	0	0	0	0	0	0	0	4	0	0	0	4	0	0	0	0		
Libya																										
Tobruk	0	0	0	0	0	0	0	0	0	0	0	0	0	0	0	1	0	0	0	0	0	0	0	0		
Tripoli	0	0	0	0	0	0	0	0	0	0	0	0	0	0	0	8	4	0	0	0	0	0	0	0		
Malta																										
Valetta	0	0	0	0	0	0	0	0	0	0	0	0	0	0	0	0	0	0	0	0	0	0	0	0	4	

[a]Some of the figures, particularly for ship days in Albanian, Egyptian, and Syrian ports, are estimates based on incompl[ete] data. This listing includes visits to ports in the Alboran, Balearic, Tyrrhenian, Adriatic, Ionian, and Aegean Seas.

Table 11 (Continued)

Soviet Naval Ship Days Spent in Mediterranean Area Ports, 1954–1980

COUNTRY/PORT	54	55	56	57	58	59	60	61	62	63	64	65	66	67	68	69	70	71	72	73	74	75	76	77	78	79	80
Spain																											
Algeciras	0	0	0	0	0	0	0	0	0	0	0	0	0	0	0	0	0	0	3	0	25	8	9	1	0	0	0
Alicante	0	0	0	0	0	0	0	0	0	0	0	0	0	0	0	0	0	0	0	0	0	0	1	0	0	0	0
Cartagena	0	0	0	0	0	0	0	0	0	0	0	0	0	0	0	0	0	0	0	0	0	0	0	0	2	0	0
Ceuta	0	0	0	0	0	0	0	0	0	0	0	0	0	0	0	0	0	0	0	0	0	12	12	23	26	18	30
Málaga	0	0	0	0	0	0	0	0	0	0	0	0	0	0	0	0	0	0	0	0	0	0	1	0	0	0	0
Syria																											
Latakia	0	0	0	77	12	0	0	0	0	0	0	0	0	423	707	97	149	163	196	75	200	0	3	0	18	0	25
Tartus	0	0	0	0	0	0	0	0	0	0	0	0	0	0	0	20	0	0	91	226	270	927	1730	2098	2234	1891	2107
Tunisia																											
Bizerte	0	0	0	0	0	0	0	0	0	0	0	0	0	0	0	0	0	0	0	0	10	10	48	32	27	33	103
La Goulette	0	0	0	0	0	0	0	0	0	0	0	0	0	0	0	0	0	0	0	0	5	19	10	0	0	0	18
Menzel-Bourguiba	0	0	0	0	0	0	0	0	0	0	0	0	0	0	0	0	0	0	0	0	0	0	0	161	392	363	294
Sfax	0	0	0	0	0	0	0	0	0	0	0	0	0	0	0	0	0	0	0	0	0	0	27	0	0	0	0
Sousse	0	0	0	0	0	0	0	0	0	0	0	0	0	0	0	0	0	0	0	0	0	0	14	0	0	0	0
Tunis	0	0	0	0	0	0	0	0	0	0	0	0	0	15	20	0	19	3	0	0	20	14	9	14	0	0	15
Turkey																											
Antalya	0	0	0	0	0	0	0	0	0	0	0	0	0	0	0	0	0	0	0	0	0	0	10	0	0	0	0
Istanbul	0	0	0	0	0	0	0	0	0	0	0	0	0	0	0	0	0	0	0	0	0	0	0	0	10	0	0
Yugoslavia																											
Bijela	0	0	0	0	0	0	0	0	0	0	0	0	0	0	0	0	0	0	0	0	0	0	217	0	142	0	0
Dubrovnik	0	0	0	0	0	0	0	0	0	0	0	0	0	0	0	0	0	18	21	24	10	20	0	43	30	35	36
Gruz	0	0	0	0	0	0	0	0	0	0	0	0	0	0	0	0	0	0	0	0	0	0	5	0	0	0	0
Hercegnovi	0	0	0	0	0	0	0	0	0	0	0	0	0	0	0	0	0	0	115	11	0	0	0	0	0	0	0
Kotor	0	0	0	10	0	0	0	0	0	0	0	0	0	24	42	24	0	24	0	0	0	8	0	0	2	0	0
Kraljevica	0	0	0	0	0	0	0	0	0	0	0	0	0	0	0	0	0	0	0	0	0	0	0	0	0	149	0
Novi Sad	0	0	0	0	0	0	0	0	0	0	0	0	0	0	0	0	0	0	0	0	0	0	0	0	0	0	20
Rijeka	0	0	0	0	0	0	0	0	0	0	0	0	0	0	0	0	0	17	0	24	15	0	0	21	40	18	0
Split	0	0	15	49	15	0	0	0	0	0	24	0	30	79	35	33	33	0	18	18	18	24	40	0	32	29	69
Tivat	0	0	0	0	0	0	0	0	0	0	0	0	0	0	102	0	0	0	0	0	27	756	844	739	810	784	801
Trogir	0	0	0	0	0	0	0	0	0	0	0	0	0	0	0	0	0	0	0	0	93	41	203	205	152	209	90
Zadar	0	0	0	0	0	0	0	0	0	0	0	0	0	0	0	0	0	0	0	78	182	0	0	0	220	0	0

Table 12

Average Length of Soviet Naval Ship Visits in Mediterranean Area Ports, 1954-1980[a]

COUNTRY/PORT	54	55	56	57	58	59	60	61	62	63	64	65	66	67	68	69	70	71	72	73	74	75	76	77	78	79	80
Albania																											
Durazzo	5	0	0	5	8	0	0	0	0	0	0	0	0	0	0	0	0	0	0	0	0	0	0	0	0	0	0
Durres	5	1	6	4	5	0	0	0	0	0	0	0	0	0	0	0	0	0	0	0	0	0	0	0	0	0	0
Valona	0	0	0	0	78	71	84	73	0	0	0	0	0	0	0	0	0	0	0	0	0	0	0	0	0	0	0
Algeria																											
Algiers	0	0	0	0	0	0	0	0	0	0	0	0	6	7	12	5	6	7	2	0	6	0	0	0	5	0	3
Annaba	0	0	0	0	0	0	0	0	0	0	0	0	0	0	0	5	6	5	6	5	6	5	6	8	9	12	12
Mers-el-Kebir	0	0	0	0	0	0	0	0	0	0	0	0	0	0	0	2	0	0	0	0	0	0	0	0	0	0	0
Oran	0	0	0	0	0	0	0	0	0	0	0	0	4	0	0	0	6	1	0	3	2	1	4	5	4	0	0
Cyprus																											
Larnaca	0	0	0	0	0	0	0	0	0	0	0	0	0	0	0	0	0	0	0	0	0	0	1	0	0	1	0
Egypt																											
Alexandria	0	0	0	8	8	11	0	11	5	0	0	4	6	31	40	41	37	36	28	21	22	23	21	0	0	0	0
Matrûh	0	0	0	0	0	0	0	0	0	0	0	0	0	0	0	0	235	18	56	37	10	6	0	0	0	0	0
Port Said	0	0	0	34	0	3	0	0	0	0	0	5	5	22	0	10	9	21	51	76	1	2	3	0	0	0	0
Ras al Kanis	0	0	0	0	0	0	0	0	0	0	0	0	0	0	0	0	0	5	5	48	6	8	0	0	0	0	0
France																											
Marseille	0	0	0	0	0	0	0	0	0	0	0	0	6	0	0	6	0	0	2	6	0	0	0	0	0	0	0
Toulon	0	0	0	0	0	0	0	0	0	0	0	0	6	0	0	0	0	0	0	0	5	0	0	0	6	0	0
Gibraltar	0	0	0	0	0	1	0	0	0	3	6	5	0	6	0	3	4	3	2	2	3	3	3	5	3	14	0
Greece																											
Ermoúpolis	0	0	0	0	0	0	0	0	0	0	0	0	0	0	0	0	0	0	0	0	0	0	0	0	0	15	71
Iraklion	0	0	0	0	0	0	0	0	0	0	0	0	0	0	0	0	0	0	1	0	0	0	1	1	1	2	2
Patrai	0	0	0	0	0	0	0	0	0	0	0	0	0	0	0	0	0	0	0	0	0	5	0	0	0	0	0
Piraeus	0	0	0	0	0	0	0	0	0	0	0	0	0	0	0	0	0	0	0	0	0	0	6	3	6	3	5
Pylos	0	0	0	0	0	0	0	0	0	0	0	0	0	0	0	0	0	0	0	0	0	0	0	0	4	5	6
Thessaloniki	0	0	0	0	0	0	0	0	0	0	0	0	0	0	0	0	0	0	0	0	0	0	0	0	0	0	5
Zakros	0	0	0	0	0	0	0	0	0	0	0	0	0	0	0	0	0	5	0	0	0	0	0	0	0	0	0
Italy																											
Augusta	0	0	0	0	0	0	0	0	0	0	0	0	0	0	0	0	0	0	0	0	0	1	0	0	0	0	0
Bari	0	0	0	0	0	0	0	0	0	0	0	0	0	0	0	0	0	0	0	0	4	5	0	0	0	0	0
Cagliari	0	0	0	0	0	0	0	0	0	0	0	0	0	0	0	0	0	0	0	0	2	1	0	5	0	6	0
Catania	0	0	0	0	0	0	0	0	0	0	0	0	0	0	0	0	0	0	0	0	2	0	0	0	0	0	0
Civitavecchia	0	0	0	0	0	0	0	0	0	0	0	0	6	6	0	0	5	0	5	5	6	5	0	0	0	0	0
Genoa	0	0	0	0	0	0	0	0	0	0	0	5	6	0	0	0	0	0	0	0	5	0	0	0	0	0	0
Livorno	0	0	0	0	0	0	0	0	0	0	0	0	0	0	0	0	0	0	0	0	0	0	6	0	0	0	0
Messina	0	0	0	0	0	0	0	0	0	0	0	0	0	0	7	0	0	0	0	0	4	0	0	6	6	4	0
Naples	0	0	0	0	0	0	0	0	0	0	0	6	6	6	0	0	1	0	0	0	0	0	0	0	0	0	0
Palermo	0	0	0	0	0	0	0	0	0	0	0	0	6	0	3	4	4	1	5	6	2	7	2	2	2	2	2

[a]Some of the figures, particularly for ship days in Albanian, Egyptian, and Syrian ports, are estimates based on incomplete data. This listing includes visits to ports in the Alboran, Balearic, Tyrrhenian, Adriatic, Ionian, and Aegean Seas.

Table 12 (Continued)

Average Length of Soviet Naval Ship Visits in Mediterranean Area Ports, 1954–1980

COUNTRY/PORT	54	55	56	57	58	59	60	61	62	63	64	65	66	67	68	69	70	71	72	73	74	75	76	77	78	79	80
Pantelleria	0	0	0	0	0	0	0	0	0	0	0	0	0	0	0	0	2	0	0	0	0	0	0	0	0	0	0
Reggio di Calabria	0	0	0	0	0	0	0	0	0	0	0	0	0	0	0	0	2	0	0	0	3	0	0	0	0	0	0
Salerno	0	0	0	0	0	0	0	0	0	0	0	0	0	0	0	5	5	0	0	5	6	5	0	0	0	0	0
Taranto	0	0	0	0	0	0	0	0	0	0	0	0	0	0	0	0	0	3	0	4	6	0	1	0	0	1	0
Trapani	0	0	0	0	0	0	0	0	0	0	0	0	0	0	0	0	0	0	0	0	6	0	0	0	0	0	0
Venice	0	0	0	0	0	0	0	0	0	0	0	0	0	0	0	4	0	0	0	0	4	0	0	0	0	0	0
Libya																											
Tobruk	0	0	0	0	0	0	0	0	0	0	0	0	0	0	0	1	0	0	0	0	0	0	0	0	0	0	0
Tripoli	0	0	0	0	0	0	0	0	0	0	0	0	0	0	0	8	4	0	0	0	0	0	0	0	0	0	0
Malta																											
Valetta	0	0	0	0	0	0	0	0	0	0	0	0	0	0	0	0	0	0	0	0	0	0	0	0	2	0	2
Spain																											
Algeciras	0	0	0	0	0	0	0	0	0	0	0	0	0	0	0	0	0	0	2	0	2	1	2	1	0	0	0
Alicante	0	0	0	0	0	0	0	0	0	0	0	0	0	0	0	0	0	0	0	0	0	0	1	0	0	0	0
Cartagena	0	0	0	0	0	0	0	0	0	0	0	0	0	0	0	0	0	0	0	0	0	0	0	0	2	0	0
Ceuta	0	0	0	0	0	0	0	0	0	0	0	0	0	0	0	0	0	0	0	0	0	2	1	2	2	2	4
Málaga	0	0	0	0	0	0	0	0	0	0	0	0	0	0	0	0	0	0	0	0	0	0	1	0	0	0	0
Syria																											
Latakia	0	0	0	11	6	0	0	0	0	0	0	0	0	24	18	11	8	9	8	5	8	0	3	0	6	0	5
Tartus	0	0	0	0	0	0	0	0	0	0	0	0	0	0	0	3	0	0	6	13	14	14	21	24	24	23	27
Tunisia																											
Bizerte	0	0	0	0	0	0	0	0	0	0	0	0	0	0	0	0	0	0	0	0	5	5	5	6	7	4	9
La Goulette	0	0	0	0	0	0	0	0	0	0	0	0	0	0	0	0	0	0	0	0	0	5	5	5	0	0	6
Menzel-Bourguiba	0	0	0	0	0	0	0	0	0	0	0	0	0	0	0	0	0	0	0	0	0	0	0	20	28	28	33
Sfax	0	0	0	0	0	0	0	0	0	0	0	0	0	0	0	0	0	0	0	0	9	0	0	0	0	0	0
Sousse	0	0	0	0	0	0	0	0	0	0	0	0	0	0	0	0	0	0	0	0	0	0	7	0	0	0	0
Tunis	0	0	0	0	0	0	0	0	0	0	0	0	0	15	4	0	5	3	0	4	5	2	5	0	0	0	5
Turkey																											
Antalya	0	0	0	0	0	0	0	0	0	0	0	0	0	0	0	0	0	0	0	0	0	0	5	0	0	0	0
Istanbul	0	0	0	0	0	0	0	0	0	0	0	0	0	0	0	0	0	0	0	0	0	0	0	5	0	0	0
Yugoslavia																											
Bijela	0	0	0	0	0	0	0	0	0	0	0	0	0	0	0	0	0	0	0	0	0	109	0	142	0	0	0
Dubrovnik	0	0	0	0	0	0	0	0	0	0	0	0	0	0	0	0	0	6	7	8	5	7	0	7	10	9	9
Gruz	0	0	0	0	0	0	0	0	0	0	0	0	0	0	0	0	0	0	0	0	0	0	0	5	0	0	0
Hercegnovi	0	0	0	0	0	0	0	0	0	0	0	0	0	0	0	0	0	0	115	11	0	0	0	0	0	0	0
Kotor	0	0	0	5	0	0	0	0	0	0	0	0	0	8	7	8	0	24	0	0	0	8	0	0	2	0	0
Kraljevica	0	0	0	0	0	0	0	0	0	0	0	0	0	0	0	0	0	0	0	0	0	0	0	0	0	149	0
Novi Sad	0	0	0	0	0	0	0	0	0	0	0	0	0	0	0	0	0	0	0	0	0	0	0	0	0	0	5
Rijeka	0	0	0	0	0	0	0	0	0	0	0	0	0	0	0	0	0	6	0	8	5	0	0	7	10	6	0
Split	0	0	5	7	5	0	0	0	0	0	8	0	6	7	35	6	6	0	6	9	5	5	6	0	8	6	8
Tivat	0	0	0	0	0	0	0	0	0	0	0	0	0	0	20	0	0	0	0	14	95	77	82	68	112	80	0
Trogir	0	0	0	0	0	0	0	0	0	0	0	0	0	0	0	0	0	0	0	93	41	102	68	76	52	30	0
Zadar	0	0	0	0	0	0	0	0	0	0	0	0	0	0	0	0	0	0	0	78	182	0	0	0	110	0	0

Table 13

Cumulative Totals of Soviet Naval Port Visits
in the Mediterranean Area By Port, 1954-1980

Port	Total Ship Days	Comments
1. Alexandria, Egypt	31,270	These visits were for operational support of the fleet and for repair and upkeep of naval ships. Some overhaul/yard work may also have been performed in Alexandria. The Soviets had routine access to the port after the June 1967 War, and many Soviet ships were permanently located there. The Soviets' use of the port ended when they were expelled in 1976.
2. Tartus, Syria	11,594	Beginning in 1969, this port was used extensively to support the Mediterranean fleet. Use became heavier in 1972, and access to Tartus became critical in 1976, after the expulsion from Alexandria. Routine use of the port has continued through 1980.
3. Valona, Albania	11,161	Use of Valona was crucial to the Soviet presence in the Mediterranean from 1958 to 1961. Valona was used as a base when the Soviets stationed a submarine force in the Mediterranean in the wake of the Lebanon crisis of 1958. The port was used extensively until the Soviets were expelled in 1961. This denial of facilities was probably a major cause for the cessation of Soviet naval operations in the Mediterranean from 1961 to 1964.
4. Tivat, Yugoslavia	4,863	Overhaul/yard work on Soviet ships.
5. Matrûh, Egypt	4,431	Routine access/semi-permanent presence from 1970 to 1975.
6. Port Said, Egypt	3,161	Routine access/semi-permanent presence from 1967 to 1973. Soviet ships were probably stationed here to protect the port from possible Israeli attacks.
7. Latakia, Syria	2,145	This port was used extensively for fleet support from 1967 to 1974.
8. Annaba, Algeria	1,498	Good will/operational visits which began in 1969.
9. Menzel-Bourguiba, Tunisia	1,210	Overhaul/yard work began on Soviet ships in 1977 and was constant through 1980.
10. Trogir, Yugoslavia	993	Overhaul/yard work began on Soviet ships in 1974 and was constant through 1980.
11. Algiers, Algeria	663	Good will/operational visits, which began in 1966.
12. Ermoúpolis, Greece	562	Overhaul/yard work on Soviet auxiliary ships since 1979.
13. Split, Yugoslavia	561	Official visits which began in 1956.
14. Zadar, Yugoslavia	480	Overhaul/yard work on Soviet ships since 1973.
15. Gibraltar	425	Good will/operational visits, primarily by auxiliary ships to support naval operations in the western Mediterranean and the Atlantic Ocean since 1959.
16. Bijela, Yugoslavia	359	Overhaul/yard work on Soviet ships since 1976.
17. Palermo, Italy	328	Good will/operational visits, primarily by auxiliaries, to support fleet operations in the central Mediterranean.
18. Bizerte, Tunisia	263	These good will/operational visits, which began in 1974, reflect Soviet interest in Tunisia as their access to Egyptian ports was threatened.
19. Dubrovnik, Yugoslavia	237	Good will/operational visits, which began in 1971.
20. Kraljevica, Yugoslavia	149	Overhaul/yard work on a Soviet auxiliary ship in 1979.

Table 13 (Continued)

Cumulative Totals of Soviet Naval Port Visits
in the Mediterranean Area By Port, 1954-1980

Port	Total Ship Days	Comments
21. Rijeka, Yugoslavia	135	Good will/operational visits, which began in 1971.
22. Kotor, Yugoslavia	134	Good will/operational visits, which began in 1957.
23. Tunis, Tunisia	129	Good will/operational visits, which began in 1968.
24. Hercegnovi, Yugoslavia	126	Good will/operational visits in 1973 and 1974.
25. Ceuta, Spain	121	Good will/operational visits by Soviet auxiliaries to support fleet operations in the western Mediterranean.
26. Ras al Kanis, Egypt	104	Routine access from 1971 to 1975.
27. Oran, Algeria	89	Good will/operational visits, which began in 1966.
28. Iráklion, Greece	86	Good will/operational visits, primarily by auxiliary ships, in support of fleet operations in the eastern Mediterranean.
29. Durres, Albania	79	Good will/operational visits which occurred from 1954 to 1958.
30. Piraeus, Greece	64	Official and good will/operational visits since 1976.
31. Civitavecchia, Italy	60	Good will/operational visits by hydrographic ships.
32. La Goulette, Tunisia	52	Good will/operational visits, which began in 1974.
33. Algeciras, Spain	46	See entry 25.
34. Durazzo, Albania	43	Good will/operational visits, which occurred from 1954 to 1958.
35. Marseille, France	38	Official and good will/operational visits.
36. Salerno, Italy	37	See entry 31.
37. Messina, Italy	37	Official and good will/operational visits since 1968.
38. Toulon, France	34	Official visits, which began in 1966.
39. Sfax, Tunisia	27	Good will/operational visit in 1976.
40. Genoa, Italy	27	See entry 31.
41. Naples, Italy	25	See entry 31.
42. Novi Sad, Yugoslavia	20	Good will/operational visit in 1980.
43. Taranto, Italy	19	Official and good will/operational visits, which began in 1971.
44. Cagliari, Italy	18	See entry 17.
45. Pylos, Greece	15	Good will/operational visits, which began in 1978.
46. Bari, Italy	14	See entry 31.
47. Sousse, Tunisia	14	Good will/operational visit in 1976.
48. Tripoli, Libya	12	Good will/operational visits in 1969 and 1970.
49. Antalya, Turkey	10	Good will/operational visit in 1976.
50. Istanbul, Turkey	10	Official visit in 1978.
51. Reggio di Calabria, Italy	9	See entry 17.

Table 13 (Continued)

Cumulative Totals of Soviet Naval Port Visits
in the Mediterranean Area By Port, 1954–1980

	Port	Total Ship Days	Comments
52.	Venice, Italy	8	See entry 31.
53.	Trapani, Italy	6	See entry 31.
54.	Livorno, Italy	6	Good will/operational visit in 1977.
55.	Pantelleria, Italy	6	See entry 17.
56.	Valetta, Malta	6	Good will/operational visits in 1978 and 1980.
57.	Zakros, Greece	5	Good will/operational visit in 1972.
58.	Gruz, Yugoslavia	5	Good will/operational visit in 1976.
59.	Patrai, Greece	5	Good will/operational visit in 1975.
60.	Thessaloniki, Greece	5	Good will/operational visit in 1980.
61.	Catania, Italy	2	See entry 17.
62.	Mers-el-Kebir, Algeria	2	Good will/operational visit in 1969.
63.	Cartagena, Spain	2	See entry 25.
64.	Larnaca, Cyprus	2	Evacuation of Soviet personnel from Cyprus in 1976 and a good will/operational visit in 1979.
65.	Malaga, Spain	1	See entry 25.
66.	Alicante, Spain	1	See entry 25.
67.	Tobruk, Libya	1	Good will/operational visit in 1969.
68.	Augusta, Italy	1	See entry 17.

Table 14

Cumulative Totals of Soviet Naval Port Visits
in the Mediterranean Area By Country, 1954-1980

	Country	Total Ship Days
1.	Egypt (Mediterranean coast only)	38,966
2.	Syria	13,739
3.	Albania	11,283
4.	Yugoslavia	8,062
5.	Algeria	2,252
6.	Tunisia	1,695
7.	Greece	742
8.	Italy	603
9.	Gibraltar	425
10.	Spain (Mediterranean coast only)	171
11.	France (Mediterranean coast only)	72
12.	Turkey (Mediterranean coast only)	20
13.	Libya	13
14.	Malta	6
15.	Cyprus	2

Table 15

Number of Soviet Naval Ships Visiting Pacific Area Ports, 1956–1980[a]

COUNTRY/PORT	56	57	58	59	60	61	62	63	64	65	66	67	68	69	70	71	72	73	74	75	76	77	78	79	80
Australia																									
Cairns	0	0	0	0	0	0	0	0	0	0	0	0	0	0	0	0	0	1	0	1	0	0	0	0	0
Cambodia																									
Sihanoukville	0	0	0	0	0	0	0	0	0	0	0	0	0	1	0	0	0	0	0	0	0	0	0	0	0
Canada																									
Vancouver	0	0	0	0	0	0	0	0	1	3	2	4	0	2	3	0	2	1	0	0	3	0	0	0	0
Chile																									
Valparaiso	0	0	0	0	0	0	0	0	0	0	0	0	0	1	0	0	0	0	1	0	0	0	0	0	0
China																									
Shanghai	3	0	0	0	0	0	0	0	0	0	0	0	0	0	0	0	0	0	0	0	0	0	0	0	0
Colombia																									
Buenaventura	0	0	0	0	0	0	0	0	0	0	0	0	0	0	0	0	0	0	0	0	0	0	0	2	0
Ecuador																									
Guayaquil	0	0	0	0	0	0	0	0	0	0	0	0	0	0	0	0	0	2	0	1	0	0	0	2	0
Fiji Islands																									
Suva	0	0	0	0	0	0	0	0	0	0	0	0	0	0	2	4	0	0	0	0	2	0	0	0	0
Indonesia																									
Djakarta	0	0	0	4	0	0	0	0	0	0	0	0	0	0	0	0	0	0	0	0	0	0	0	0	0
Japan																									
Chiba	0	0	0	0	0	0	0	0	0	0	0	0	0	0	0	0	0	0	0	0	0	0	3	3	0
Tokyo	0	0	0	0	0	0	0	0	0	0	1	0	2	2	0	0	0	0	1	0	0	0	0	0	0
Yokohama	0	0	0	0	0	0	0	0	0	0	0	0	0	0	0	0	0	0	1	0	0	1	4	2	0
Kampuchea																									
Kompong Som	0	0	0	0	0	0	0	0	0	0	0	0	0	0	0	0	0	0	0	0	0	0	0	0	4
Mexico																									
Acapulco	0	0	0	0	0	0	0	0	0	0	0	0	0	0	0	0	0	0	0	0	0	0	0	6	0
Mazatlán	0	0	0	0	0	0	0	0	0	0	0	2	0	0	2	0	0	0	0	0	0	0	0	0	0
New Caledonia																									
Nouméa	0	0	0	0	0	0	0	0	0	0	0	0	0	0	2	0	0	0	0	0	0	0	0	0	0
New Zealand																									
Auckland	0	0	0	0	0	0	0	0	0	0	0	0	0	0	0	0	0	1	0	0	0	0	0	0	0
Wellington	0	0	0	0	0	0	0	0	0	0	0	0	0	0	0	1	0	0	0	0	0	0	0	0	0
North Korea																									
Nampo	0	0	0	0	0	0	0	0	0	0	0	0	0	0	1	0	1	2	2	3	4	2	0	0	0
Peru																									
Callao	0	0	0	0	0	0	0	0	0	0	0	0	0	0	2	0	0	2	4	1	0	0	0	0	1
Samoa																									
Apia	0	0	0	0	0	0	0	0	0	0	0	0	0	0	0	0	0	3	0	0	0	0	0	0	0
Singapore	0	0	0	0	0	0	0	0	0	0	0	0	0	9	17	16	19	33	31	24	19	32	24	24	8
Tahiti																									
Papeete	0	0	0	0	0	0	0	0	0	0	0	0	0	0	0	2	0	0	0	0	0	0	0	0	0
Tasmania																									
Hobart	0	0	0	0	0	0	0	0	0	0	0	0	0	0	0	0	0	0	0	0	0	0	2	0	0
United States																									
Honolulu	0	0	0	0	0	0	0	0	0	0	0	0	0	0	0	0	0	0	1	0	0	0	0	0	0
San Francisco	0	0	0	0	0	0	0	0	0	0	1	0	0	0	0	0	0	0	1	0	0	0	0	0	0
Seattle	0	0	0	0	0	0	0	0	0	0	0	0	0	0	0	0	0	0	1	0	0	0	0	0	0
Vietnam																									
Cam Ranh Bay	0	0	0	0	0	0	0	0	0	0	0	0	0	0	0	0	0	0	0	0	0	0	0	28	110
Da Nang	0	0	0	0	0	0	0	0	0	0	0	0	0	0	0	0	0	0	0	0	0	0	0	39	23
Haiphong	0	0	0	0	0	0	0	0	0	0	0	0	0	0	0	0	0	0	0	0	0	0	0	11	7
Ho Chi Minh City	0	0	0	0	0	0	0	0	0	0	0	0	0	0	0	0	0	0	0	0	0	0	0	1	3

[a]Includes port visits in the Yellow Sea, Sea of Japan, East and South China Seas, Java Sea, and Tasman Sea.

Table 16

Soviet Naval Ship Days Spent in Pacific Area Ports, 1956–1980[a]

COUNTRY/PORT	56	57	58	59	60	61	62	63	64	65	66	67	68	69	70	71	72	73	74	75	76	77	78	79	80
Australia																									
Cairns	0	0	0	0	0	0	0	0	0	0	0	0	0	0	0	0	0	6	0	6	0	0	0	0	0
Cambodia																									
Sihanoukville	0	0	0	0	0	0	0	0	0	0	0	0	0	6	0	0	0	0	0	0	0	0	0	0	0
Canada																									
Vancouver	0	0	0	0	0	0	0	0	6	13	2	20	0	11	18	0	10	5	0	0	15	0	0	0	0
Chile																									
Valparaiso	0	0	0	0	0	0	0	0	0	0	0	0	0	5	0	0	0	5	0	0	0	0	0	0	0
China																									
Shanghai	18	0	0	0	0	0	0	0	0	0	0	0	0	0	0	0	0	0	0	0	0	0	0	0	0
Colombia																									
Buenaventura	0	0	0	0	0	0	0	0	0	0	0	0	0	0	0	0	0	0	0	0	0	0	0	6	0
Ecuador																									
Guayaquil	0	0	0	0	0	0	0	0	0	0	0	0	0	0	0	0	0	12	0	6	0	0	0	11	0
Fiji Islands																									
Suva	0	0	0	0	0	0	0	0	0	0	0	0	0	0	0	12	32	0	0	0	11	0	0	0	0
Indonesia																									
Djakarta	0	0	0	20	0	0	0	0	0	0	0	0	0	0	0	0	0	0	0	0	0	0	0	0	0
Japan																									
Chiba	0	0	0	0	0	0	0	0	0	0	0	0	0	0	0	0	0	0	0	0	0	0	143	62	0
Tokyo	0	0	0	0	0	0	0	0	0	0	6	0	2	8	0	0	0	0	4	0	0	0	0	0	0
Yokohama	0	0	0	0	0	0	0	0	0	0	0	0	0	0	0	0	0	3	0	0	0	30	27	45	0
Kampuchea																									
Kompong Som	0	0	0	0	0	0	0	0	0	0	0	0	0	0	0	0	0	0	0	0	0	0	0	0	34
Mexico																									
Acapulco	0	0	0	0	0	0	0	0	0	0	0	0	0	0	0	0	0	0	0	0	0	0	0	24	0
Mazatlán	0	0	0	0	0	0	0	0	0	0	0	6	0	0	12	0	0	0	0	0	0	0	0	0	0
New Caledonia																									
Nouméa	0	0	0	0	0	0	0	0	0	0	0	0	0	10	0	0	0	0	0	0	0	0	0	0	0
New Zealand																									
Auckland	0	0	0	0	0	0	0	0	0	0	0	0	0	0	0	0	0	2	0	0	0	0	0	0	0
Wellington	0	0	0	0	0	0	0	0	0	0	0	0	0	0	0	4	0	0	0	0	0	0	0	0	0
North Korea																									
Nampo	0	0	0	0	0	0	0	0	0	0	0	0	0	5	0	4	12	12	16	23	10	0	0	0	0
Peru																									
Callao	0	0	0	0	0	0	0	0	0	0	0	0	0	0	4	0	0	12	22	6	0	0	0	0	4
Samoa																									
Apia	0	0	0	0	0	0	0	0	0	0	0	0	0	0	0	0	0	12	0	0	0	0	0	0	0
Singapore	0	0	0	0	0	0	0	0	0	0	0	0	0	43	66	42	209	559	933	748	439	659	657	463	260
Tahiti																									
Papeete	0	0	0	0	0	0	0	0	0	0	0	0	0	0	0	0	10	0	0	0	0	0	0	0	0
Tasmania																									
Hobart	0	0	0	0	0	0	0	0	0	0	0	0	0	0	0	0	0	0	0	0	0	0	8	0	0
United States																									
Honolulu	0	0	0	0	0	0	0	0	0	0	0	0	0	0	0	0	0	4	0	0	0	0	0	0	0
San Francisco	0	0	0	0	0	0	0	0	0	0	7	0	0	0	0	0	0	6	0	0	0	0	0	0	0
Seattle	0	0	0	0	0	0	0	0	0	0	0	0	0	0	0	0	0	6	0	0	0	0	0	0	0
Vietnam																									
Cam Ranh Bay	0	0	0	0	0	0	0	0	0	0	0	0	0	0	0	0	0	0	0	0	0	0	0	342	1657
Da Nang	0	0	0	0	0	0	0	0	0	0	0	0	0	0	0	0	0	0	0	0	0	0	0	331	435
Haiphong	0	0	0	0	0	0	0	0	0	0	0	0	0	0	0	0	0	0	0	0	0	0	0	54	27
Ho Chi Minh City	0	0	0	0	0	0	0	0	0	0	0	0	0	0	0	0	0	0	0	0	0	0	0	4	16

[a]Includes port visits in the Yellow Sea, Sea of Japan, East and South China Seas, Java Sea, and Tasman Sea.

Table 17

Average Length of Soviet Naval Ship Visits in Pacific Area Ports, 1956-1980[a]

COUNTRY/PORT	56	57	58	59	60	61	62	63	64	65	66	67	68	69	70	71	72	73	74	75	76	77	78	79	80
Australia																									
Cairns	0	0	0	0	0	0	0	0	0	0	0	0	0	0	0	0	0	6	0	6	0	0	0	0	
Cambodia																									
Sihanoukville	0	0	0	0	0	0	0	0	0	0	0	0	0	0	6	0	0	0	0	0	0	0	0	0	
Canada																									
Vancouver	0	0	0	0	0	0	0	0	6	4	1	5	0	6	6	0	5	5	0	0	5	0	0	0	
Chile																									
Valparaiso	0	0	0	0	0	0	0	0	0	0	0	5	0	0	0	5	0	0	0	5	0	0	0	0	
China																									
Shanghai	6	0	0	0	0	0	0	0	0	0	0	0	0	0	0	0	0	0	0	0	0	0	0	0	
Colombia																									
Buenaventura	0	0	0	0	0	0	0	0	0	0	0	0	0	0	0	0	0	0	0	0	0	0	0	3	
Ecuador																									
Guayaquil	0	0	0	0	0	0	0	0	0	0	0	0	0	0	0	0	0	6	0	6	0	0	0	6	
Fiji Islands																									
Suva	0	0	0	0	0	0	0	0	0	0	0	0	0	0	6	8	0	0	0	0	6	0	0	0	
Indonesia																									
Djakarta	0	0	0	5	0	0	0	0	0	0	0	0	0	0	0	0	0	0	0	0	0	0	0	0	
Japan																									
Chiba	0	0	0	0	0	0	0	0	0	0	0	0	0	0	0	0	0	0	0	0	0	0	48	21	
Tokyo	0	0	0	0	0	0	0	0	0	0	6	0	1	4	0	0	0	0	4	0	0	0	0	0	
Yokohama	0	0	0	0	0	0	0	0	0	0	0	0	0	0	0	0	0	3	0	0	0	30	7	23	
Kampuchea																									
Kompong Som	0	0	0	0	0	0	0	0	0	0	0	0	0	0	0	0	0	0	0	0	0	0	0	0	
Mexico																									
Acapulco	0	0	0	0	0	0	0	0	0	0	0	0	0	0	0	0	0	0	0	0	0	0	0	4	
Mazatlán	0	0	0	0	0	0	0	0	0	0	0	3	0	0	6	0	0	0	0	0	0	0	0	0	
New Caledonia																									
Nouméa	0	0	0	0	0	0	0	0	0	0	0	0	0	5	0	0	0	0	0	0	0	0	0	0	
New Zealand																									
Auckland	0	0	0	0	0	0	0	0	0	0	0	0	0	0	0	0	0	2	0	0	0	0	0	0	
Wellington	0	0	0	0	0	0	0	0	0	0	0	0	0	0	4	0	0	0	0	0	0	0	0	0	
North Korea																									
Nampo	0	0	0	0	0	0	0	0	0	0	0	0	0	5	0	4	6	6	5	6	5	0	0	0	
Peru																									
Callao	0	0	0	0	0	0	0	0	0	0	0	0	0	2	0	0	6	6	6	0	0	0	0	0	
Samoa																									
Apia	0	0	0	0	0	0	0	0	0	0	0	0	0	0	0	0	0	4	0	0	0	0	0	0	
Singapore	0	0	0	0	0	0	0	0	0	0	0	0	0	5	4	3	11	17	30	31	23	21	27	19	3
Tahiti																									
Papeete	0	0	0	0	0	0	0	0	0	0	0	0	0	5	0	0	0	0	0	0	0	0	0	0	
Tasmania																									
Hobart	0	0	0	0	0	0	0	0	0	0	0	0	0	0	0	0	0	0	0	0	0	0	4	0	
United States																									
Honolulu	0	0	0	0	0	0	0	0	0	0	0	0	0	0	0	0	0	4	0	0	0	0	0	0	
San Francisco	0	0	0	0	0	0	0	0	0	0	0	7	0	0	0	0	0	6	0	0	0	0	0	0	
Seattle	0	0	0	0	0	0	0	0	0	0	0	0	0	0	0	0	0	6	0	0	0	0	0	0	
Vietnam																									
Cam Ranh Bay	0	0	0	0	0	0	0	0	0	0	0	0	0	0	0	0	0	0	0	0	0	0	0	12	1
Da Nang	0	0	0	0	0	0	0	0	0	0	0	0	0	0	0	0	0	0	0	0	0	0	0	8	1
Haiphong	0	0	0	0	0	0	0	0	0	0	0	0	0	0	0	0	0	0	0	0	0	0	0	5	
Ho Chi Minh City	0	0	0	0	0	0	0	0	0	0	0	0	0	0	0	0	0	0	0	0	0	0	0	4	

[a]Includes port visits in the Yellow Sea, Sea of Japan, East and South China Seas, Java Sea, and Tasman Sea.

Table 18

Cumulative Totals of Soviet Naval Port Visits
in the Pacific Area By Port, 1956-1980

	Port	Total Ship Days	Comments
1.	Singapore	5,078	Overhaul and yard work on Soviet ships. This access was probably denied in 1980, possibly as part of a reaction to the Soviet invasion of Afghanistan.
2.	Cam Ranh Bay, Vietnam	1,999	The heavy use of Vietnamese ports began after the conclusion of the Sino-Vietnamese War in 1979. The Soviets probably intend to
3.	Da Nang, Vietnam	766	maintain a constant naval presence in Vietnam and may develop a forward base at one or more ports. This would ease considerably the logistical problem of supporting the Indian Ocean Squadron and would enable the Soviets to respond more quickly to Indian Ocean crises. The bases would also further isolate the People's Republic of China and would increase the Soviet maritime threat against Japan and the U.S. Seventh Fleet.
4.	Chiba, Japan	205	Overhaul/yard work on Soviet auxiliary ships which probably began in 1978.
5.	Yokohama, Japan	105	Overhaul/yard work that began in 1977.
6.	Vancouver, Canada	100	Good will/operational visits by hydrographic ships, which began in 1964. An official visit took place in 1976.
7.	Nampo, North Korea	82	Good will/operational visits by hydrographic ships.
8.	Haiphong, Vietnam	81	See entry 2.
9.	Suva, Fiji Islands	55	Good will/operational visits which began in 1970 and are associated with naval operations in the South Pacific.
10.	Callao, Peru	48	Good will/operational visits, which began in 1970.
11.	Kompong Som, Kampuchea	34	Good will/operational visits, which began in 1980.
12.	Guayaquil, Ecuador	29	Good will/operational visits, which began in 1973.
13.	Acapulco, Mexico	24	Good will/operational visits in 1979.
14.	Tokyo, Japan	20	See entry 7.
15.	Djakarta, Indonesia	20	These official visits occurred in 1959. There have been no visits since that year.
16.	Ho Chi Minh City, Vietnam	20	See entry 2.
17.	Shanghai, People's Republic of China	18	All of these official visits occurred in 1956.
18.	Mazatlán, Mexico	18	See entry 7.
19.	San Francisco, United States	13	See entry 7.
20.	Apia, Samoa	12	Good will/operational visit in 1973.
21.	Cairns, Australia	12	See entry 7.
22.	Nouméa, New Caledonia	10	Good will/operational visit in 1970.
23.	Papeete, Tahiti	10	See entry 7.
24.	Valparaiso, Chile	10	Good will/operational visits in 1969 and 1973.
25.	Hobart, Tasmania	8	See entry 7.
26.	Sihanoukville, Cambodia	6	Good will/operational visit in 1969.
27.	Seattle, United States	6	See entry 7.
28.	Buenaventura, Colombia	6	See entry 7.
29.	Wellington, New Zealand	4	Good will/operational visit in 1971.
30.	Honolulu, United States	4	Good will/operational visit in 1974.
31.	Auckland, New Zealand	2	Good will/operational visit in 1973.

Table 19

Cumulative Totals of Soviet Naval Port Visits
in the Pacific Area By Country, 1956–1980

	Country	Total Ship Days
1.	Singapore	5,078
2.	Vietnam	2,866
3.	Japan	330
4.	Canada (Pacific coast only)	100
5.	North Korea	82
6.	Fiji Islands	55
7.	Peru	48
8.	Mexico (Pacific coast only)	42
9.	Kampuchea	34
10.	Ecuador	29
11.	United States (Pacific coast only)	23
12.	Indonesia	20
13.	People's Republic of China	18
14.	Samoa	12
15.	Australia	12
16.	Chile	10
17.	New Caledonia	10
18.	Tahiti	10
19.	Tasmania	8
20.	Cambodia	6
21.	New Zealand	6
22.	Colombia (Pacific coast only)	6

Table 20

Number of Soviet Naval Ships Visiting Indian Ocean Area Ports, 1962–1980[a]

COUNTRY/PORT	62	63	64	65	66	67	68	69	70	71	72	73	74	75	76	77	78	79	80
Bangladesh																			
Chittagong	0	0	0	0	0	0	0	2	0	0	9	10	11	0	0	0	0	0	0
Egypt																			
Berenice	0	0	0	0	0	0	3	0	0	0	0	0	0	0	0	0	0	0	0
Hurghada	0	0	0	0	0	0	0	0	0	0	0	0	23	0	0	0	0	0	0
Ras Shukheir	0	0	0	0	0	0	0	0	1	0	0	0	0	0	0	0	0	0	0
Safâga	0	0	0	0	0	0	0	2	0	0	0	0	0	0	0	0	0	0	0
Ethiopia																			
Assab	0	0	0	0	0	0	0	0	0	0	0	0	0	0	0	1	17	3	1
Dahlak Island	0	0	0	0	0	0	0	0	0	0	0	0	0	0	0	0	40	50	95
Massawa	0	0	0	1	1	1	2	2	1	2	1	1	1	0	1	0	7	0	10
India																			
Bombay	0	0	0	0	2	0	6	3	7	2	2	3	2	4	3	5	2	1	3
Cochin	0	0	0	0	0	0	0	0	0	0	0	0	0	0	2	0	0	0	3
Madras	0	0	0	0	0	0	5	0	0	0	0	3	0	2	0	0	0	1	0
Vishakhapatnam	0	0	0	0	0	0	0	0	3	0	0	0	0	1	0	0	0	0	0
Iran																			
Bandar ʿAbbas	0	0	0	0	0	0	3	9	0	0	3	0	0	0	3	0	0	0	0
Iraq																			
Basra	0	0	0	0	0	0	3	0	0	2	3	2	8	2	8	3	0	0	0
Khawr al Amaya	0	0	0	0	0	0	0	0	0	0	0	1	0	0	0	0	0	0	0
Umm Qasr	0	0	0	0	0	0	0	8	3	4	7	15	11	8	7	4	4	8	0
Kenya																			
Mombasa	0	0	0	0	0	0	5	3	7	0	2	5	4	1	0	3	0	2	0
Kerguelen Islands																			
Port-aux-Français	0	0	0	0	0	0	0	0	0	0	1	0	1	1	0	1	0	0	0
Kuwait																			
Mīnā' al-Ahmadī	0	0	0	0	0	0	2	1	0	0	0	0	0	0	0	0	0	0	0
Malagasy Republic																			
Tamatave	0	0	0	0	0	0	1	5	1	0	0	0	0	0	0	0	0	0	1

[a]Includes port visits in the Gulf of Aden, Red Sea, Persian Gulf, Arabian Sea, and Bay of Bengal.

Table 20 (Continued)

Number of Soviet Naval Ships Visiting Indian Ocean Area Ports, 1962-1980

COUNTRY/PORT	62	63	64	65	66	67	68	69	70	71	72	73	74	75	76	77	78	79	80
Maldive Islands																		
Male	0	0	0	0	0	0	0	0	1	0	5	1	4	1	0	1	0	0	0
Mauritius																		
Port Louis	0	0	0	0	0	3	4	12	21	11	26	11	15	10	11	7	3	14	5
Mozambique																		
Beira	0	0	0	0	0	0	0	0	0	0	0	0	0	0	0	1	1	4	4
Maputo	0	0	0	0	0	0	0	0	0	0	0	0	0	0	0	9	2	5	0
Nacala	0	0	0	0	0	0	0	0	0	0	0	0	0	0	0	4	0	2	0
Pakistan																		
Karachi	0	0	0	0	0	0	3	3	2	0	0	0	0	2	5	0	0	2	0
People's Dem. Rep. of Yemen																		
Aden	0	0	0	0	0	0	5	18	10	23	6	15	46	36	28	38	74	40	88
Perim Island	0	0	0	0	0	0	0	0	0	0	0	0	0	0	0	0	0	1	0
Seychelles																		
Victoria	0	0	0	0	0	4	0	0	0	0	0	0	0	0	0	1	3	8	4
Somalia																		
Berbera	0	0	0	0	0	0	0	8	9	15	17	44	60	48	75	52	0	0	0
Chisimaio(Kismayu)	0	0	0	0	0	0	0	2	0	2	0	0	0	5	9	9	0	0	0
Mogadiscio	0	0	0	0	0	0	3	8	4	6	13	5	7	5	6	3	0	0	0
Sri Lanka																		
Colombo	1	0	0	0	0	6	5	9	3	3	17	8	10	10	11	10	7	3	16
Sudan																		
Port Sudan	0	0	0	0	0	0	0	2	1	2	0	0	0	0	0	2	0	0	0
Tanzania																		
Dar es Salaam	0	0	0	0	0	0	4	0	2	0	0	0	0	0	0	0	0	0	0
Zanzibar	0	0	0	0	0	0	0	2	0	0	0	0	0	0	0	0	0	0	0
Terr. Afars & Issas																		
Djibouti	0	0	0	0	0	0	0	0	0	0	0	0	0	0	0	0	1	0	7
United Arab Emirates																		
Dubai	0	0	0	0	0	0	0	0	0	0	0	0	0	0	1	0	1	0	1
Yemen Arab Republic																		
Hodeida	0	3	0	0	0	0	0	2	3	0	0	0	1	2	5	3	1	3	10

Table 21

Soviet Naval Ship Days Spent in Indian Ocean Area Ports, 1962–1980[a]

COUNTRY/PORT	62	63	64	65	66	67	68	69	70	71	72	73	74	75	76	77	78	79	80
Bangladesh																			
Chittagong	0	0	0	0	0	0	0	9	0	0	644	2222	1045	0	0	0	0	0	0
Egypt																			
Berenice	0	0	0	0	0	0	15	0	0	0	0	0	0	0	0	0	0	0	0
Hurghada	0	0	0	0	0	0	0	0	0	0	0	0	1574	0	0	0	0	0	0
Ras Shukheir	0	0	0	0	0	0	0	0	2	0	0	0	0	0	0	0	0	0	0
Safaga	0	0	0	0	0	0	0	8	0	0	0	0	0	0	0	0	0	0	0
Ethiopia																			
Assab	0	0	0	0	0	0	0	0	0	0	0	0	0	0	0	3	216	8	3
Dahlak Island	0	0	0	0	0	0	0	0	0	0	0	0	0	0	0	0	815	1336	2175
Massawa	0	0	0	4	11	6	14	10	7	8	5	5	7	0	5	0	83	0	91
India																			
Bombay	0	0	0	0	12	0	26	12	42	20	14	18	14	32	21	28	9	5	15
Cochin	0	0	0	0	0	0	0	0	0	0	0	0	0	0	8	0	0	0	13
Madras	0	0	0	0	0	0	20	0	0	0	0	18	0	16	0	0	0	5	0
Vishakhapatnam	0	0	0	0	0	0	0	0	21	0	0	0	0	5	0	0	0	0	0
Iran																			
Bandar 'Abbas	0	0	0	0	0	0	18	49	0	0	20	0	0	0	14	0	0	0	0
Iraq																			
Basra	0	0	0	0	0	0	27	0	0	83	89	6	323	26	41	14	0	0	0
Khawr al Amaya	0	0	0	0	0	0	0	0	0	0	0	9	0	0	0	0	0	0	0
Umm Qasr	0	0	0	0	0	0	0	39	15	25	63	202	115	89	77	70	23	50	0
Kenya																			
Mombasa	0	0	0	0	0	0	33	19	34	0	11	28	23	4	0	9	0	9	0
Kerguelen Islands																			
Port-aux-Français	0	0	0	0	0	0	0	0	0	0	5	0	20	46	0	6	0	0	0
Kuwait																			
Mīnā' al-Ahmadī	0	0	0	0	0	0	0	9	12	0	0	0	0	0	0	0	0	0	0
Malagasy Republic																			
Tamatave	0	0	0	0	0	0	1	13	6	0	0	0	0	0	0	0	0	0	4
Maldive Islands																			
Male	0	0	0	0	0	0	0	6	0	72	5	28	5	0	4	0	0	0	0

[a]Includes port visits in the Gulf of Aden, Red Sea, Persian Gulf, Arabian Sea, and Bay of Bengal.

Table 21 (Continued)

Soviet Naval Ship Days Spent in Indian Ocean Area Ports, 1962–1980

COUNTRY/PORT	62	63	64	65	66	67	68	69	70	71	72	73	74	75	76	77	78	79	80
Mauritius																			
Port Louis	0	0	0	0	0	9	11	81	129	49	154	139	84	80	64	45	19	64	37
Mozambique																			
Beira	0	0	0	0	0	0	0	0	0	0	0	0	0	0	0	3	14	33	33
Maputo	0	0	0	0	0	0	0	0	0	0	0	0	0	0	0	64	16	49	0
Nacala	0	0	0	0	0	0	0	0	0	0	0	0	0	0	0	37	0	12	0
Pakistan																			
Karachi	0	0	0	0	0	0	27	16	20	0	0	0	0	12	24	0	0	10	0
People's Dem. Rep. of Yemen																			
Aden	0	0	0	0	0	0	16	90	71	134	19	88	340	521	214	263	1121	542	1198
Perim Island	0	0	0	0	0	0	0	0	0	0	0	0	0	0	0	0	0	8	0
Seychelles																			
Victoria	0	0	0	0	0	12	0	0	0	0	0	0	0	0	0	7	30	56	27
Somalia																			
Berbera	0	0	0	0	0	0	0	27	74	87	153	806	851	1160	1433	938	0	0	0
Chisimaio (Kismayu)	0	0	0	0	0	0	0	7	0	22	0	0	0	61	124	45	0	0	0
Mogadiscio	0	0	0	0	0	0	27	30	41	45	96	33	40	54	33	12	0	0	0
Sri Lanka																			
Colombo	6	0	0	0	0	24	31	37	7	11	100	46	46	44	35	44	33	15	69
Sudan																			
Port Sudan	0	0	0	0	0	0	0	10	6	12	0	0	0	0	0	4	0	0	0
Tanzania																			
Dar es Salaam	0	0	0	0	0	0	32	0	16	0	0	0	0	0	0	0	0	0	0
Zanzibar	0	0	0	0	0	0	0	10	0	0	0	0	0	0	0	0	0	0	0
Terr. Afars & Issas																			
Djibouti	0	0	0	0	0	0	0	0	0	0	0	0	0	0	0	0	2	0	30
United Arab Emirates																			
Dubai	0	0	0	0	0	0	0	0	0	0	0	0	0	0	3	0	2	0	4
Yemen Arab Republic																			
Hodeida	0	11	0	0	0	0	0	8	11	0	0	0	4	6	103	22	1	17	49

Table 22

Average Length of Soviet Naval Ship Visits in Indian Ocean Area Ports, 1962–1980[a]

COUNTRY/PORT	62	63	64	65	66	67	68	69	70	71	72	73	74	75	76	77	78	79	80
Bangladesh																			
Chittagong	0	0	0	0	0	0	0	5	0	0	72	222	95	0	0	0	0	0	0
Egypt																			
Berenice	0	0	0	0	0	0	5	0	0	0	0	0	0	0	0	0	0	0	0
Hurghada	0	0	0	0	0	0	0	0	0	0	0	0	68	0	0	0	0	0	0
Ras Shukheir	0	0	0	0	0	0	0	0	2	0	0	0	0	0	0	0	0	0	0
Safâga	0	0	0	0	0	0	0	4	0	0	0	0	0	0	0	0	0	0	0
Ethiopia																			
Assab	0	0	0	0	0	0	0	0	0	0	0	0	0	0	0	3	13	3	3
Dahlak Island	0	0	0	·0	0	0	0	0	0	0	0	0	0	0	0	0	20	27	23
Massawa	0	0	0	4	11	6·	7	5	7	4	5	5	7	0	5	0	12	0	9
India																			
Bombay	0	0	0	0	6	0	4	4	6	10	7	6	7	8	7	6	5	5	5
Cochin	0	0	0	0	0	0	0	0	0	0	0	0	0	0	4	0	0	0	4
Madras	0	0	0	0	0	0	4	0	0	0	0	6	0	8	0	0	0	5	0
Vishakhapatnam	0	0	0	0	0	0	0	0	7	0	0	0	0	5	0	0	0	0	0
Iran																			
Bandar Abbas	0	0	0	0	0	0	6	5	0	0	7	0	0	0	5	0	0	0	0
Iraq																			
Basra	0	0	0	0	0	0	9	0	0	42	30	3	40	13	5	5	0	0	0
Khawr al Amaya	0	0	0	0	0	0	0	0	0	0	0	9	0	0	0	0	0	0	0
Umm Qasr	0	0	0	0	0	0	0	5	5	6	9	13	10	11	11	18	6	6	0
Kenya																			
Mombasa	0	0	0	0	0	0	7	6	5	0	6	6	6	4	0	3	0	5	0
Kerguelen Islands																			
Port-aux-Français	0	0	0	0	0	0	0	0	0	0	5	0	20	46	0	6	0	0	0
Kuwait																			
Mīnā' al-Ahmadī	0	0	0	0	0	0	0	5	12	0	0	0	0	0	0	0	0	0	0
Malagasy Republic																			
Tamatave	0	0	0	0	0	0	1	3	6	0	0	0	0	0	0	0	0	0	4
Maldive Islands																			
Male	0	0	0	0	0	0	0	6	0	14	5	7	5	0	4	0	0	0	0
Mauritius																			
Port Louis	0	0	0	0	0	3	3	7	6	4	6	13	6	8	6	6	6	5	7
Mozambique																			
Beira	0	0	0	0	0	0	0	0	0	0	0	0	0	0	0	3	14	8	8
Maputo	0	0	0	0	0	0	0	0	0	0	0	0	0	0	0	7	8	10	0
Nacala	0	0	0	0	0	0	0	0	0	0	0	0	0	0	0	9	0	6	0
Pakistan																			
Karachi	0	0	0	0	0	0	9	5	10	0	0	0	0	6	5	0	0	5	0
People's Dem. Rep. of Yemen																			
Aden	0	0	0	0	0	0	3	5	7	6	3	6	7	14	8	7	15	14	14
Perim Island	0	0	0	0	0	0	0	0	0	0	0	0	0	0	0	0	0	8	0
Seychelles																			
Victoria	0	0	0	0	0	3	0	0	0	0	0	0	0	0	0	7	10	7	7
Somalia																			
Berbera	0	0	0	0	0	0	0	3	8	6	9	18	14	24	19	18	0	0	0
Chisimaio (Kismayu)	0	0	0	0	0	0	0	4	0	11	0	0	0	12	14	5	0	0	0
Mogadiscio	0	0	0	0	0	0	9	4	10	8	7	7	6	11	6	4	0	0	0

[a]Includes port visits in the Gulf of Aden, Red Sea, Persian Gulf, Arabian Sea, and Bay of Bengal.

Table 22 (Continued)

Average Length of Soviet Naval Ship Visits in Indian Ocean Area Ports, 1962–1980

COUNTRY/PORT	62	63	64	65	66	67	68	69	70	71	72	73	74	75	76	77	78	79	80
Sri Lanka																			
Colombo	6	0	0	0	0	4	6	4	2	4	6	6	5	4	3	4	5	5	4
Sudan																			
Port Sudan	0	0	0	0	0	0	0	5	6	6	0	0	0	0	0	2	0	0	0
Tanzania																			
Dar es Salaam	0	0	0	0	0	0	8	0	8	0	0	0	0	0	0	0	0	0	0
Zanzibar	0	0	0	0	0	0	0	5	0	0	0	0	0	0	0	0	0	0	0
Terr. Afars & Issas																			
Djibouti	0	0	0	0	0	0	0	0	0	0	0	0	0	0	0	0	2	0	4
United Arab Emirates																			
Dubai	0	0	0	0	0	0	0	0	0	0	0	0	0	0	3	0	2	0	4
Yemen Arab Republic																			
Hodeida	0	4	0	0	0	0	0	4	4	0	0	0	4	3	21	7	1	6	5

Table 23

Cumulative Totals of Soviet Naval Port Visits
in the Indian Ocean Area By Port, 1962-1980

Port	Total Ship Days	Comments
1. Berbera, Somalia	5,529	The Soviet presence in Somalia began in 1968. In the early 1970s, the Soviets began an almost constant presence in Berbera and used this port for fleet logistical support. Berbera remained a forward base supporting the Indian Ocean Squadron until 1977, when the Somalis evicted the Soviets because of the latter's support of Ethiopia in the Ethiopian-Somali War. The loss of these facilities was a setback for the Soviets. The alternative facilities they developed in Ethiopia were less ideally located than Berbera.
2. Aden, People's Democratic Republic of Yemen (South Yemen)	4,617	Port visits to Aden were significant as early as 1969 and were quite heavy in the early 1970s, indicating that the port was used to support the Indian Ocean Squadron. Visits increased after the Soviet expulsion from Somalia, reflecting the logistical problems associated with the loss of Berbera.
3. Dahlak Island, Ethiopia	4,326	The intense naval activity at this island indicates that the Soviets are developing a logistical base here for support to their squadron. This base should provide the same degree of support that Berbera did, although Dhalak is not as ideally located.
4. Chittagong, Bangladesh	3,920	This activity reflects Soviet assistance in clearing Bengali ports, which had been damaged during the Indo-Pakistani War. It does not appear that the Soviet Navy was granted concessions for this assistance, since there have been no port visits to Bangladesh since 1974.
5. Hurghada, Egypt	1,574	This activity reflects Soviet mineclearing of the Gulf of Suez in 1974. No visits have been made to the port since the operation was completed, and no visits have been made to Egypt since the expulsion in 1976.
6. Port Louis, Mauritius	965	Good will/operational visits, which began in 1967 and were in support of naval operations in the southern Indian Ocean.
7. Umm Qasr, Iraq	768	Good will/operational visits, probably to maintain Soviet influence and an occasional naval presence in the Persian Gulf. These visits led to speculation that the Soviets were developing a forward base in Iraq, but there is little evidence to support such speculation.
8. Basra, Iraq	609	See entry 7.
9. Colombo, Sri Lanka	548	Good will/operational visits, which began in 1962.
10. Mogadiscio, Somalia	411	Good will/operational visits from 1968 to 1977. These visits ended when the Soviets were expelled from Berbera. (See entry 1.)
11. Bombay, India	268	Good will/operational visits, which began in 1966.
12. Chisimaio (Kismayu), Somalia	259	See entry 10.
13. Massawa, Ethiopia	256	Official and good will/operational visits, which began in 1965. Many of these were for participation in Ethiopian Navy Day, a holiday of considerable regional significance. These visits became more frequent in 1978, when the Soviets, as a result of their assistance to the Marxist Ethiopian government in its war with Somalia, began using Ethiopia to support their Indian Ocean Squadron.
14. Hodeida, Yemen Arab Republic (North Yemen)	232	These visits, which began in 1963, became more frequent in 1976, possibly reflecting Soviet assistance to the Yemeni Navy.

Table 23 (Continued)

Cumulative Totals of Soviet Naval Port Visits
in the Indian Ocean Area By Port, 1962-1980

Port	Total Ship Days	Comments
15. Assab, Ethiopia	230	Good will/operational visits, which began in 1977.
16. Mombasa, Kenya	170	Good will/operational visits, which began in 1968.
17. Victoria, Seychelles	132	Official and good will/operational visits, which began in 1967.
18. Maputo, Mozambique	129	Good will/operational visits from 1977 onward, possibly a show of support for Mozambique.
19. Male, Maldive Islands	120	Good will/operational visits from 1969 onward.
20. Karachi, Pakistan	109	Official and good will/operational visits, which began in 1968.
21. Bandar 'Abbas, Iran	101	Good will/operational visits from 1968 to 1976.
22. Beira, Mozambique	83	See entry 18.
23. Port-aux-Français, Kerguelen Islands	77	Good will/operational visits, which began in 1972.
24. Madras, India	59	Good will/operational visits, which began in 1968.
25. Nacala, Mozambique	49	See entry 18.
26. Dar es Salaam, Tanzania	48	Good will/operational visits, which began in 1968.
27. Port Sudan, Sudan	32	Good will/operational visits, which began in 1969.
28. Djibouti, Territory of Afars and Issas	32	Good will/operational visits, which began in 1978.
29. Vishakhapatnam, India	26	Good will/operational visits in 1970 and 1975.
30. Tamatave, Malagasy Republic	24	Good will/operational visits, which began in 1968.
31. Cochin, India	21	Good will/operational visits in 1976 and 1980.
32. Mīnā' al-Ahmadī	21	Good will/operational visits in 1969 and 1970.
33. Berenice, Egypt	15	Official and good will/operational visits in 1968.
34. Zanzibar, Tanzania	10	Good will/operational visit in 1969.
35. Khawr al Amaya, Iraq	9	Good will/operational visit in 1973.
36. Dubai, United Arab Emirates	9	Good will/operational visits, which began in 1976.
37. Safâga, Egypt	8	Good will/operational visit in 1969.
38. Perim Island, People's Democratic Republic of Yemen	8	Operational visit in 1979.
39. Ras Shukheir, Egypt	2	Good will/operational visit in 1970.

Table 24

Cumulative Totals of Soviet Naval Port Visits
in the Indian Ocean Area By Country, 1962–1980

	Country	Total Ship Days
1.	Somalia	6,199
2.	Ethiopia	4,812
3.	People's Democratic Republic of Yemen (South Yemen)	4,625
4.	Bangladesh	3,920
5.	Egypt (Red Sea coast only)	1,599
6.	Iraq	1,386
7.	Mauritius	965
8.	Sri Lanka	548
9.	India	374
10.	Mozambique	261
11.	Yemen Arab Republic (North Yemen)	232
12.	Kenya	170
13.	Seychelles	132
14.	Maldive Islands	120
15.	Pakistan	109
16.	Iran	101
17.	Kerguelen Islands	77
18.	Tanzania	58
19.	Sudan	32
20.	Territory of Afars and Issas	32
21.	Malagasy Republic	24
22.	Kuwait	21
23.	United Arab Emirates	9

Table 25

Cumulative Totals of Soviet Naval Port Visits
by Country, Worldwide, 1953-1980

	Country	Total Ship Days	Comments
1.	Egypt	40,565	Following the loss of the Arab-Israeli War in June 1967, Egypt opened its ports to the Soviet Navy and granted the Soviets other concessions in return for assistance. From that time until 1976, Alexandria was crucial to the support of the Soviet Mediterranean Fleet. The Soviet naval presence was also heavy at Port Said and Matruh, possibly reflecting port security measures. The Soviets also visited Egyptian ports on the Red Sea and assisted in mine-clearing of the Gulf of Suez in 1974. Due to deteriorating Soviet-Egyptian relations, the Soviet Navy was evicted from Alexandria in 1976 and has been denied use of Egyptian ports since that time. No Soviet port visits to Egypt have occurred since 1976.
2.	Syria	13,739	The Soviets began using Syrian ports for support of their Mediterranean Fleet and for ship repair after the June 1967 Arab-Israeli War. Soviet use was heavier after expulsion from Alexandria in 1976. Tartus remains the center of logistical support for the Mediterranean Fleet through 1980. Although it is not as ideally located as Alexandria, it appears adequate for such purposes.
3.	Albania	11,283	Albanian ports were used to stage a Soviet submarine force in the Mediterranean Sea from 1958 until 1961. This force was discontinued after the Albanians evicted the Soviets in 1961. No visits to Albania have occurred since that time.
4.	Guinea	8,488	The Soviet naval presence in Conakry began in 1970, when a patrol was established in response to Guinean pleas for assistance. Since that time it has been a focal point of Soviet naval activity along West Africa. Conakry was used as a staging area for Soviet naval forces during the Angolan Civil War in 1975 and 1976. It remained open to Soviet naval ships through 1980.
5.	Yugoslavia	8,062	Soviet use of Yugoslav ports for overhaul and yard work, which began in 1973, continued through 1980.
6.	Cuba	7,781	Since the first Soviet naval combatant deployment to Cuba in 1969 until May 1981, twenty-one deployments occurred. The Soviets also established a modest but constant non-combatant naval presence in the area. A host of Cuban ports have been visited, but Soviet activity centered around Havana, Cienfuegos, a major Cuban naval port on the southern coast, and Mariel, on the northern coast. Activity in Cienfuegos prompted speculation that the Soviets are establishing a facility at this port. However, such a Soviet base was not operational in 1981.
7.	Somalia	6,199	The Soviet presence in Somalia began in 1968. In the early 1970s, the Soviets began an almost constant presence in the vicinity of Somalia and used Berbera to support this operation. Berbera remained a forward base supporting the Indian Ocean Squadron until 1977, when the Somalis evicted the Soviets because of the latter's support of Ethiopia in the Ethiopian-Somali War. Access to two other Somali ports, Mogadiscio and Chisimaio, was also denied at that time. The loss of access to these ports was a setback for the Soviets. Although they developed alternative facilities in Ethiopia and Aden, these were less ideally located than the Somalian facilities at Berbera.
8.	Singapore	5,078	Overhaul/yard work on auxilary ships. This access ended in 1980 possibly as part of a reaction to the Soviet invasion of Afghanistan

Table 25 (Continued)

Cumulative Totals of Soviet Naval Port Visits
by Country, Worldwide, 1953–1980

Country	Total Ship Days	Comments
9. Ethiopia	4,812	The intense Soviet naval activity at Ethiopian ports since 1977 indicates that the Soviets intend to use Ethiopia as a primary logistical base for supporting their Indian Ocean Squadron. These ports should provide the same degree of support as Berbera did, although their location in the southern Red Sea is not as ideal.
10. People's Democratic Republic of Yemen (South Yemen)	4,625	Port visit activity to Aden in the early 1970s was quite heavy, indicating that the port was used to support the Indian Ocean Squadron. Use of Aden increased after the Soviet expulsion from Somalia.
11. Bangladesh	3,920	Soviet assistance in clearing Bengali ports which were damaged in the Indo-Pakistani War of 1971. It does not appear that the Soviets were granted concessions for this assistance, since there have been no visits to Bengali ports since 1974.
12. Angola	3,394	Since the conclusion of the Angolan Civil War, the Soviet naval presence in Angola has been fairly constant, indicating that the Soviets have unrestricted access to the port and intend to use it as a base of operations in the Gulf of Guinea. The base is ideal for such operations, particularly those that might be launched against South Africa.
13. People's Democratic Republic of Vietnam	2,866	The heavy use of Vietnamese ports began in 1979, after the end of the Sino-Vietnamese War. This probably indicates Soviet intentions to maintain a constant naval presence here and possibly to develop a forward base at one or more Vietnamese ports. These would ease the logistical problems of the Indian Ocean Squadron and would enable the Soviets to react more quickly to Indian Ocean crises. They would also contribute to the Soviet aim of isolating the People's Republic of China and would increase the maritime threat posed against Japan and the U.S. Seventh Fleet.
14. Algeria	2,252	This activity reflects a routine but rather heavy use of Algerian ports for supply of the Mediterranean Fleet since 1967.
15. Tunisia	1,695	Soviet visits to Tunisian ports became more frequent in 1976, when the Soviets were expelled from Alexandria. Overhaul/yard work on Soviet ships began in Menzel-Bourguiba in 1977 and was constant through 1980.
16. Iraq	1,386	Good will visits and some assistance rendered at Umm Qasr. The intention of the visits is probably to maintain Soviet influence in the nation and an occasional presence in the Persian Gulf. This activity has led to speculation that the Soviets were developing a forward base at Umm Qasr, but in 1980, there was little evidence to support this speculation.
17. Canary Islands	1,011	Ports in the Canary Islands have been used since 1969 to support naval operations along West Africa and elsewhere in the Atlantic.
18. Mauritius	965	A heavy use of Port Louis to support Soviet naval operations in the southern Indian Ocean since 1967.
19. Greece	742	Good will/operational visits since 1972. Since the loss of access to Alexandria, the Soviets have made greater use of Greek ports to support the Mediterranean fleet and use Ermoúpolis for overhaul/yard work on auxiliary ships.
20. Morocco	666	Good will/operational visits in support of naval operations in the Atlantic and off West Africa, which began in 1964.
21. Italy	603	Good will/operational visits in support of fleet operations in the central Mediterranean, which began in 1964.

Table 25 (Continued)

Cumulative Totals of Soviet Naval Port Visits
By Country, Worldwide, 1953–1980

	Country	Total Ship Days	Comments
22.	Sri Lanka	548	Good will/operational visits which began in 1962.
23.	Sweden	540	Overhaul/yard work on auxiliary ships is accomplished in Gothenburg, while many official visits have been made to Stockholm since 1954.
24.	Benin	462	Good will/operational visits to Cotonou.
25.	Senegal	446	Good will/operational visits by hydrographic and space support ships to support their operations in the Atlantic.
26.	Gibraltar	425	Good will/operational visits in support of naval operations in the western Mediterranean and the Atlantic.
27.	Canada	417	Official and good will/operational visits to both the Atlantic and Pacific coasts of Canada.
28.	India	374	Good will/operational visits, which began in 1966.
29.	Japan	330	Good will/operational visits to Japan began in 1966. Overhaul/yard work on auxiliary ships probably began in 1977.
30.	Uruguay	300	Good will/operational visits by space support ships operating in the Atlantic.
31.	Mozambique	261	Good will/operational visits, which began in 1977, possibly as a show of support for Mozambique.
32.	Finland	258	Official visits which began in 1954. Rauma has been used for overhaul/yard work.
33.	Yemen Arab Republic	232	These visits, which began in 1963, became more frequent in 1976, possibly reflecting Soviet assistance to the Yemeni Navy.
34.	Spain	213	Good will/operational visits to both the Atlantic and Mediterranean ports of Spain in support of naval operations.
35.	France	192	Official and good will/operational visits to the Atlantic and Mediterranean ports of France.
36.	United Kingdom	170	Official and good will/operational visits, probably a part of the port visit program to NATO nations discussed in Chapter 2.
37.	Kenya	170	Good will/operational visits, which began in 1968.
38.	Iceland	159	Good will/operational visits by hydrographic ships.
39.	Norway	136	See entry 36.
40.	Seychelles	132	Good will/operational visits, which began in 1967.
41.	Faeroe Islands	130	See entry 38.
42.	Mexico	121	Good will/operational visits to both the Atlantic and Pacific ports of Mexico.
43.	Maldive Islands	120	Good will/operational visits, which began in 1969.
44.	Sierra Leone	119	Official and good will/operational visits, which began in 1959.
45.	Pakistan	109	Good will/operational visits, which began in 1968.
46.	São Thomé	103	Good will/operational visits, which began in 1978.

Table 25 (Continued)

Cumulative Totals of Soviet Naval Port Visits
By Country, Worldwide, 1953-1980

	Country	Total Ship Days	Comments
47.	Iran	101	Good will/operational visits, which began in 1968.
48.	Nigeria	89	Good will/operational visits from 1969 to 1976.
49.	Ivory Coast	89	See entry 30.
50.	United States	83	Good will/operational visits to the Atlantic and Pacific ports of the United States. An official visit was made to Boston in 1975.
51.	North Korea	82	See entry 38.
52.	Denmark	79	See entry 36.
53.	Kerguelen Islands	77	Good will/operational visits, which began in 1972.
54.	Curaçao	74	See entry 38.
55.	Bermuda	70	See entry 38.
56.	Equatorial Guinea	66	Good will/operational visits by naval combatants from 1970 to 1974.
57.	Brazil	61	See entry 38.
58.	Tanzania	58	Good will/operational visits, which began in 1968.
59.	Netherlands	56	See entry 36.
60.	Fiji Islands	55	Good will/operational visits associated with naval operations in the South Pacific.
61.	St. Helena	49	Good will/operational visits, mostly by space support ships.
62.	Colombia	49	See entry 38.
63.	Peru	48	Good will/operational visits, which began in 1970.
64.	Congo	47	Good will/operational visits by naval combatants from 1972 to 1976.
65.	Kampuchea	34	Good will/operational visits, which began in 1980.
66.	Sudan	32	Good will/operational visits, which began in 1969.
67.	Territory of Afars and Issas	32	Good will/operational visits in 1978 and 1980.
68.	Ecuador	29	Good will/operational visits, which began in 1973.
69.	Ireland	26	See entry 38.
70.	Cape Verde Islands	25	Good will/operational visits by naval combatant groups.
71.	Malagasy Republic	24	Good will/operational visits, which began in 1968.
72.	Kuwait	21	Good will/operational visits in 1969 and 1970.
73.	Indonesia	20	Official visits in 1959.
74.	Turkey	20	An official and a good will/operational visit.
75.	Venezuela	20	See entry 38.
76.	People's Republic of China	18	Official visits in 1956.

Table 25 (Continued)

Cumulative Totals of Soviet Naval Port Visits

By Country, Worldwide, 1953–1980

Country	Total Ship Days	Comments
77. Guinea–Bissau	16	Official and good will/operational visits by naval combatants from 1976 to 1979.
78. Jamaica	13	Good will/operational visits, which began in 1962.
79. Libya	13	Good will/operational visits, which began in 1969.
80. Liberia	13	See entry 25.
81. Samoa	12	Good will/operational visit in 1973.
82. Australia	12	See entry 38.
83. Falkland Islands	12	Good will/operational visit by hydrographic ships in 1972.
84. Argentina	12	See entry 38.
85. Barbados	10	Good will/operational visits, which began in 1969.
86. Chile	10	Good will/operational visits in 1969 and 1973.
87. New Caledonia	10	Good will/operational visit in 1970.
88. Tahiti	10	See entry 38.
89. Azores	9	See entry 38.
90. United Arab Emirates	9	Good will/operational visits, which began in 1976.
91. Southwest Africa	8	Good will/operational visit in 1972.
92. Trinidad	8	See entry 25.
93. Tasmania	8	See entry 38.
94. Cambodia	6	Good will/operational visit in 1969.
95. Martinique	6	Good will/operational visit by naval combatants in 1969.
96. New Zealand	6	Good will/operational visits in 1971 and 1973.
97. Malta	6	Good will/operational visits in 1978 and 1980.
98. Mauritania	5	Good will/operational visit in 1972.
99. Cameroon	5	Good will/operational visit by a naval combatant in 1975.
100. Gambia	3	Good will/operational visit in 1971.
101. Surinam	3	See entry 30.
102. Aruba	2	Good will/operational visit in 1978.
103. Cyprus	2	Evacuation of Soviet citizens in 1976 and a good will/operational visit in 1979.

Bibliography
and Recommended Reading

"About 30 Soviet Backfire Bombers Stationed in Far East, JDA's View." *Mainichi* (Tokyo), 15 July 1980, p. 2.

"Angolan Faction Is Said to Push Deep into South Against Little Resistance." *New York Times,* 15 February 1976, p. 52.

Baker, A. J. *The Yom Kippur War.* New York: Random House, Inc., 1974.

Binder, David. "Aid to Angolans Ended by House in Rebuff to Ford." *New York Times,* 28 January 1976, pp. 1, 3.

Blechman, Barry M., and Levinson, Stephanie E. "Soviet Submarine Visits to Cuba." *U.S. Naval Institute Proceedings* 101:9 (September 1975):30–39.

Bradsher, Henry S. "Soviets Post Ships Off Viet Coast." *Washington Star,* 7 February 1979, pp. 1, 8.

Breyer, Siegfried. *Guide to the Soviet Navy.* Annapolis, Md.: Naval Institute Press, 1970.

Burt, Richard. "Soviet Places Ships Off Vietnam Coast." *New York Times,* 8 February 1979, p. 13.

_____. "Soviet Ships Arrive at Cam Ranh Bay." *New York Times,* 29 March 1979, p. 7.

"Castro Says Cuba Is Open to Soviet." *New York Times,* 29 July 1969, p. 19.

Churchill, Randolph S., and Churchill, Winston S. *The Six Day War.* Boston: Houghton Mifflin Company, 1967.

Cooley, John. "Soviets Beefing Up Reconnaissance in Far East." *Christian Science Monitor,* 22 February 1979, p. 10.

Corddry, Charles W. "Soviet Sends Warships to Vietnam Base." *Baltimore Sun,* 28 March 1979, p. 1.

Cottrell, Alvin J., and Moorer, Thomas H. *U.S. Overseas Bases: Problems of Projecting American Military Power Abroad.* Washington Papers, vol. 47. Washington, D.C.: Center for Strategic and International Studies, Georgetown University, 1977.

"Cuban MiG May Be Attack Plane." *Baltimore Sun,* 1 November 1978, p. A2.

"Cubans Said to Fight in Eritrea." *New York Times,* 17 March 1978, p. A7.

"Cuban Troops Counterbalance to South African Contingents." *Herald* (Salisbury), 29 March 1979, p. 6.

Dismukes, Bradford, and McConnell, James, eds. *Soviet Naval Diplomacy.* New York: Pergamon Press, 1979.

Dragnich, George S. _The Soviet Union's Quest for Access to Naval Facilities in Egypt Prior to the June War of 1967._ Arlington, Va.: Center for Naval Analyses, 1974.

Ellis, Harry B. _Challenge in the Middle East._ New York: Ronald Press Company, 1960.

"Ethiopia Says It Now Holds Entire Ogaden Region." _New York Times,_ 25 March 1978, p. 4.

"Expansion of Soviet Pacific Fleet Enumerated, Discussed." Broadcast on Beijing _Xinhua_ in English, 7 July 1979. Cited in _Foreign Broadcast Information Service Daily Report: Vol. 2, People's Republic of China,_ no. 132, 9 July 1979, p. C1.

Fairhall, David. _Russian Sea Power._ Boston: Gambit, Inc., 1971.

_____. "Transformed Role for the Soviet Navy." _Manchester Guardian Weekly,_ 29 January 1978, p. 7.

George, James L., ed. _Problems of Sea Power As We Approach the Twenty-First Century._ Washington, D.C.: American Enterprise Institute for Public Policy Research, 1978.

Golan, Galia. _Yom Kippur and After: The Soviet Union and the Middle East Crisis._ Cambridge: Cambridge University Press, 1977.

Gorshkov, Sergei G. "For the Security of Navigation on the High Seas." _Izvestiya,_ 8 July 1972, p. 4.

_____. "Greeting the Twenty-fifth Congress of the CPSU." _Morskoy sbornik_ 2 (1976):8–13.

_____. "Long Voyages Are a School for Naval Training." _Red Star,_ 16 April 1970, p. 2.

_____. "Loyal Sons of the Motherland." _Pravda,_ 24 July 1965, p. 2.

_____. "The Maritime Might of the Land of the Soviets." _Pravda,_ 28 July 1974, p. 2.

_____. _Morskaya moshch gosudarstva [Sea Power of the State]._ Moscow: Voyennoye Izdatel'stvo, 1976.

_____. "A Most Important Factor of the Navy's Combat Readiness and Combat Efficiency." _Tyl i snabzheniye sovetskikh vooruzhennykh sil_ 7 (1976):3–9.

_____. "Navies in War and Peace." _Morskoy sbornik_ 2 (1972):20–29.

_____. "Navies in War and Peace." _Morskoy sbornik_ 12 (1972):14–22.

_____. "Navy Day Speech on Moscow Domestic Television Service, 27 July 1975."

_____. "The Navy on a Big Cruise." _Tekhnika i vooruzheniye_ 7 (1970):1–3.

_____. "The Oceanic Guard of the Homeland." _Agitator_ 13 (July 1974):30–33.

_____. "On Ocean Watch." _Red Star,_ 11 February 1976, p. 2.

_____. "On the High Seas and Oceans." _Pravda,_ 14 February 1968, p. 3.

_____. "Ruggedness of Naval Life." _Ogonek_ 31 (July 1972):5.

_____. _Sea Power of the State._ See _Morskaya moshch gosudarstva._

Gwertzman, Bernard. "Soviet Proposes Plan to Resolve Arms Pact Snag." _New York Times,_ 24 January 1976, pp. 1, 3.

Hackett, General Sir John, and Other Top Ranking Generals and Advisors. _The Third World War, August 1985._ New York: Berkley Books, 1980.

Herrick, R. W. _Soviet Naval Strategy._ Annapolis, Md.: Naval Institute Press, 1968.

Holzman, Franklyn D. "Soviet Trade and Aid Policies." In _Soviet-American Rivalry_ *in the Middle East,* edited by J. C. Hurewitz, pp. 104–120. New York: Frederick A. Praeger, 1969.

Homan, Richard L. "New Soviet Base Perturbs Hill Unit." *Washington Post,* 9 July 1975, p. A31.

Hoskins, H. L. *Soviet Economic Penetration in the Middle East.* Washington, D.C.: Government Printing Office, 1959.

Hovey, Graham. "Brzezinski Asserts That Soviet General Leads Ethiopia Units." *New York Times,* 25 February 1978, pp. 1, 5.

_____. "Soviet Assures U.S. Ethiopians Will Stop at Somalia's Border." *New York Times,* 11 February 1978, pp. 1, 3.

_____. "Tough Job for Cuba in Eritrea Seen." *New York Times,* 2 April 1978, p. 7.

_____. "U.S. Officials Say Soviet Mounts a Major Arms Airlift to Ethiopia." *New York Times,* 14 December 1977, pp. 1, 10.

"How to View Emergence of Soviet Navy." *Nihon keizai,* 17 November 1979, p. 2.

Hurewitz, J. C. *Middle East Politics: The Military Dimension.* New York: Frederick A. Praeger, 1969.

Interview with Admiral Elmo R. Zumwalt, U.S. Navy (Retired). Arlington, Virginia, 22 October 1977.

Interview with Admiral Thomas H. Moorer, U.S. Navy (Retired). Washington, D.C., 9 January 1978.

"Japan-Soviet Relations." *Daily Yomiuri* (Tokyo), 9 December 1979, p. 2.

"Japan Warns of USSR in Far East." *Christian Science Monitor,* 7 August 1980, p. 5.

Ji Yanfeng. "Soviet Expansionist Strategy in the 'Dumbbell' Area." *Renmin Ribao* (Beijing), 22 June 1979, p. 6. Translated in *Foreign Broadcast Information Service Daily Report: Vol. 1, People's Republic of China,* no. 127, 29 June 1979, pp. C2–C4.

Kaufman, Michael. "Somalis Abandoning Northern Ogaden." *New York Times,* 9 March 1978, p. A4.

Kelly, Anne M. *Port Visits and the "Internationalist Mission" of the Soviet Navy.* Arlington, Va.: Center for Naval Analyses, 1976.

Kilmarx, R. A. *Soviet–United States Naval Balance.* Washington, D.C.: Center for Strategic and International Studies, Georgetown University, 1975.

Kimche, David, and Bawly, Dan. *The Sandstorm: The Arab-Israeli War of 1967, Prelude and Aftermath.* New York: Stein and Day, 1968.

Kramer, Barry. "Regulars of China, Vietnam May Clash, Raising Specter of War Involving Soviets." *Wall Street Journal,* 22 February 1979, p. 3.

Lan Hai. "The Special Task Force of the Soviet Union Is Striving to Dominate the Seas." *Renmin Ribao* (Beijing), 5 July 1979, p. 6. Translated in *Foreign Broadcast Information Service Daily Report: Vol. 1, People's Republic of China,* no. 137, 16 July 1979, pp. C1–C2.

Lenin, V. I. "Speech Delivered at a Meeting of Activists of the Moscow Organization of the RCP(B), December 6, 1920." In *Lenin Collected Works,* vol. 31, pp. 438–459. Moscow: Progress Publishers, 1966.

Luttwak, Edward N. *The Political Uses of Seapower.* Baltimore: Johns Hopkins University Press, 1975.

McCGwire, Michael, ed. *Soviet Naval Developments: Capability and Context*. New York: Praeger Publishers, Inc., 1973.

McCGwire, Michael; Booth, Ken; and McDonnell, John, eds. *Soviet Naval Policy: Objectives and Constraints*. New York: Praeger Publishers, Inc., 1975.

McCGwire, Michael, and McDonnell, John, eds. *Soviet Naval Influence: Domestic and Foreign Dimensions*. New York: Praeger Publishers, Inc., 1977.

McConnell, James M., and Kelly, Anne M. *Naval Diplomacy in the Indo-Pakistani Crisis*. Arlington, Va.: Center for Naval Analyses, 1973.

McGruther, Kenneth R. *The Evolving Soviet Navy*. Newport, R.I.: Naval War College Press, 1978.

Markham, James M. "U.S. Evacuates 263 from Beirut on Naval Vessel." *New York Times*, 21 June 1976, pp. 1, 14.

Middleton, Drew. "Egypt Begins a Hurried Search to Add to Sources of Weapons." *New York Times*, 28 March 1976, pp. 1, 8.

_____. "New Soviet Role in Africa Alleged." *New York Times*, 10 December 1975, p. 11.

_____. "Soviet Extends Power of Navy to All Oceans." *New York Times*, 20 March 1979, p. 7.

_____. "Soviet Foothold Is Worrying NATO." *New York Times*, 19 January 1976, p. 11.

_____. "Soviet Position in Aden and Kabul Seen Improving." *New York Times*, 31 July 1978, p. A2.

Moore, John E., ed. *Jane's Fighting Ships, 1980–1981*. New York: Franklin Watts, Inc., 1980.

"More Cubans Reported on Way." *New York Times*, 8 February 1978, p. A5.

"Moscow Beefs Up Its Pacific Fleet." *Beijing Review* (10 August 1979):26–27.

"Movement Loses Port." *New York Times*, 15 August 1975, p. 5.

Murphy, Paul J., ed. *Naval Power in Soviet Policy*. Studies in Communist Affairs, vol. 2. Washington, D.C.: Government Printing Office, 1978.

"'Myth' Cannot Cover Up Reality." Broadcast on Beijing *Xinhua* in English, 19 July 1979. Cited in *Foreign Broadcast Information Service Daily Report: Vol. 1, People's Republic of China*, no. 118, 20 June 1979, p. C1.

"Neto Visits Soviet Ships in Luanda Harbor." *Jornal de Angola*, 6 April 1979, pp. 1, 6. Translated in *Joint Publications Research Service: Translations on Sub-Saharan Africa*, 10 May 1979, pp. 19–20.

Nitze, Paul H.; Sullivan, Leonard, Jr.; and the Atlantic Council Working Group on Securing the Seas. *Securing the Seas: The Soviet Naval Challenge and Western Alliance Options*. Boulder, Colo.: Westview Press, 1979.

"Not Regarded as Actual Threat, JDA Cautions." *Mainichi* (Tokyo), 2 October 1979, p. 1.

Oberdorfer, Don. "Somalia Agrees to Let U.S. Use Ports, Airfields." *Washington Post*, 22 August 1980, pp. A1, A20.

_____. "U.S. Concern Grows over Da Nang Visit by Soviet Vessels." *Washington Post*, 10 March 1979, p. A16.

_____. "U.S. Sees Little Likelihood of Soviet Attack." *Washington Post*, 22 February 1979, pp. A1, A12.

Petersen, Charles C. *The Soviet Port Clearing Operation in Bangladesh, March 1972–December 1973.* Arlington, Va.: Center for Naval Analyses, 1974.

———. *The Soviet Union and the Reopening of the Suez Canal: Mineclearing Operations in the Gulf of Suez.* Arlington, Va.: Center for Naval Analyses, 1975.

Polmar, Norman. *Soviet Naval Power: Challenge for the 1970s.* Rev. ed. New York: Crane, Russak and Co., 1974.

"President Ahmed and Sékou Touré in Benin." *Horoya,* 7 March 1979, pp. 2–5. Translated in *Joint Publications Research Service: Translations on Sub-Saharan Africa,* 8 June 1979, pp. 20–23.

Prina, L. Edgar. "U.S. Says Hanoi Opens Ports to Soviet Ships." *San Diego Union,* 22 March 1979, p. 2.

"Red Ships 'Sighted' Off SA's West Caost." *Cape Times,* 11 April 1979, p. 1.

Report on Luanda Domestic Service in Portuguese, 3 April 1979. Translated in *Foreign Broadcast Information Service: Vol. 8, Southern Africa Daily Report,* 4 April 1979, p. E1.

Rivero, Horacio. "Why a U.S. Fleet in the Mediterranean?" *U.S. Naval Institute Proceedings* 103 (May 1977):66–89.

Russia in the Caribbean: Part I, Panelists' Findings, Recommendations, and Comments. Washington, D.C.: Center for Strategic and International Studies, Georgetown University, 1973.

"Russians Give Cuba Its Second Submarine." *Washington Star,* 26 April 1979, p. A7.

"Russian Ships Cross Frigate's Firing Line." *Washington Star,* 13 April 1979, p. A10.

"Sadat Says Soviet Pilots Are Flying for Ethiopia in Fighting with Somalia." *New York Times,* 7 February 1978, p. 4.

Safire, William. "Brezhnev's Big Ear." *New York Times,* 6 September 1979, p. 21.

Savichev, G. "Soviet Ships' Mozambique Call." *Red Star,* 22 April 1979, p. 3.

———. "Soviet Ships Visit Angola." *Red Star,* 11 April 1979, p. 3.

Schiebel, Joseph. "Convergence or Confrontation." *Intercollegiate Review* (Winter 1968–1969):101–113.

———. "The USSR in World Affairs: New Tactics, New Strategy." In *The Soviet Union: The Seventies and Beyond,* edited by Bernard Eissenstat, pp. 71–92. Lexington, Mass.: Lexington Books, 1975.

Scott, Harriet Fast, and Scott, William F. *The Armed Forces of the USSR.* Boulder, Colo.: Westview Press, 1979.

"Seven Soviet Warships Arrive for Week's Visit in Cuba." *New York Times,* 21 July 1969, pp. 19, 27.

Sheehan, Neil. "Admiral Says Soviet Shadowing Often Imperils Ships in Sixth Fleet." *New York Times,* 1 June 1967, p. 18.

———. "U.S. Sees Gain in Nuclear Submarine Operations Off East Coast." *New York Times,* 4 October 1970, p. 23.

"Showing the Soviet Flag." *New York Times,* 26 July 1969, p. 2.

Smith, Hedrick. "U.S. Says Castro Has Transferred 60's Policy of Intervention to Africa." *New York Times,* 17 November 1977, pp. A1, A11.

Smith, Robert M. "U.S. Warns Soviet Not to Build Base for Subs in Cuba." *New York Times,* 26 September 1970, pp. 1, 8.

Sokolovskiy, V. D. *Soviet Military Strategy*. Edited by Harriet Fast Scott. New York: Crane, Russak and Company, Inc., 1975.

"Somalis Abandoning Northern Ogaden." *New York Times*, 9 March 1978, p. A4.

"Somalis Say They Killed 1000 in Ogaden Battles." *New York Times*, 16 April 1978, p. 8.

"Soviet Aircraft Carrier Reported in the South China Sea." Broadcast on Beijing *Xinhua* in Chinese, 20 June 1979. Translated in *Foreign Broadcast Information Service Daily Report: Vol. 1, People's Republic of China*, no. 123, 25 June 1979, p. C1.

"Soviet Carrier at Aden." *New York Times*, 31 May 1979. Cited in *U.S. Naval Institute Proceedings* 105 (August 1979):124.

"Soviet Fleet Heads for Gulf." *New York Times*, 29 July 1969, p. 74.

"Soviet Reported to Yield on Cuba." *New York Times*, 19 October 1970, p. 9.

"Soviet Said to Begin Airlift to Vietnam." *Baltimore Sun*, 23 February 1979, p. 2.

"Soviet Ships Linger Off Vietnam." *Christian Science Monitor*, 8 February 1979, p. 2.

"Soviet Ships Sighted Off SA Coast." *Rand Daily Mail*, 12 April 1979, p. 4.

"Soviet Ships with Cuban Force Reported 30 Miles Off Angola." *New York Times*, 6 February 1976, p. 2.

"Soviet Spy Ship Stays Nine Days Off Tsugaru." *Daily Yomiuri*, 30 July 1980, p. 2.

"Soviets Reported Building Submarine Base in Cuba." *Aerospace Daily*, 3 April 1979, p. 166.

"Soviet Warships Anchor 75 Miles Off Key West." *New York Times*, 15 July 1969, p. 77.

"Soviet Warship Visits Luanda." *Rand Daily Mail*, 4 April 1979, p. 3.

Stockholm International Peace Research Institute. *The Arms Trade Registers: The Arms Trade with the Third World*. Cambridge, Mass.: M.I.T. Press, 1975.

"Surprising Buildup of Soviet Warships: Eight Additional Warships of 80,000 Tons Deployed in Far East; Pushing to Three Times 7th Fleet." *Sankei*, 22 December 1979, p. 1.

Szulc, Tad. "White House Charge on Cuba Puzzles U.S. Officials." *New York Times*, 30 September 1970, p. 2.

Tahtinen, Dale. *Arms in the Persian Gulf*. Washington, D.C.: American Enterprise Institute for Public Policy Research, 1974.

Tan Feng. "Why Does the Minsk Sail the Ocean?" *Renmin Ribao* (Beijing), 26 June 1979, p. 6. Translated in *Foreign Broadcast Information Service Daily Report: Vol. 1, People's Republic of China*, no. 130, 5 July 1979, pp. C1–C2.

Tanner, Henry. "Sadat Acts to End Pact with Soviets Cairo Signed in 1971." *New York Times*, 15 March 1976, pp. 1, 5.

Taylor, John W. R. *Jane's All the World's Aircraft, 1980–1981*. New York: Franklin Watts, Inc., 1980.

Theberge, James T. *Russia in the Caribbean: Part II, A Special Report*. Washington, D.C.: Center for Strategic and International Studies, Georgetown University, 1973.

_____. *Soviet Seapower in the Caribbean: Political and Strategic Implications*. New York: Praeger Publishers, 1972.

"Three Soviet Vessels Begin 17-Day Cuba Visit Tomorrow." *New York Times,* 6 December 1970, p. 5.

United Nations, Security Council. "Exchange of Communications with the Deputy Permanent Representative of Saudi Arabia to the United Nations," (S/7842), 6 April 1967.

"Urges Prudence on 'Soviet Threat' Theory; Unnecessary Subjective Feeling of Fear; Efforts for Friendship Rather Than Emphasis Urged; Peace and Security Institute Executive Director Takuya Kubo." *Asahi,* 15 October 1979, p. 3.

U.S., Department of the Navy, Office of the Chief of Naval Operations. *Understanding Soviet Naval Developments.* 4th ed. Washington, D.C.: Government Printing Office, 1981.

"U.S. Jets Intercept Soviet Aircraft." *Washington Star,* 27 April 1980, p. 16.

"U.S. Warns Soviet over Fleet's Use of Vietnam Base." *Baltimore Sun,* 29 March 1979, p. A4.

Watson, Bruce W. "Comments on Gorshkov's *Sea Power of the State.*" *U.S. Naval Institute Proceedings* 103 (April 1977):41–47.

_____. "Maritime Problems in the Mediterranean Sea As We Approach the Twenty-First Century." In *Problems of Sea Power As We Approach the Twenty-First Century,* edited by James L. George, pp. 97–122. Washington, D.C.: American Enterprise Institute for Public Policy Research, 1978.

Watson, Bruce W., and Walton, Margurite A. "Okean-75." *U.S. Naval Institute Proceedings* 102 (July 1976):93–97.

Welles, Benjamin. "Soviet's Removal of Vessel in Cuba Is Awaited by U.S." *New York Times,* 15 November 1970, pp. 1, 22.

_____. "U.S. Now Dubious on Cuba Sub Base." *New York Times,* 14 October 1970, pp. 1, 4.

_____. "U.S. Officials Say Soviet Has Given Assurances That Nuclear Arms Will Be Kept Out of Hemisphere." *New York Times,* 18 November 1970, p. 11.

Wells, Michael. "Russians Shelling Massawa?" *Manchester Guardian Weekly,* 29 January 1978, p. 7.

"White Paper on Defense Stresses Soviet Threats." Broadcast on Tokyo *Kyodo* in English, 18 June 1979. Cited in *Foreign Broadcast Information Service Daily Report: Vol. 4, Asia and Pacific,* no. 119, 19 June 1979, p. C4.

Wylie, J. C. "The Sixth Fleet and American Diplomacy." In *Soviet-American Rivalry in the Middle East,* edited by J. C. Hurewitz, pp. 55–60. New York: Frederick A. Praeger, 1969.

Zumwalt, Elmo R., Jr. *On Watch: A Memoir.* New York: Quadrangle/New York Times Book Company, Inc., 1976.

Index

Page numbers in italics indicate references to photo captions.